PRENTICE HALL

WORLD STUDIES
AFRICA

Geography • History • Culture

In association with
DK

PEARSON

Prentice
Hall

Boston, Massachusetts
Upper Saddle River, New Jersey

Program Consultants

Heidi Hayes Jacobs

Heidi Hayes Jacobs, Ed.D., has served as an education consultant to more than 1,000 schools across the nation and abroad. Dr. Jacobs serves as an adjunct professor in the Department of Curriculum on Teaching at Teachers College, Columbia University. She has written two best-selling books and numerous articles on curriculum reform. She received an M.A. from the University of Massachusetts, Amherst, and completed her doctoral work at Columbia University's Teachers College in 1981. The core of Dr. Jacobs' experience comes from her years teaching high school, middle school, and elementary school students. As an educational consultant, she works with K–12 schools and districts on curriculum reform and strategic planning.

Michal L. LeVasseur

Michal LeVasseur is the Executive Director of the National Council for Geographic Education. She is an instructor in the College of Education at Jacksonville State University and works with the Alabama Geographic Alliance. Her undergraduate and graduate work were in the fields of anthropology (B.A.), geography (M.A.), and science education (Ph.D.). Dr. LeVasseur's specialization has moved increasingly into the area of geography education. Since 1996 she has served as the Director of the National Geographic Society's Summer Geography Workshops. As an educational consultant, she has worked with the National Geographic Society as well as with schools and organizations to develop programs and curricula for geography.

Senior Reading Consultants

Kate Kinsella

Kate Kinsella, Ed.D., is a faculty member in the Department of Secondary Education at San Francisco State University. A specialist in second-language acquisition and content area literacy, she consults nationally on school-wide practices that support adolescent English learners and striving readers to make academic gains. Dr. Kinsella earned her M.A. in TESOL from San Francisco State University, and her Ed.D. in Second Language Acquisition from the University of San Francisco.

Kevin Feldman

Kevin Feldman, Ed.D., is the Director of Reading and Early Intervention with the Sonoma County Office of Education (SCOE) and an independent educational consultant. At the SCOE, he develops, organizes, and monitors programs related to K–12 literacy. Dr. Feldman has an M.A. from the University of California, Riverside in Special Education, Learning Disabilities and Instructional Design. He earned his Ed.D. in Curriculum and Instruction from the University of San Francisco.

Acknowledgments appear on page 249, which constitutes an extension of this copyright page.

ISBN 0-13-204143-X
5678910 V057 15 14 13 12 11

Cartography Consultant
 Andrew Heritage

Andrew Heritage has been publishing atlases and maps for more than 25 years. In 1991, he joined the leading illustrated nonfiction publisher Dorling Kindersley (DK) with the task of building an international atlas list from scratch. The DK atlas list now includes some 10 titles, which are constantly updated and appear in new editions either annually or every other year.

Academic Reviewers

Africa
Barbara B. Brown, Ph.D.
African Studies Center
Boston University
Boston, Massachusetts

Ancient World
Evelyn DeLong Mangie, Ph.D.
Department of History
University of South Florida
Tampa, Florida

Central Asia and the Middle East
Pamela G. Sayre
History Department,
    Social Sciences Division
Henry Ford Community College
Dearborn, Michigan

East Asia
Huping Ling, Ph.D.
History Department
Truman State University
Kirksville, Missouri

Eastern Europe
Robert M. Jenkins, Ph.D.
Center for Slavic, Eurasian and
    East European Studies
University of North Carolina
Chapel Hill, North Carolina

Latin America
Dan La Botz
Professor, History Department
Miami University
Oxford, Ohio

Medieval Times
James M. Murray
History Department
University of Cincinnati
Cincinnati, Ohio

North Africa
Barbara E. Petzen
Center for Middle Eastern Studies
Harvard University
Cambridge, Massachusetts

Religion
Charles H. Lippy, Ph.D.
Department of Philosophy
    and Religion
University of Tennessee
    at Chattanooga
Chattanooga, Tennessee

Russia
Janet Vaillant
Davis Center for Russian
    and Eurasian Studies
Harvard University
Cambridge, Massachusetts

United States and Canada
Victoria Randlett
Geography Department
University of Nevada, Reno
Reno, Nevada

Western Europe
Ruth Mitchell-Pitts
Center for European Studies
University of North Carolina
    at Chapel Hill
Chapel Hill, North Carolina

Reviewers

Sean Brennan
Brecksville-Broadview Heights
    City School District
Broadview Heights, Ohio

Stephen Bullick
Mt. Lebanon School District
Pittsburgh, Pennsylvania

Louis P. De Angelo, Ed.D.
Archdiocese of Philadelphia
Philadelphia, Pennsylvania

Paul Francis Durietz
Social Studies
    Curriculum Coordinator
Woodland District #50
Gurnee, Illinois

Gail Dwyer
Dickerson Middle School,
    Cobb County
Marietta, Georgia

Michal Howden
Social Studies Consultant
Zionsville, Indiana

Rosemary Kalloch
Springfield Public Schools
Springfield, Massachusetts

Deborah J. Miller
Office of Social Studies,
    Detroit Public Schools
Detroit, Michigan

Steven P. Missal
Plainfield Public Schools
Plainfield, New Jersey

Catherine Fish Petersen
Social Studies Consultant
Saint James, Long Island, New York

Joe Wieczorek
Social Studies Consultant
Baltimore, Maryland

AFRICA

Develop Skills

Use these pages to develop your reading, writing, and geography skills.

Build a Regional Background

Learn about the geography, history, and culture of the region.

Focus on Countries

Create an understanding of the region by focusing on specific countries.

MAP MASTER

- Learn map skills with the MapMaster Skills Handbook.
- Practice your skills with every map in this book.
- Interact with every map online and on CD-ROM.

DK

Maps and illustrations created by DK help build your understanding of the world. The DK World Desk Reference Online keeps you up to date.

interactive Textbook

The *World Studies* Interactive Textbook online and on CD-ROM uses interactive maps and other activities to help you learn.

COUNTRY DATABANK

Read about all the countries that make up Africa.

Literature

A selection by an African author brings social studies to life.

Links

See the fascinating links between social studies and other disciplines.

COUNTRY PROFILES

Theme-based maps and charts provide a closer look at countries, regions, and provinces.

MAP★MASTER™ Interactive

Go online to find an interactive version of every MapMaster map in this book. Use the Web Code provided to gain direct access to these maps.

How to Use Web Codes:

1. Go to www.PHSchool.com.
2. Enter the Web Code.
3. Click Go!

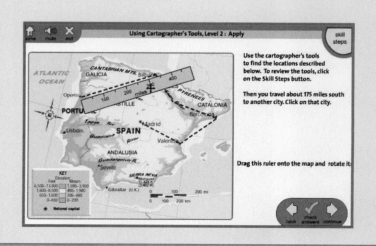

Charts, Graphs, and Tables

Building Geographic Literacy

Learning about a country often starts with finding it on a map. The MapMaster™ system in *World Studies* helps you develop map skills you will use throughout your life. These three steps can help you become a MapMaster!

The MAP✦MASTER™ System

1 Learn

You need to learn geography tools and concepts before you explore the world. Get started by using the MapMaster Skills Handbook to learn the skills you need for success.

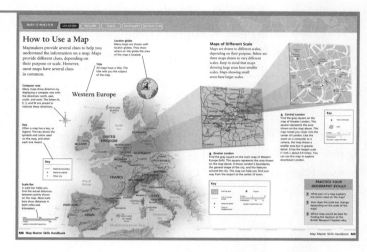

MAP✦MASTER™
Skills Activity

Location The Equator runs through parts of Latin America, but it is far from other parts of the region.

Locate Find the Equator on the map. Which climates are most common in Latin America, and how far is each climate region from the Equator?

Draw Conclusions How do climates change as you move away from the Equator?

Go Online
PHSchool.com Use Web Code lfp-1142 for step-by-step map skills practice.

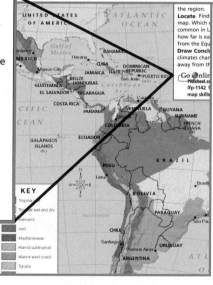

2 Practice

You need to practice and apply your geography skills frequently to be a MapMaster. The maps in *World Studies* give you the practice you need to develop geographic literacy.

3 Interact

Using maps is more than just finding places. Maps can teach you many things about a region, such as its climate, its vegetation, and the languages that the people who live there speak. Every MapMaster map is online at **PHSchool.com,** with interactive activities to help you learn the most from every map.

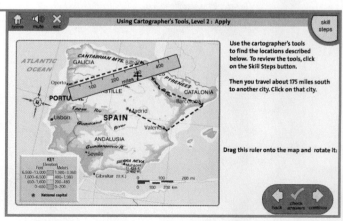

Learning With Technology

You will be making many exciting journeys across time and place in *World Studies*. Technology will help make what you learn come alive.

Go Online
PHSchool.com

For: An activity on the cultures of West Africa
Visit: PHSchool.com
Web Code: lad-5302

Go Online at PHSchool.com

Use the Web Codes listed below and in each Go Online box to access exciting information or activities.

How to Use the Web Code:
1. Go to **www.PHSchool.com.**
2. Enter the Web Code.
3. Click Go!

For a complete list of features for this book, use Web Code lak-1000.

Africa Activities

Web Code	Activity
	History Interactive
lap-5803	5 Pillars of Islam
lap-5812	Tour of Egyptian Pyramids
lap-5814	Learn More About Ancient Writing
lap-5816	Inside a Mosque
lap-5817	Investigating Ancient Trade
	MapMaster
lap-5801	Geography of Ancient Egypt
lap-5802	Fossil Finds in Africa
lap-5804	Continental Drift
lap-5806	West African Empires
lap-5807	Trade Routes of Ghana
lap-5809	Origins of Agriculture
lap-5810	Early River Valley Civilizations
lap-5811	Environments of Africa
lap-5813	The Spread of Islam
lap-5815	The Fertile Crescent
lap-5818	The Seasons

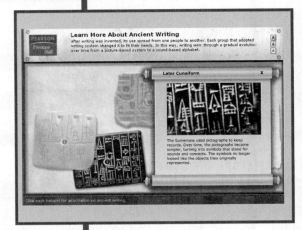

World Desk Reference Online

There are more than 190 countries in the world. To learn about them, you need the most up-to-date information and statistics. The **DK World Desk Reference Online** gives you instant access to the information you need to explore each country.

Reading Informational Texts

Reading a magazine, an Internet page, or a textbook is not the same as reading a novel. The purpose of reading nonfiction texts is to acquire new information. On page M18 you'll read about some ⤵ **Target Reading Skills** that you'll have a chance to practice as you read this textbook. Here we'll focus on a few skills that will help you read nonfiction with a more critical eye.

Analyze the Author's Purpose

Different types of materials are written with different purposes in mind. For example, a textbook is written to teach students information about a subject. The purpose of a technical manual is to teach someone how to use something, such as a computer. A newspaper editorial might be written to persuade the reader to accept a particular point of view. A writer's purpose influences how the material is presented. Sometimes an author states his or her purpose directly. More often, the purpose is only suggested, and you must use clues to identify the author's purpose.

Distinguish Between Facts and Opinions

It's important when reading informational texts to read actively and to distinguish between fact and opinion. A fact can be proven or disproven. An opinion cannot—it is someone's personal viewpoint or evaluation.

For example, the editorial pages in a newspaper offer opinions on topics that are currently in the news. You need to read newspaper editorials with an eye for bias and faulty logic. For example, the newspaper editorial at the right shows factual statements in blue and opinion statements in red. The underlined words are examples of highly charged words. They reveal bias on the part of the writer.

More than 5,000 people voted last week in favor of building a new shopping center, but the opposition won out. The margin of victory is irrelevant. Those <u>radical</u> voters who opposed the center are obviously <u>self-serving elitists</u> who do not care about anyone but themselves.

This month's unemployment figure for our area is 10 percent, which represents an increase of about 5 percent over the figure for this time last year. These figures mean that unemployment is getting worse. But the people who voted against the mall probably do not care about creating new jobs.

Identify Evidence

Before you accept an author's conclusion, you need to make sure that the author has based the conclusion on enough evidence and on the right kind of evidence. An author may present a series of facts to support a claim, but the facts may not tell the whole story. For example, what evidence does the author of the newspaper editorial on the previous page provide to support his claim that the new shopping center would create more jobs? Is it possible that the shopping center might have put many small local businesses out of business, thus increasing unemployment rather than decreasing it?

Evaluate Credibility

Whenever you read informational texts, you need to assess the credibility of the author. This is especially true of sites you may visit on the Internet. All Internet sources are not equally reliable. Here are some questions to ask yourself when evaluating the credibility of a Web site.

- ☐ Is the Web site created by a respected organization, a discussion group, or an individual?
- ☐ Does the Web site creator include his or her name as well as credentials and the sources he or she used to write the material?
- ☐ Is the information on the site balanced or biased?
- ☐ Can you verify the information using two other sources?
- ☐ Is there a date telling when the Web site was created or last updated?

Writing for Social Studies

Writing is one of the most powerful communication tools you will ever use. You will use it to share your thoughts and ideas with others. Research shows that writing about what you read actually helps you learn new information and ideas. A systematic approach to writing—including prewriting, drafting, revising, and proofing—can help you write better, whether you're writing an essay or a research report.

Narrative Essays

Writing that tells a story about a personal experience

1 Select and Narrow Your Topic

A narrative is a story. In social studies, it might be a narrative essay about how an event affected you or your family.

2 Gather Details

Brainstorm a list of details you'd like to include in your narrative.

3 Write a First Draft

Start by writing a simple opening sentence that conveys the main idea of your essay. Continue by writing a colorful story that has interesting details. Write a conclusion that sums up the significance of the event or situation described in your essay.

4 Revise and Proofread

Check to make sure you have not begun too many sentences with the word *I*. Replace general words with more colorful ones.

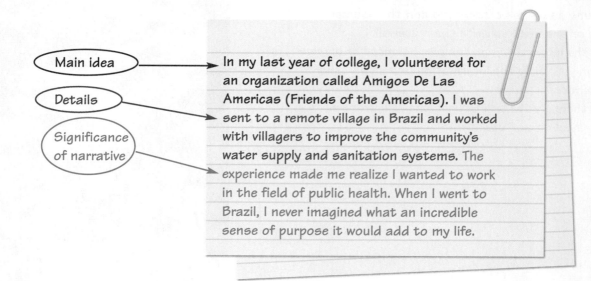

Main idea → In my last year of college, I volunteered for an organization called Amigos De Las Americas (Friends of the Americas). I was

Details → sent to a remote village in Brazil and worked with villagers to improve the community's water supply and sanitation systems. The

Significance of narrative → experience made me realize I wanted to work in the field of public health. When I went to Brazil, I never imagined what an incredible sense of purpose it would add to my life.

Persuasive Essays

Writing that supports an opinion or position

1 Select and Narrow Your Topic

Choose a topic that provokes an argument and has at least two sides. Choose a side. Decide which argument will appeal most to your audience and persuade them to understand your point of view.

2 Gather Evidence

Create a chart that states your position at the top and then lists the pros and cons for your position below, in two columns. Predict and address the strongest arguments against your stand.

3 Write a First Draft

Write a strong thesis statement that clearly states your position. Continue by presenting the strongest arguments in favor of your position and acknowledging and refuting opposing arguments.

4 Revise and Proofread

Check to make sure you have made a logical argument and that you have not oversimplified the argument.

Main Idea

Supporting (pro) argument

Opposing (con) argument

Transition words

It is vital to vote in elections. When people vote, they tell public officials how to run the government. Not every proposal is carried out; however, politicians do their best to listen to what the majority of people want. Therefore, every vote is important.

Expository Essays

Writing that explains a process, compares and contrasts, explains causes and effects, or explores solutions to a problem

❶ Identify and Narrow Your Topic

Expository writing is writing that explains something in detail. It might explain the similarities and differences between two or more subjects (compare and contrast). It might explain how one event causes another (cause and effect). Or it might explain a problem and describe a solution.

❷ Gather Evidence

Create a graphic organizer that identifies details to include in your essay.

Cause 1	Cause 2	Cause 3
Most people in the Mexican countryside work on farms.	The population in Mexico is growing at one of the highest rates in the world.	There is not enough farm work for so many people.

Effect

As a result, many rural families are moving from the countryside to live in Mexico City.

❸ Write Your First Draft

Write a topic sentence and then organize the essay around your similarities and differences, causes and effects, or problem and solutions. Be sure to include convincing details, facts, and examples.

❹ Revise and Proofread

Research Papers

Writing that presents research about a topic

❶ Narrow Your Topic

Choose a topic you're interested in and make sure that it is not too broad. For example, instead of writing a report on Panama, write about the construction of the Panama Canal.

❷ Acquire Information

Locate several sources of information about the topic from the library or the Internet. For each resource, create a source index card like the one at the right. Then take notes using an index card for each detail or subtopic. On the card, note which source the information was taken from. Use quotation marks when you copy the exact words from a source.

Source #1
McCullough, David. *The Path Between the Seas: The Creation of the Panama Canal, 1870-1914.* N.Y., Simon and Schuster, 1977.

❸ Make an Outline

Use an outline to decide how to organize your report. Sort your index cards into the same order.

Outline
I. Introduction
II. Why the canal was built
III. How the canal was built
  A. Physical challenges
  B. Medical challenges
IV. Conclusion

Introduction

Building the Panama Canal

Ever since Christopher Columbus first explored the Isthmus of Panama, the Spanish had been looking for a water route through it. They wanted to be able to sail west from Spain to Asia without sailing around South America. However, it was not until 1914 that the dream became a reality.

Conclusion

It took eight years and more than 70,000 workers to build the Panama Canal. It remains one of the greatest engineering feats of modern times.

4 Write a First Draft

Write an introduction, a body, and a conclusion. Leave plenty of space between lines so you can go back and add details that you may have left out.

5 Revise and Proofread

Be sure to include transition words between sentences and paragraphs. Here are some examples:

To show a contrast—*however, although, despite.*

To point out a reason—*since, because, if.*

To signal a conclusion—*therefore, consequently, so, then.*

Evaluating Your Writing

Use this table to help you evaluate your writing.

	Excellent	Good	Acceptable	Unacceptable
Purpose	Achieves purpose—to inform, persuade, or provide historical interpretation—very well	Informs, persuades, or provides historical interpretation reasonably well	Reader cannot easily tell if the purpose is to inform, persuade, or provide historical interpretation	Purpose is not clear
Organization	Develops ideas in a very clear and logical way	Presents ideas in a reasonably well-organized way	Reader has difficulty following the organization	Lacks organization
Elaboration	Explains all ideas with facts and details	Explains most ideas with facts and details	Includes some supporting facts and details	Lacks supporting details
Use of Language	Uses excellent vocabulary and sentence structure with no errors in spelling, grammar, or punctuation	Uses good vocabulary and sentence structure with very few errors in spelling, grammar, or punctuation	Includes some errors in grammar, punctuation, and spelling	Includes many errors in grammar, punctuation, and spelling

CONTENTS

Go Online PHSchool.com Use Web Code **lap-0000** for all of the maps in this handbook.

Five Themes of Geography

Studying the geography of the entire world is a huge task. You can make that task easier by using the five themes of geography: location, regions, place, movement, and human-environment interaction. The themes are tools you can use to organize information and to answer the where, why, and how of geography.

▲ **Location**
This museum in England has a line running through it. The line marks its location at 0° longitude.

LOCATION

1 Location answers the question, "Where is it?" You can think of the location of a continent or a country as its address. You might give an absolute location such as 40° N and 80° W. You might also use a relative address, telling where one place is by referring to another place. *Between school and the mall* and *eight miles east of Pleasant City* are examples of relative locations.

REGIONS

2 Regions are areas that share at least one common feature. Geographers divide the world into many types of regions. For example, countries, states, and cities are political regions. The people in any one of these places live under the same government. Other features, such as climate and culture, can be used to define regions. Therefore the same place can be found in more than one region. For example, the state of Hawaii is in the political region of the United States. Because it has a tropical climate, Hawaii is also part of a tropical climate region.

MOVEMENT

4 Movement answers the question, "How do people, goods, and ideas move from place to place?" Remember that what happens in one place often affects what happens in another. Use the theme of movement to help you trace the spread of goods, people, and ideas from one location to another.

PLACE

3 Place identifies the natural and human features that make one place different from every other place. You can identify a specific place by its landforms, climate, plants, animals, people, language, or culture. You might even think of place as a geographic signature. Use the signature to help you understand the natural and human features that make one place different from every other place.

INTERACTION

5 Human-environment interaction focuses on the relationship between people and the environment. As people live in an area, they often begin to make changes to it, usually to make their lives easier. For example, they might build a dam to control flooding during rainy seasons. Also, the environment can affect how people live, work, dress, travel, and communicate.

◄ **Interaction**
These Congolese women interact with their environment by gathering wood for cooking.

PRACTICE YOUR GEOGRAPHY SKILLS

1 Describe your town or city, using each of the five themes of geography.

2 Name at least one thing that comes into your town or city and one that goes out. How is each moved? Where does it come from? Where does it go?

Understanding Movements of Earth

The planet Earth is part of our solar system. Earth revolves around the sun in a nearly circular path called an orbit. A revolution, or one complete orbit around the sun, takes 365¼ days, or one year. As Earth orbits the sun, it also spins on its axis, an invisible line through the center of Earth from the North Pole to the South Pole. This movement is called a rotation.

▼ **Spring begins**
On March 20 or 21, the sun is directly overhead at the Equator. The Northern and Southern Hemispheres receive almost equal hours of sunlight and darkness.

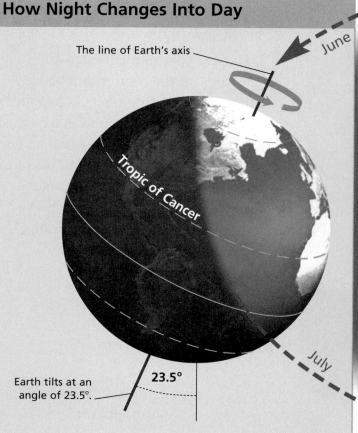

How Night Changes Into Day

The line of Earth's axis

Tropic of Cancer

Earth tilts at an angle of 23.5°.

23.5°

Earth takes about 24 hours to make one full rotation on its axis. As Earth rotates, it is daytime on the side facing the sun. It is night on the side away from the sun.

Equator

April
May
June
July
August
September

◀ **Summer begins**
On June 21 or 22, the sun is directly overhead at the Tropic of Cancer. The Northern Hemisphere receives the greatest number of sunlight hours.

The Seasons

Earth's axis is tilted at an angle. Because of this tilt, sunlight strikes different parts of Earth at different times in the year, creating seasons. The illustration below shows how the seasons are created in the Northern Hemisphere. In the Southern Hemisphere, the seasons are reversed.

PRACTICE YOUR GEOGRAPHY SKILLS

1 What causes the seasons in the Northern Hemisphere to be the opposite of those in the Southern Hemisphere?

2 During which two days of the year do the Northern Hemisphere and Southern Hemisphere have equal hours of daylight and darkness?

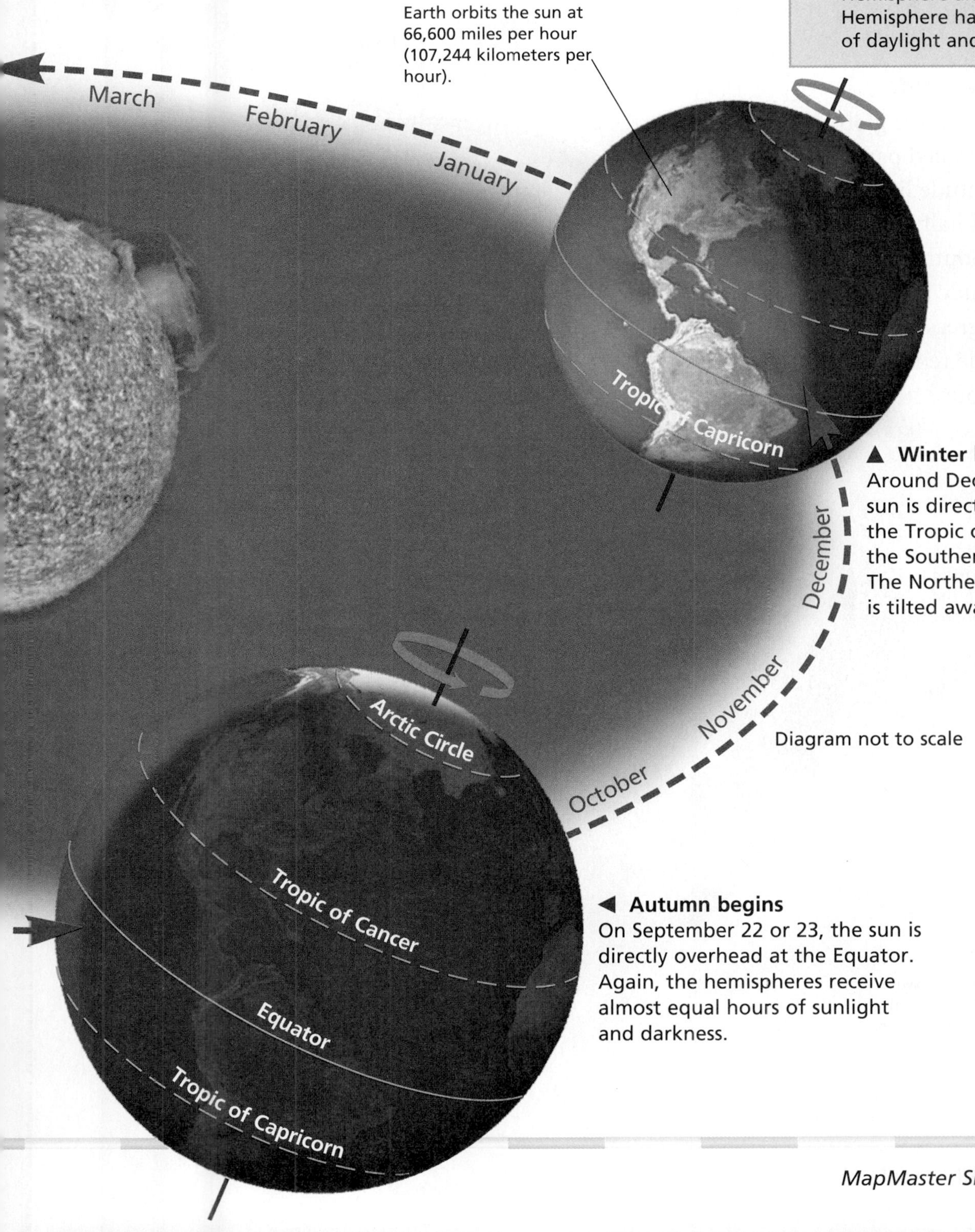

March
February
January

Earth orbits the sun at 66,600 miles per hour (107,244 kilometers per hour).

Tropic of Capricorn

December

November

October

Diagram not to scale

▲ **Winter begins**
Around December 21, the sun is directly overhead at the Tropic of Capricorn in the Southern Hemisphere. The Northern Hemisphere is tilted away from the sun.

Arctic Circle

Tropic of Cancer

Equator

Tropic of Capricorn

◄ **Autumn begins**
On September 22 or 23, the sun is directly overhead at the Equator. Again, the hemispheres receive almost equal hours of sunlight and darkness.

Understanding Globes

A globe is a scale model of Earth. It shows the actual shapes, sizes, and locations of all Earth's landmasses and bodies of water. Features on the surface of Earth are drawn to scale on a globe. This means that a small unit of measure on the globe stands for a large unit of measure on Earth.

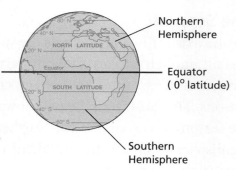

Northern Hemisphere

Equator (0° latitude)

Southern Hemisphere

Parallels of Latitude

Geographers divide the globe along imaginary horizontal lines called parallels of latitude. One of these latitude lines is the Equator, located halfway between the North and South Poles. Parallels of latitude are measured in degrees (°). One degree of latitude represents a distance of about 69 miles (111 kilometers).

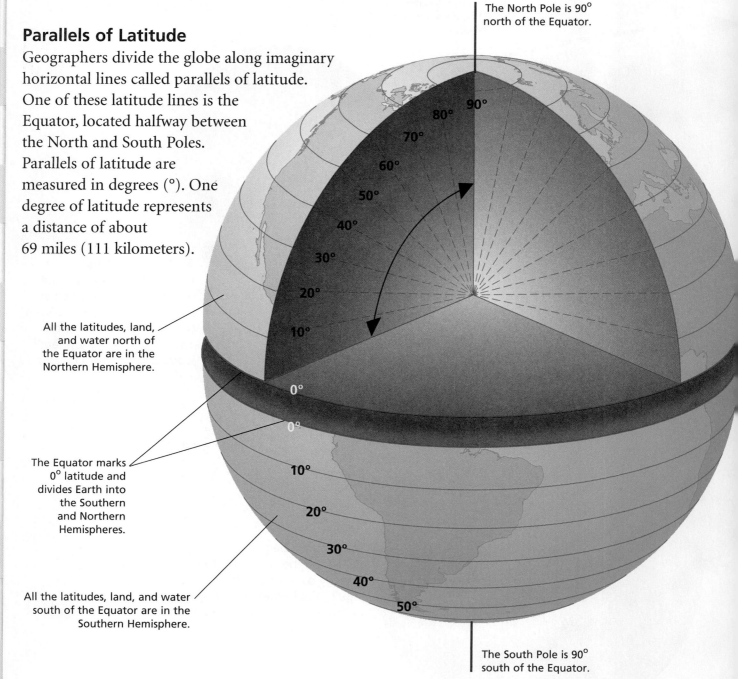

The North Pole is 90° north of the Equator.

All the latitudes, land, and water north of the Equator are in the Northern Hemisphere.

The Equator marks 0° latitude and divides Earth into the Southern and Northern Hemispheres.

All the latitudes, land, and water south of the Equator are in the Southern Hemisphere.

The South Pole is 90° south of the Equator.

Meridians of Longitude

Geographers also divide the globe along imaginary vertical lines called meridians of longitude, which are measured in degrees (°). The longitude line called the Prime Meridian runs from pole to pole through Greenwich, England. All meridians of longitude come together at the North and South Poles.

PRACTICE YOUR GEOGRAPHY SKILLS

1 Which continents lie completely in the Northern Hemisphere? In the Western Hemisphere?

2 Is there land or water at 20° S latitude and the Prime Meridian? At the Equator and 60° W longitude?

All the longitudes, land, and water west of the Prime Meridian are in the Western Hemisphere.

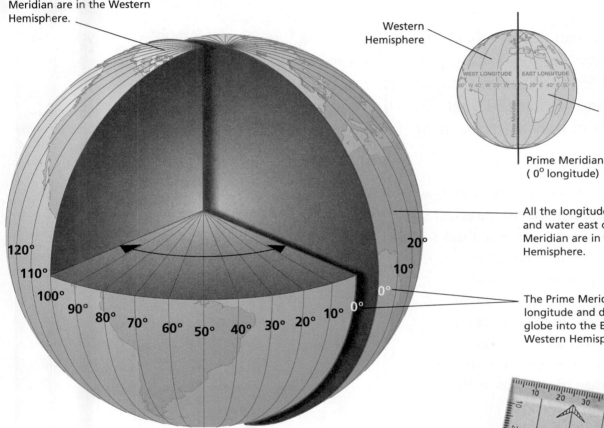

Western Hemisphere

WEST LONGITUDE   EAST LONGITUDE

Eastern Hemisphere

Prime Meridian (0° longitude)

All the longitudes, land, and water east of the Prime Meridian are in the Eastern Hemisphere.

120° 110° 100° 90° 80° 70° 60° 50° 40° 30° 20° 10° 0°
20° 10° 0°

The Prime Meridian marks 0° longitude and divides the globe into the Eastern and Western Hemispheres.

The Global Grid

Together, the pattern of parallels of latitude and meridians of longitude is called the global grid. Using the lines of latitude and longitude, you can locate any place on Earth. For example, the location of 30° north latitude and 90° west longitude is usually written as 30° N, 90° W. Only one place on Earth has these coordinates—the city of New Orleans, in the state of Louisiana.

▲ **Compass**
Wherever you are on Earth, a compass can be used to show direction.

Map Projections

Maps are drawings that show regions on flat surfaces. Maps are easier to use and carry than globes, but they cannot show the correct size and shape of every feature on Earth's curved surface. They must shrink some places and stretch others. To make up for this distortion, mapmakers use different map projections. No one projection can accurately show the correct area, shape, distance, and direction for all of Earth's surface. Mapmakers use the projection that has the least distortion for the information they are presenting.

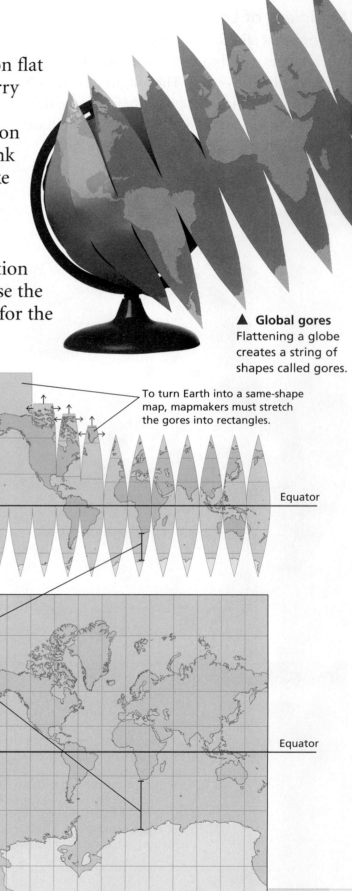

▲ **Global gores**
Flattening a globe creates a string of shapes called gores.

Same-Shape Maps

Map projections that accurately show the shapes of landmasses are called same-shape maps. However, these projections often greatly distort, or make less accurate, the size of landmasses as well as the distance between them. In the projection below, the northern and southern areas of the globe appear more stretched than the areas near the Equator.

To turn Earth into a same-shape map, mapmakers must stretch the gores into rectangles.

Equator

Stretching the gores makes parts of Earth larger. This enlargement becomes greater toward the North and South Poles.

Mercator projection ▶
One of the most common same-shape maps is the Mercator projection, named for the mapmaker who invented it. The Mercator projection accurately shows shape and direction, but it distorts distance and size. Because the projection shows true directions, ships' navigators use it to chart a straight-line course between two ports.

Equator

Equal-Area Maps

Map projections that show the correct size of landmasses are called equal-area maps. In order to show the correct size of landmasses, these maps usually distort shapes. The distortion is usually greater at the edges of the map and less at the center.

PRACTICE YOUR GEOGRAPHY SKILLS

1 What feature is distorted on an equal-area map?

2 Would you use a Mercator projection to find the exact distance between two locations? Tell why or why not.

To turn Earth's surface into an equal-area map, mapmakers have to squeeze each gore into an oval.

Equator

The tips of all the gores are then joined together. The points at which they join form the North and South Poles. The line of the Equator stays the same.

North Pole

Equator

South Pole

Robinson Maps

Many of the maps in this book use the Robinson projection, which is a compromise between the Mercator and equal-area projections. The Robinson projection gives a useful overall picture of the world. It keeps the size and shape relationships of most continents and oceans, but distorts the size of the polar regions.

The entire top edge of the map is the North Pole.

The map is least distorted at the Equator.

Equator

The entire bottom edge of the map is the South Pole.

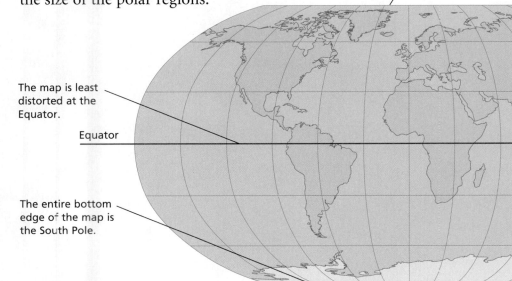

How to Use a Map

Mapmakers provide several clues to help you understand the information on a map. Maps provide different clues, depending on their purpose or scale. However, most maps have several clues in common.

Locator globe
Many maps are shown with locator globes. They show where on the globe the area of the map is located.

Title
All maps have a title. The title tells you the subject of the map.

Compass rose
Many maps show direction by displaying a compass rose with the directions north, east, south, and west. The letters N, E, S, and W are placed to indicate these directions.

Key
Often a map has a key, or legend. The key shows the symbols and colors used on the map, and what each one means.

Scale bar
A scale bar helps you find the actual distances between points shown on the map. Most scale bars show distances in both miles and kilometers.

Western Europe

Key

——	National border
⊛	National capital
•	Other city

0 miles 300
0 kilometers 300
Lambert Azimuthal Equal Area

Glasgow, North Sea, Copenhagen, DENMARK, UNITED KINGDOM, Dublin, Hamburg, Berlin, IRELAND, NETHERLANDS, Amsterdam, London, The Hague, GERMANY, Brussels, Frankfurt, Prague, BELGIUM, CZECH REPUBLIC, LUXEMBOURG, English Channel, Paris, Luxembourg, Munich, Vienna, AUSTRIA, FRANCE, Bern, LIECHTENSTEIN, SWITZERLAND, Lyon, Bay of Biscay, Milan, SAN MARINO, Toulouse, MONACO, ITALY, Adriatic Sea, Marseille, VATICAN CITY, ANDORRA, CORSICA (France), Rome, PORTUGAL, Madrid, Barcelona, SARDINIA (Italy), Lisbon, SPAIN, BALEARIC ISLANDS (Spain), Tyrrhenian Sea, Seville, Mediterranean Sea, SICILY (Italy), SHETLAND ISLANDS (U.K.)

10° E, 0°, 60° N, 20° E, 60° N, 10° W, 50° N, 50° N, 40° N, 10° W

Maps of Different Scales

Maps are drawn to different scales, depending on their purpose. Here are three maps drawn to very different scales. Keep in mind that maps showing large areas have smaller scales. Maps showing small areas have larger scales.

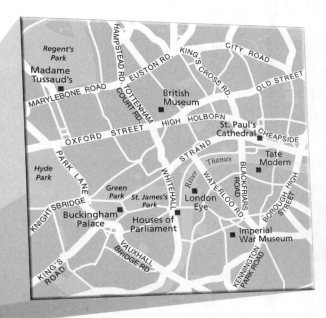

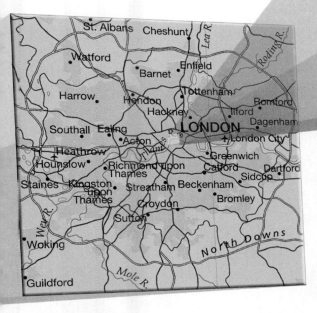

▲ **Greater London**

Find the gray square on the main map of Western Europe (left). This square represents the area shown on the map above. It shows London's boundaries, the general shape of the city, and the features around the city. This map can help you find your way from the airport to the center of town.

▲ **Central London**

Find the gray square on the map of Greater London. This square represents the area shown on the map above. This map moves you closer into the center of London. Like the zoom on a computer or a camera, this map shows a smaller area but in greater detail. It has the largest scale (1 inch represents about 0.9 mile). You can use this map to explore downtown London.

Key

■ Point of interest

Park

0 miles   0.5   1
0 kilometers   1

Key

Built-up area

✈ Airport

—— City or county border

0 miles   10   20
0 kilometers   20
Lambert Conformal Conic

⊛ National capital

• Town or neighborhood

PRACTICE YOUR GEOGRAPHY SKILLS

1 What part of a map explains the colors used on the map?

2 How does the scale bar change depending on the scale of the map?

3 Which map would be best for finding the location of the British Museum? Explain why.

Political Maps

Political maps show political borders: continents, countries, and divisions within countries, such as states or provinces. The colors on political maps do not have any special meaning, but they make the map easier to read. Political maps also include symbols and labels for capitals, cities, and towns.

PRACTICE YOUR GEOGRAPHY SKILLS

1 What symbols show a national border, a national capital, and a city?

2 What is Angola's capital city?

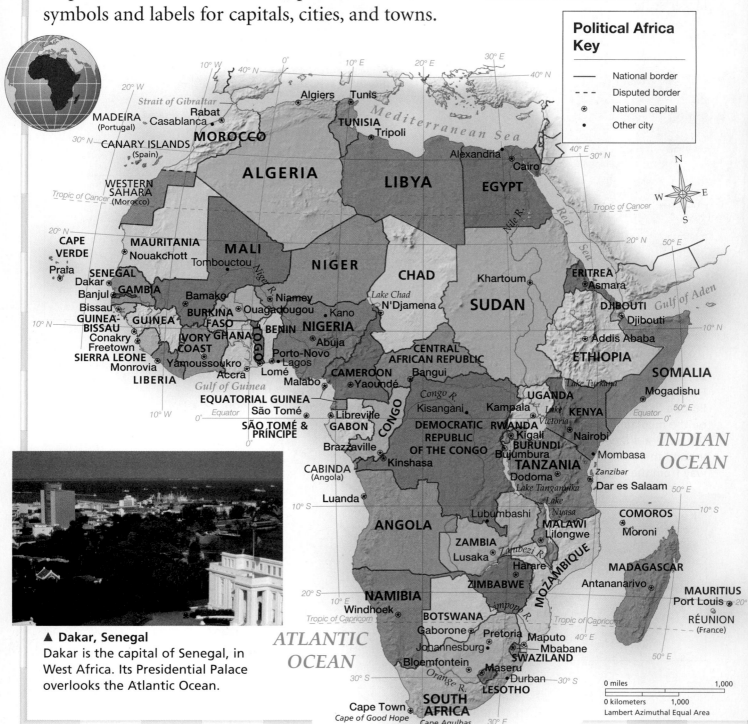

Political Africa Key

——	National border
- - -	Disputed border
⊛	National capital
•	Other city

▲ **Dakar, Senegal**
Dakar is the capital of Senegal, in West Africa. Its Presidential Palace overlooks the Atlantic Ocean.

Physical Maps

Physical maps represent what a region looks like by showing its major physical features, such as hills and plains. Physical maps also often show elevation and relief. Elevation, indicated by colors, is the height of the land above sea level. Relief, indicated by shading, shows how sharply the land rises or falls.

PRACTICE YOUR GEOGRAPHY SKILLS

1 Which areas of Africa have the highest elevation?

2 How can you use relief to plan a hiking trip?

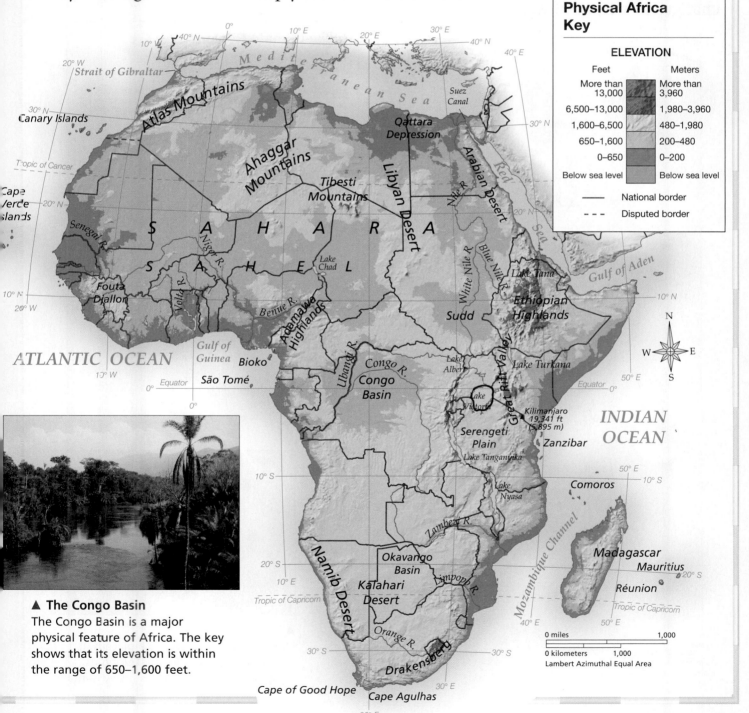

Physical Africa Key

ELEVATION

Feet	Meters
More than 13,000	More than 3,960
6,500–13,000	1,980–3,960
1,600–6,500	480–1,980
650–1,600	200–480
0–650	0–200
Below sea level	Below sea level

—— National border

- - - Disputed border

▲ **The Congo Basin**

The Congo Basin is a major physical feature of Africa. The key shows that its elevation is within the range of 650–1,600 feet.

Lambert Azimuthal Equal Area

Special-Purpose Maps: Climate

Unlike the boundary lines on a political map, the boundary lines on climate maps do not separate the land into exact divisions. For example, in this climate map of India, a tropical wet climate gradually changes to a tropical wet and dry climate.

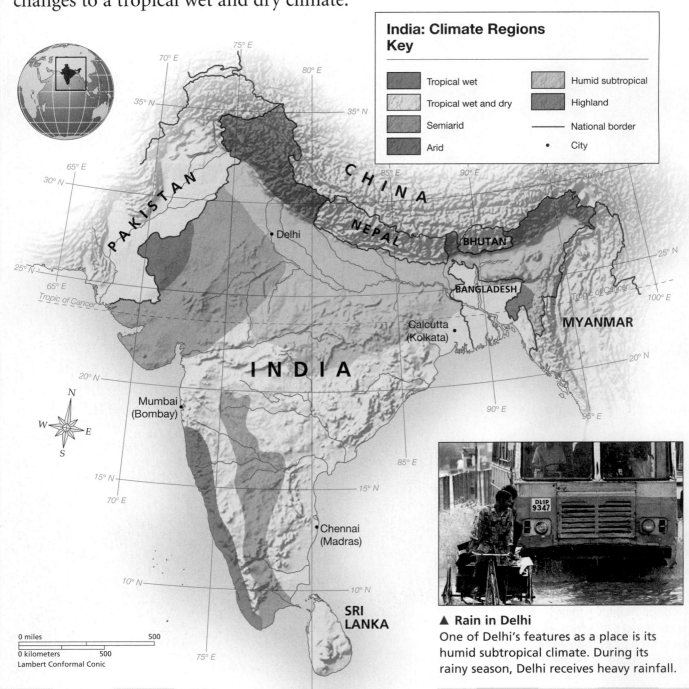

India: Climate Regions Key

- Tropical wet
- Tropical wet and dry
- Semiarid
- Arid
- Humid subtropical
- Highland
- National border
- • City

▲ **Rain in Delhi**
One of Delhi's features as a place is its humid subtropical climate. During its rainy season, Delhi receives heavy rainfall.

0 miles 500
0 kilometers 500
Lambert Conformal Conic

Special-Purpose Maps: Language

This map shows the official languages of India. An official language is the language used by the government. Even though a region has an official language, the people there may speak other languages as well. As in other special-purpose maps, the key explains how the different languages appear on the map.

PRACTICE YOUR GEOGRAPHY SKILLS

1 What color represents the Malayalam language on this map?

2 Where in India is Tamil the official language?

The Hindi language ▶
Hindi is the most widely spoken language in India. It is also the most popular language in Delhi.

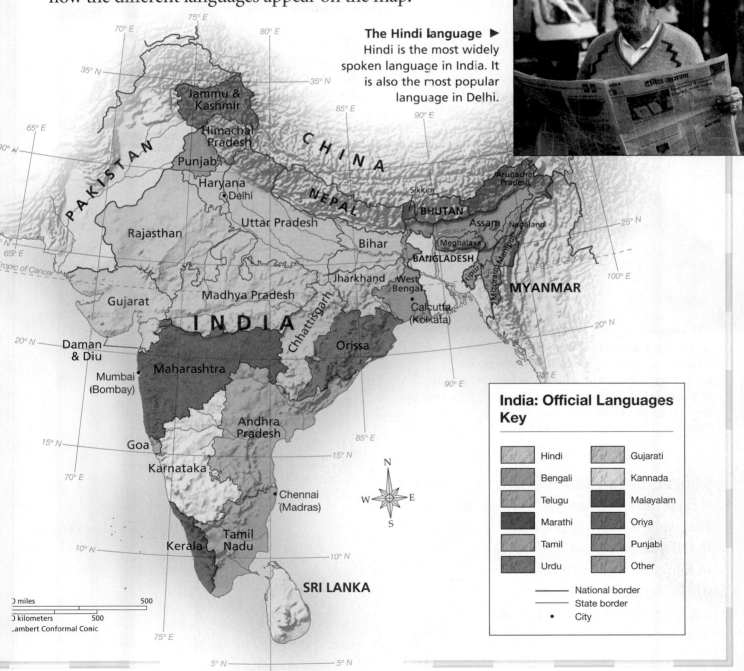

India: Official Languages Key

	Hindi		Gujarati
	Bengali		Kannada
	Telugu		Malayalam
	Marathi		Oriya
	Tamil		Punjabi
	Urdu		Other

——— National border
——— State border
• City

miles 500
kilometers 500
Lambert Conformal Conic

Human Migration

Migration is an important part of the study of geography. Since the beginning of history, people have been on the move. As people move, they both shape and are shaped by their environments. Wherever people go, the culture they bring with them mixes with the cultures of the place in which they have settled.

Explorers arrive ▼
In 1492, Christopher Columbus set sail from Spain for the Americas with three ships. The ships shown here are replicas of those ships.

▲ **Native American pyramid**
When Europeans arrived in the Americas, the lands they found were not empty. Diverse groups of people with distinct cultures already lived there. The temple-topped pyramid shown above was built by Mayan Indians in Mexico, long before Columbus sailed.

Migration to the Americas, 1500–1800

A huge wave of migration from the Eastern Hemisphere began in the 1500s. European explorers in the Americas paved the way for hundreds of years of European settlement there. Forced migration from Africa started soon afterward, as Europeans began to import enslaved Africans to work in the Americas. The map to the right shows these migrations.

ATLANTIC OCEAN

NEW SPAIN
(Spain)
Mexico City

Caribbean Sea

Panama City

DUTCH GUIANA
(Netherlands)

NEW GRENADA
(Spain)

FRENCH GUIANA
(France)

Amazon R.

PERU
(Spain)
Lima
Cuzco

BRAZIL
(Portugal)

Potosí

RIO DE LA PLATA
(Spain)

Concepción

Buenos Aires

0 miles   1,000
0 kilometers   1,000
Wagner VII

1 Where did the Portuguese settle in the Americas?

2 Would you describe African migration at this time as a result of both push factors and pull factors? Explain why or why not.

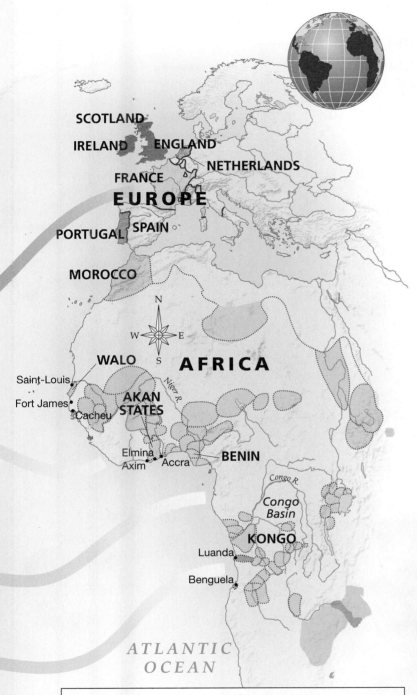

SCOTLAND
IRELAND   ENGLAND
FRANCE   NETHERLANDS
EUROPE
PORTUGAL SPAIN
MOROCCO
WALO   **AFRICA**
Saint-Louis
Fort James
AKAN STATES
Cacheu
Niger R.
Elmina
Axim   Accra   **BENIN**
Congo R.
Congo Basin
KONGO
Luanda
Benguela
ATLANTIC OCEAN

"Push" and "Pull" Factors

Geographers describe a people's choice to migrate in terms of "push" factors and "pull" factors. Push factors are things in people's lives that push them to leave, such as poverty and political unrest. Pull factors are things in another country that pull people to move there, including better living conditions and hopes of better jobs.

▲ **Elmina, Ghana**
Elmina, in Ghana, is one of the many ports from which enslaved Africans were transported from Africa. Because slaves and gold were traded here, stretches of the western African coast were known as the Slave Coast and the Gold Coast.

Migration to Latin America, 1500–1800
Key

⬅ European migration	Spain and possessions
⬅ African migration	Portugal and possessions
── National or colonial border	Netherlands and possessions
⋯⋯ Traditional African border	France and possessions
African State	England and possessions

World Land Use

People around the world have many different economic structures, or ways of making a living. Land-use maps are one way to learn about these structures. The ways that people use the land in each region tell us about the main ways that people in that region make a living.

World Land Use Key

	Nomadic herding
	Hunting and gathering
	Forestry
	Livestock raising
	Commercial farming
	Subsistence farming
	Manufacturing and trade
	Little or no activity
——	National border
- - - -	Disputed border

▲ **Wheat farming in the United States**
Developed countries practice commercial farming rather than subsistence farming. Commercial farming is the production of food mainly for sale, either within the country or for export to other countries. Commercial farmers like these in Oregon often use heavy equipment to farm.

Levels of Development

Notice on the map key the term *subsistence farming*. This term means the production of food mainly for use by the farmer's own family. In less-developed countries, subsistence farming is often one of the main economic activities. In contrast, in developed countries there is little subsistence farming.

▲ **Growing barley in Ecuador**
These farmers in Ecuador use hand tools to harvest barley. They will use most of the crop they grow to feed themselves or their farm animals.

NORTH AMERICA

SOUTH AMERICA

0 miles   2,000
0 kilometers   2,000
Robinson

▲ Growing rice in Vietnam
Women in Vietnam plant rice in wet rice paddies, using the same planting methods their ancestors did.

PRACTICE YOUR GEOGRAPHY SKILLS

1 In what parts of the world is subsistence farming the main land use?

2 Locate where manufacturing and trade are the main land use. Are they found more often near areas of subsistence farming or areas of commercial farming? Why might this be so?

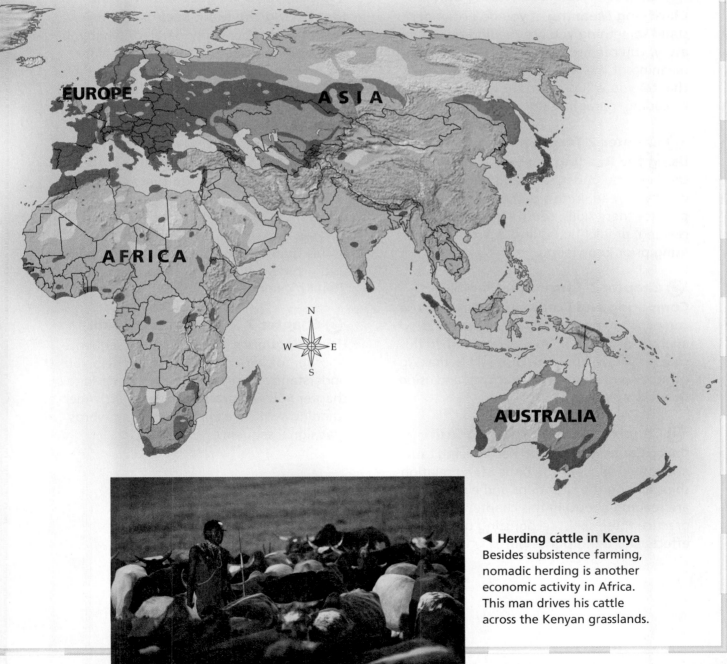

EUROPE

ASIA

AFRICA

AUSTRALIA

◀ Herding cattle in Kenya
Besides subsistence farming, nomadic herding is another economic activity in Africa. This man drives his cattle across the Kenyan grasslands.

How to Read Social Studies

 ## Target Reading Skills

The Target Reading Skills introduced on this page will help you understand the words and ideas in this book and in other social studies reading you do. Each chapter focuses on one of these reading skills. Good readers develop a bank of reading strategies, or skills. Then they draw on the particular strategies that will help them understand the text they are reading.

Chapter 1 Target Reading Skill
Clarifying Meaning If you do not understand something you are reading right away, you can use several skills to clarify the meaning of the word or idea. In this chapter you will practice these strategies: rereading, paraphrasing, and summarizing.

Chapter 2 Target Reading Skill
Using the Reading Process Previewing can help you understand and remember what you read. In this chapter you will practice these skills: setting a purpose for reading, predicting, asking questions, and using prior knowledge.

Chapter 3 Target Reading Skill
Comparing and Contrasting You can use comparison and contrast to sort out and analyze information you are reading. In this chapter you will practice these skills: making comparisons, identifying contrasts, and using signal words.

Chapter 4 Target Reading Skill
Using Cause and Effect Recognizing cause and effect will help you understand relationships among the situations and events you are reading about. In this chapter you will practice these skills: recognizing causes and effects and using signal words.

Chapter 5 Target Reading Skill
Identifying the Main Idea Since you cannot remember every detail of what you read, it is important to identify the main ideas. In this chapter you will practice these skills: identifying main ideas, identifying implied main ideas, and identifying supporting details.

Chapter 6 Target Reading Skill
Using Context Using the context of an unfamiliar word can help you understand its meaning. Context includes the words, phrases, and sentences surrounding a word. In this chapter you will practice these skills: using context clues and interpreting non-literal meanings.

Chapter 7 Target Reading Skill
Using Sequence Identifying the sequence, or order, of important events can help you understand and remember the events. In this chapter you will practice these skills: understanding sequence and recognizing words that signal sequence.

AFRICA

The name *Africa* may have come from the Latin word *aprica*, which means "sunny." In much of Africa, the sun does shine brightly. Each morning, the African sunrise awakens one eighth of the world's population, in more than fifty different countries. In the chapters that follow, you will spend the day with some of these people.

Guiding Questions

The text, photographs, maps, and charts in this book will help you discover answers to these Guiding Questions.

1. **Geography** What are the main physical features of Africa?

2. **History** How have historical events affected the cultures and nations of Africa?

3. **Culture** What features help define different African cultures?

4. **Government** What factors led to the development of different governments across Africa?

5. **Economics** What factors influence the ways in which Africans make a living?

Project Preview

You can also discover answers to the Guiding Questions by working on projects. Several project possibilities are listed on page 216 of this book.

Investigate Africa

Africa is the second-largest continent in the world after Asia. Africa's climate and physical geography are diverse, ranging from flat, arid deserts to tropical wet rain forests and high mountains. Africa also has a wide range of peoples with their own distinctive languages and cultures. It is a continent potentially rich in natural resources.

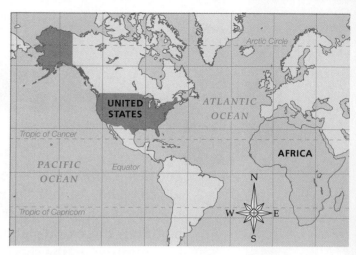

LOCATION

1 Explore Africa's Location
How would you describe Africa's location? One way would be to compare where it is to where the United States is. What ocean lies between Africa and the United States? Find the Equator. What do you know about the climate of countries near the Equator? How do you think the climates of the United States might differ from the climates of Africa?

▲ **Tanzania**
The vast, flat grasslands of the savannas support a diverse population of animals.

REGIONS

2 Estimate the Size of Africa
The United States is 3,500,000 square miles (9,064,958 square kilometers) in land area. How does Africa's size compare to that of the continental United States (all states except Alaska and Hawaii)? Measure mainland Africa at its widest point from east to west. Measure Africa from north to south. Now measure the United States the same way. How do they compare? Estimate Africa's area in square miles.

Political Africa

LOCATION

3 Predict How Location Affects Economics

When a country does not border any large body of water, it is described as being landlocked. Make a list of the African countries that are landlocked. Think about how being landlocked might limit the ability of a country to trade with other countries. How might being landlocked affect the economy of a country? How might landlocked countries trade in other ways?

▲ **Farafenni Market, Gambia**
This thriving street market is an important part of the local economy. Farmers sell their produce at such local markets, benefiting themselves and the community.

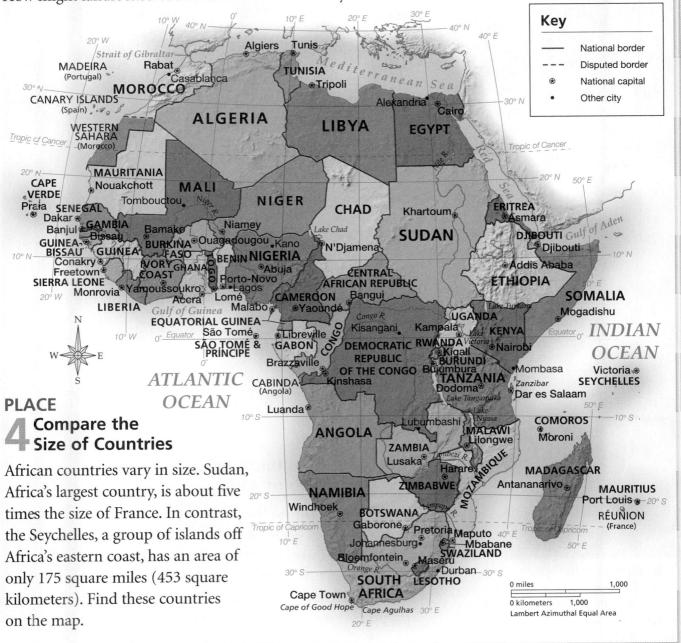

Key

——	National border
- - -	Disputed border
⊛	National capital
•	Other city

PLACE

4 Compare the Size of Countries

African countries vary in size. Sudan, Africa's largest country, is about five times the size of France. In contrast, the Seychelles, a group of islands off Africa's eastern coast, has an area of only 175 square miles (453 square kilometers). Find these countries on the map.

Physical Africa

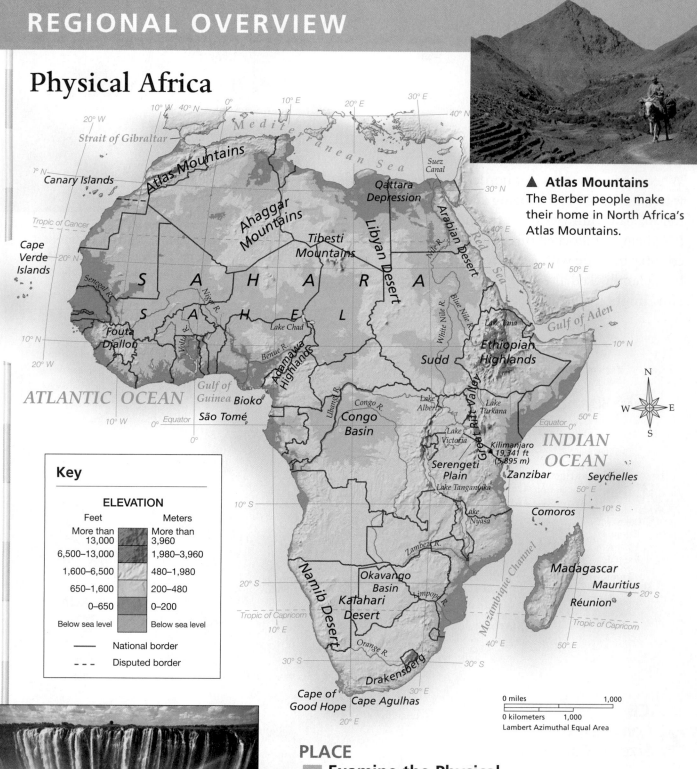

ELEVATION

Feet		Meters
More than 13,000		More than 3,960
6,500–13,000		1,980–3,960
1,600–6,500		480–1,980
650–1,600		200–480
0–650		0–200
Below sea level		Below sea level

— National border
--- Disputed border

Key

▲ **Atlas Mountains**
The Berber people make their home in North Africa's Atlas Mountains.

▲ **Victoria Falls**
The Zambezi River tumbles over Victoria Falls between Zambia and Zimbabwe in Southern Africa.

PLACE

5 Examine the Physical Features of Africa

Check the key on the physical map and you will see that some of the coastline of Africa has narrow strips of low plains. The interior is a flat plateau covered by the Sahara in the north. On the coast of Southern Africa there are many steep cliffs. Find other places where the plateau comes close to the ocean.

Africa: Land Use

▲ **Flower farming, South Africa**
People harvest "water flowers," a plant used in traditional cooking.

Mediterranean Sea

ATLANTIC
OCEAN

INDIAN
OCEAN

Key

	Nomadic herding
	Livestock raising
	Commercial farming
	Subsistence farming
	Manufacturing and trade
	Little or no activity
——	National border
- - -	Disputed border

0 miles 1,500
0 kilometers 1,500
Lambert Azimuthal Equal Area

INTERACTION

6 Investigate Natural Vegetation and Land Use

How people use the land is influenced by rainfall, temperature, the quality of the soil, landforms, politics, and many other factors. Along the Mediterranean coast, moisture from the sea makes some agriculture possible. In the vast Sahara, most people live as nomadic herders. Where on the continent is livestock raised?

PRACTICE YOUR GEOGRAPHY SKILLS

1 You are in Egypt. A river meets the sea near the country's capital. What is the name of the river?

2 Flying east from the mouth of the Zambezi River, you come to an island. What is its name, and how is land used there?

3 Now you are traveling west by ship toward the southern tip of Africa. You stop at a port near the Tropic of Capricorn. What country are you in?

▲ **Camels are still used as a means of transportation in parts of Egypt.**

Focus on Countries in Africa

Now that you've investigated the geography of Africa, take a closer look at some of the countries that make up this continent. The map shows all of the countries of Africa. The ten countries you will study in depth in the second half of this book are shown in yellow on the map.

Go Online
PHSchool.com Use Web Code **lap-5020** for the **interactive maps** on these pages.

▲ Nigeria
The Hausa-Fulani, Igbo, Yoruba, and a number of other, smaller ethnic groups make up Nigeria, where more than 200 languages are spoken. Nigeria is a major oil-producing country.

Democratic Republic of the Congo ▶
The Democratic Republic of the Congo is Africa's third-largest country. It is rich in minerals including diamonds, petroleum, cobalt, and copper.

◀ **Egypt**
Almost all of the people of Egypt live in the fertile valley of the Nile. The vast desert on either side of this river is almost completely unpopulated.

Key

—— National border

- - - Disputed border

Countries with in-depth coverage

Non-feature countries

▲ **Kenya**
Two thirds of Kenya's people live in the countryside. Many Kenyan women raise cash crops or work on plantations, while the men work in the cities.

▲ **South Africa**
South Africa, at Africa's southern tip, is bordered by oceans on three sides. It is a resource-rich country with a strong economy.

0 miles 1,000
0 kilometers 1,000
Lambert Azimuthal Equal Area

Africa: Physical Geography

Chapter Preview

This chapter will introduce you to the geography of Africa and show you how geography affects the people of the continent.

Section 1
Land and Water

Section 2
Climate and Vegetation

Section 3
Resources and Land Use

Target Reading Skill

Clarifying Meaning In this chapter you will focus on clarifying, or better understanding, the meaning of what you read. Rereading, paraphrasing, and summarizing can help you better understand sentences and passages.

▶ Elephants walk across the plains below Africa's tallest mountain, Mount Kilimanjaro.

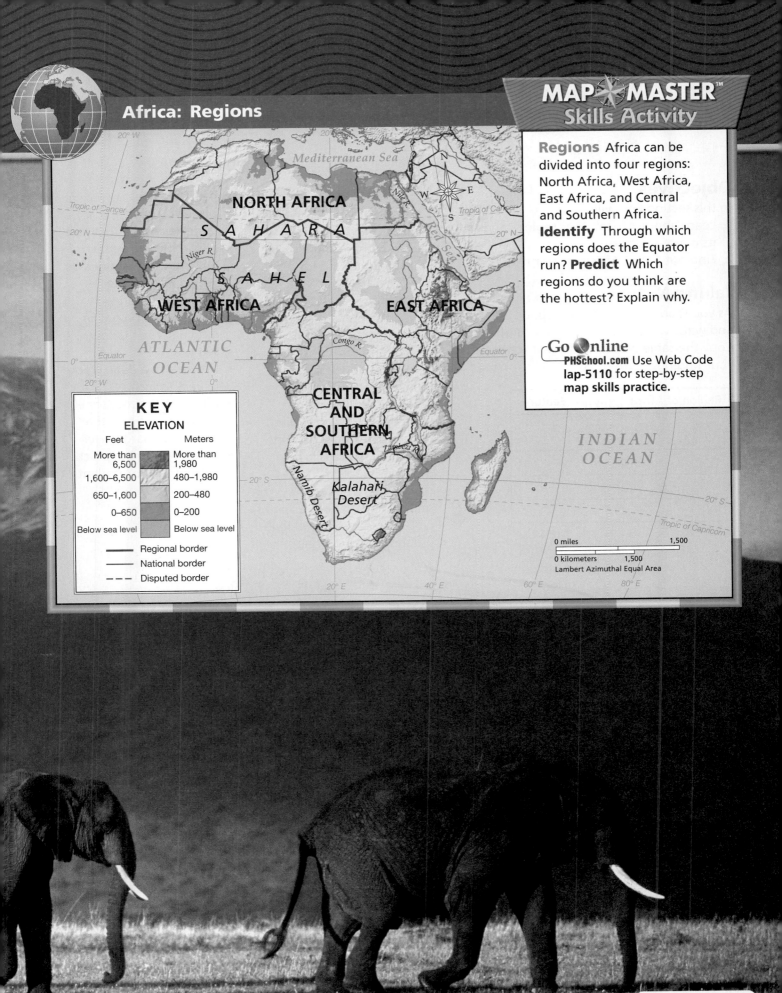

NORTH AFRICA

S A H A R A

Mediterranean Sea

Nile R.

Tropic of Cancer

Niger R.

S A H E L

WEST AFRICA

EAST AFRICA

ATLANTIC OCEAN

Congo R.

Equator

CENTRAL AND SOUTHERN AFRICA

Zambezi R.

INDIAN OCEAN

Namib Desert

Kalahari Desert

Tropic of Capricorn

Regions Africa can be divided into four regions: North Africa, West Africa, East Africa, and Central and Southern Africa. **Identify** Through which regions does the Equator run? **Predict** Which regions do you think are the hottest? Explain why.

Go Online
PHSchool.com Use Web Code lap-5110 for step-by-step map skills practice.

KEY
ELEVATION

Feet		Meters
More than 6,500		More than 1,980
1,600–6,500		480–1,980
650–1,600		200–480
0–650		0–200
Below sea level		Below sea level

——— Regional border
——— National border
– – – Disputed border

0 miles 1,500
0 kilometers 1,500
Lambert Azimuthal Equal Area

Prepare to Read

Objectives

In this section you will

1. Learn about Africa's four regions and its major landforms.
2. Find out about Africa's major rivers.

Taking Notes

As you read, look for details about the land and waterways of the four regions of Africa. Copy the table below, and use it to record your findings.

Region of Africa	Physical Features
North	• Land: • Water:

🎯 Target Reading Skill

Reread Rereading is a strategy that can help you clarify words and ideas in the text. If you do not understand a certain passage, reread it to look for connections among the words and sentences.

In the following example, you may not know what *level* means. "Much of Africa is made up of raised, mostly level areas of land. Not all of Africa is level, however. Each of Africa's four regions has mountains." If you reread, you will see that level land is land without mountains.

Key Terms

* **plateau** (pla TOH) *n.* a large, level area that rises above the surrounding land; has at least one side with a steep slope
* **elevation** (el uh VAY shun) *n.* the height of land above or below sea level
* **rift** (rift) *n.* a deep crack in Earth's surface
* **tributary** (TRIB yoo tehr ee) *n.* a river or stream that flows into a larger river
* **fertile** (FUR tul) *adj.* rich in the substances plants need to grow well

Dinosaurs like this allosaurus once lived in Africa.

Scientists believe that more than 200 million years ago, dinosaurs were able to walk from Africa to South America. They could do that because Africa and South America were connected then. Turn to page 220 of the Atlas. Find Africa on the map titled The World: Physical. As you can see, it would be impossible to walk from Africa to South America today.

How did Africa and South America become separated? At least 65 million years ago, forces on our planet's surface caused South America and Africa to move apart, forming the southern part of the Atlantic Ocean. In the process, Africa became the second-largest continent on Earth. To learn more about this vast continent, first examine the geography of Africa's regions.

Africa's Regions and Landforms

Africa includes more than 50 countries. This large continent can be divided into four regions: North Africa, West Africa, East Africa, and Central and Southern Africa. Each region contains several different climates and landforms. Turn to the map on page 9 to see the physical features of the four regions.

The Four Regions The region of North Africa is marked in places by rocky mountains. It is also home to seemingly endless stretches of the world's largest desert, the Sahara (suh HA ruh). West Africa, the continent's most populated region, consists mostly of grassland. The soil in the grassland is good for farming. The region of East Africa has many mountains and a few **plateaus,** which are large, raised areas of mostly level land. Grasslands and hills are also found there. Much of Central and Southern Africa is flat or rolling grassland. The region also has thick rain forests, mountains, and swamps. The Namib (NAH mib) Desert and the Kalahari (kah luh HAH ree) Desert are in Southern Africa.

The Plateau Continent Africa is often called the plateau continent because much of the continent is made up of raised, mostly level areas of land that drop off sharply near the sea. Much of this land has a high **elevation,** or height above or below sea level.

Mountains Not all of Africa is level, however. All of Africa's four regions have mountains. The highest are in East Africa. Mount Kilimanjaro in Tanzania is Africa's tallest mountain. It rises to a height of 19,341 feet (5,895 meters).

Rising Up From Flat Land
The Kassala Mountains in the East African country of Sudan rise up from flat land that the people farm. **Analyze Images** *Do these mountains prevent people from farming the land?*

Place The steep walls of the Great Rift Valley open out into a valley that can be 30 to 40 miles (50 to 65 kilometers) wide.

Locate Name the northernmost country and the southernmost country through which the Great Rift Valley runs.

Analyze Information What effects do you think the Great Rift Valley has on communication and travel between countries on either side of the valley?

Go Online
PHSchool.com Use Web Code **lap-5111** for step-by-step **map skills practice.**

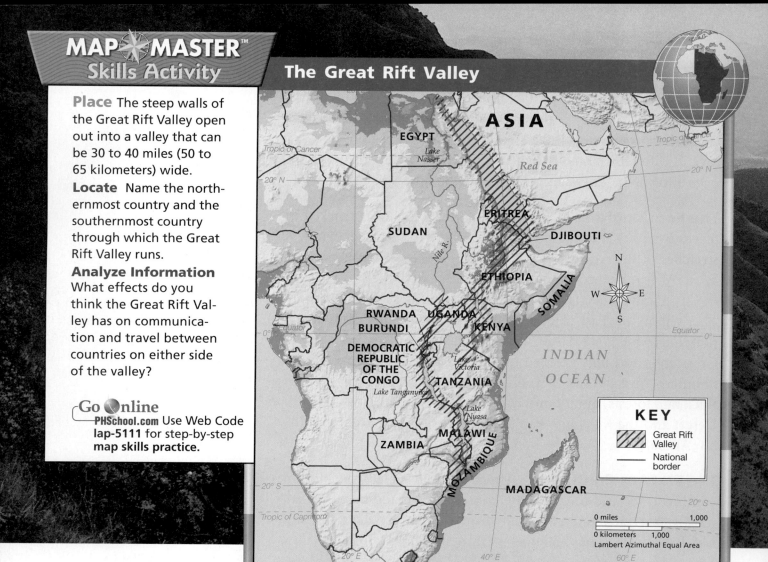

KEY
▨ Great Rift Valley
— National border

0 miles 1,000
0 kilometers 1,000
Lambert Azimuthal Equal Area

Coastal Plains Edge the Continent There is a strip of coastal plain that runs along much of Africa's coast. This land is dry and sandy in some places and marshy and moist in other places. Turn to the political map of Africa on page 3 of the Regional Overview. Find the West African country of Ghana (GAH nuh). The western edge of the coastal strip in Ghana is only about 5 miles (8 kilometers) wide. There, the coastal strip ends in a long, steep slope that rises to a plateau.

The Great Rift Valley Mount Kilimanjaro, Africa's highest peak, is located in East Africa on the edge of the Great Rift Valley. This valley was formed millions of years ago, when the continents pulled apart and left a **rift,** or deep trench. The rift that cuts through East Africa is 4,000 miles (6,400 kilometers) long. Most of Africa's major lakes are located in or near the Great Rift Valley.

✓ **Reading Check** Why is Africa called the plateau continent?

The Great Rift Valley

Africa's Rivers

Four large rivers carry water from the mountains of Africa's plateaus to the sea. They are the Nile (nyl), the Congo (KAHNG goh),
the Zambezi (zam BEE zee), and the Niger (NY jur). Turn again to
page 4 and find these rivers on the physical map of Africa. Sections of these four rivers may be used for travel. But the rivers are
broken in places by large waterfalls or steep rapids. These obstacles make it impossible for ships to sail the whole way between
Africa's interior and the sea.

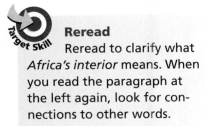

Reread
Reread to clarify what
Africa's interior means. When
you read the paragraph at
the left again, look for connections to other words.

The Nile River   The Nile is the longest river in the world. Its
length, more than 4,000 miles (6,400 kilometers), is almost twice
the length of the Mississippi River. The White Nile in Sudan and
the Blue Nile in the highlands of Ethiopia are tributaries of the
Nile. **Tributaries** are rivers and streams that flow into a larger
river. After the White Nile and Blue Nile combine to form the
Nile, the river flows north into the Mediterranean Sea.

Farming on the Banks
Farmers planted the crops shown above near the banks of the Nile River. **Summarize** *What are the benefits of farming near a river?*

Links to
Science

A River Without a Delta
A delta is a plain that forms at the mouth of a river. The Congo River's current is so strong that it does not form a delta. Instead, the river has cut a deep, wide canyon beneath the sea for a distance of about 125 miles (200 kilometers).

Farming Along the Nile   People have farmed the land surrounding the Nile for thousands of years. At one time, the Nile flooded its banks regularly. Farmers planted their crops to match the flood cycle of the river. The floods provided water for the crops and left behind a layer of silt, tiny bits of rock and dirt carried downstream by the river. Silt helps make soil **fertile,** or rich in the substances that plants need to grow well.

In the 1960s, Egypt's government built the Aswan High Dam to control the flooding of the Nile. As the water backed up behind the dam, Lake Nasser was created. Waters from the lake are channeled to water crops that grow in the desert. Water rushing through the dam produces electricity. Since the dam was built, the Nile no longer floods the land.

The Congo River   The Congo River flows through the rain forests of the Central African countries of the Congo and the Democratic Republic of the Congo. At 2,900 miles (4,677 kilometers), the Congo River is Africa's second-longest river. It is fed by hundreds of tributaries. Many farmers in this region grow yams and cassava (kuh SAH vuh), a starchy plant that is a bit like a potato. They also catch many different types of fish in the Congo River.

The Niger River   The third-longest river in Africa, the Niger, begins its journey in Guinea (GIH nee). For 2,600 miles (4,180 kilometers), the river flows north and then bends south. It provides water for farms in the river valley. Many people make their living fishing in the river.

The Zambezi River   Africa's fourth-longest river, the Zambezi, is in Southern Africa. It runs through or forms the border of six countries: Angola (ang GOH luh), Zambia (ZAM bee uh), Namibia (nuh MIB ee uh), Botswana (baht SWAH nuh), Zimbabwe (zim BAHB way), and Mozambique (moh zum BEEK). The river is 2,200 miles (3,540 kilometers) long, but boats can travel only on about 460 miles (740 kilometers) of it because of its waterfalls and rapids.

People have used the Zambezi's strong current to produce electricity. About halfway to its outlet in the Indian Ocean, the Zambezi plunges into a canyon, creating the spectacular waterfall known as Victoria Falls. Tourists from around the world visit these falls. People can sometimes see the mist and spray of Victoria Falls from as far away as 40 miles (65 kilometers).

✓ **Reading Check**   What effect has the Aswan High Dam had on Egypt and on the waters of the Nile?

Victoria Falls is located on the border between Zambia and Zimbabwe.

Section 1 Assessment

Key Terms
Review the key terms at the beginning of this section. Use each term in a sentence that explains its meaning.

Target Reading Skill
Name a word or an idea that you were able to clarify on your own by rereading. Explain it in your own words.

Comprehension and Critical Thinking
1. (a) **Identify** Name the four regions of Africa.

(b) **Compare** What physical features do all of the regions have in common?
(c) **Draw Conclusions** Why might West Africa be the continent's most populated region?
2. (a) **Describe** Describe the course traveled by each of Africa's major rivers.
(b) **Identify Effects** How do Africa's four major rivers affect the lives of its people?
(c) **Draw Inferences** How did farming on the Nile change after the Aswan High Dam was built?

Writing Activity
List several landforms and rivers in Africa that you would like to visit. Explain why you would like to visit them and what you would do on your trip.

Writing Tip Use vivid details to describe your trip. These will help support your explanation of the reasons you chose the landforms you did.

Section 2 Climate and Vegetation

Prepare to Read

Objectives

In this section you will
1. Discover the factors that influence Africa's climate.
2. Learn the characteristics of each of Africa's vegetation regions.
3. Find out how climate can affect the health of people in Africa.

Taking Notes

Copy the outline below. As you read, find details about Africa's climate and vegetation, and record them in your outline.

I. Africa's climate factors
   A. Distance from the Equator
      1.
      2.
   B.
II. Vegetation regions

Target Reading Skill

Paraphrase Paraphrasing can help you understand what you read. You paraphrase by restating what you have read in your own words.

For example, you could paraphrase the first paragraph on page 20 this way: "Africa has different kinds of vegetation in different parts of the continent. It has rain forests, savannas, and deserts."

As you read this section, paraphrase, or restate, the information following each red or blue heading.

Key Terms

- **irrigate** (IHR uh gayt) v. to supply with water through a ditch, pipe, channel, or sprinkler
- **drought** (drowt) n. a long period of little or no rain
- **oasis** (oh AY sis) n. a fertile place in a desert where there is water and vegetation
- **savanna** (suh VAN uh) n. a region of tall grasses with scattered trees
- **nomad** (NOH mad) n. a person who has no permanent, settled home and who instead moves from place to place

A home in a forest region of Uganda

If you were to travel throughout Africa, you would experience many different climates. Deserts would feel hot and dry. The highlands would feel cool and moist. In some places close to the Equator, hot weather and rainfall would occur throughout the year.

Africa's vegetation is as diverse as its climate. Forest regions are filled with trees and a great variety of plant life. Grasslands are dotted with low trees and scrub bushes. Low mountain areas support plant life, while the highest mountains are covered with snow and ice. A region's climate has a great influence on its vegetation. But what influences climate?

What Influences Climate?

Although people sometimes think of Africa as a hot place, not all parts of it are hot. That is because there are several geographic factors that influence climate. Some key factors are distance from the Equator and elevation. Nearness to large bodies of water and major landforms also affects climate.

MAP MASTER™
Skills Activity

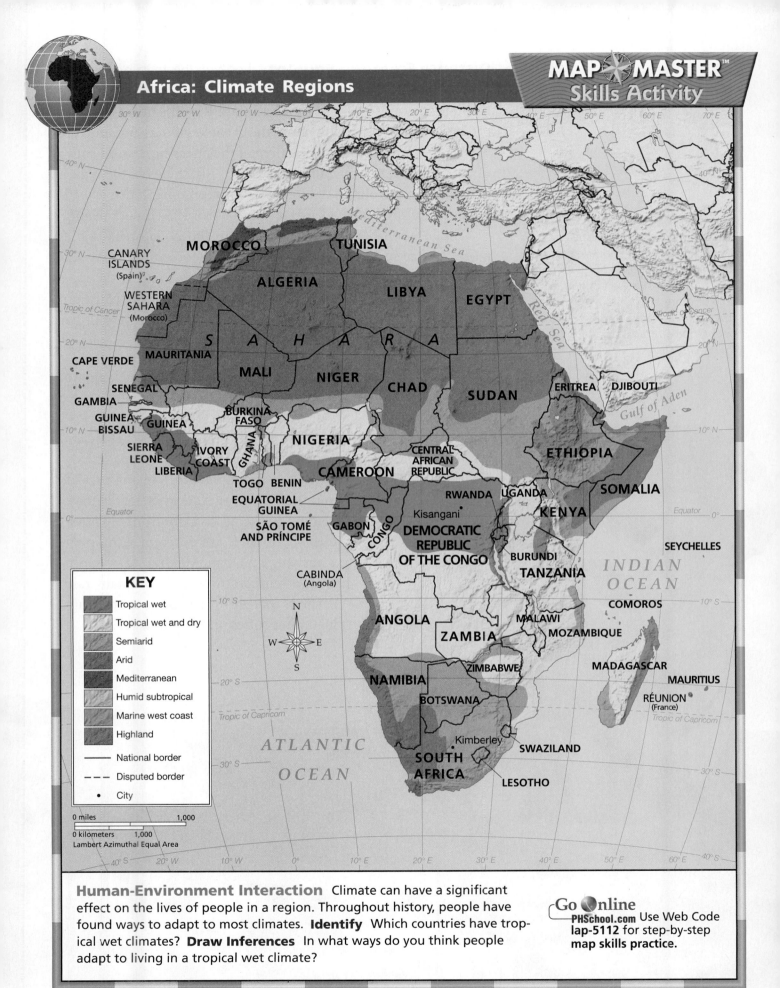

CANARY ISLANDS (Spain)

MOROCCO

TUNISIA

Mediterranean Sea

WESTERN SAHARA (Morocco)

ALGERIA

LIBYA

EGYPT

Tropic of Cancer

S A H A R A

MAURITANIA

MALI

NIGER

CHAD

SUDAN

Red Sea

Tropic of Cancer

CAPE VERDE

SENEGAL

GAMBIA

GUINEA-BISSAU

GUINEA

SIERRA LEONE

LIBERIA

IVORY COAST

GHANA

BURKINA FASO

TOGO BENIN

EQUATORIAL GUINEA

SÃO TOMÉ AND PRÍNCIPE

NIGERIA

CAMEROON

CENTRAL AFRICAN REPUBLIC

ERITREA DJIBOUTI

Gulf of Aden

ETHIOPIA

SOMALIA

RWANDA UGANDA

KENYA

Equator

CABINDA (Angola)

GABON

CONGO

Kisangani

DEMOCRATIC REPUBLIC OF THE CONGO

BURUNDI

TANZANIA

SEYCHELLES

INDIAN OCEAN

Equator

KEY

Tropical wet
Tropical wet and dry
Semiarid
Arid
Mediterranean
Humid subtropical
Marine west coast
Highland
—— National border
- - - Disputed border
• City

ANGOLA

ZAMBIA

MALAWI

MOZAMBIQUE

COMOROS

MADAGASCAR

MAURITIUS

NAMIBIA

ZIMBABWE

BOTSWANA

RÉUNION (France)

Tropic of Capricorn

ATLANTIC OCEAN

Kimberley

SOUTH AFRICA

SWAZILAND

LESOTHO

Tropic of Capricorn

0 miles 1,000
0 kilometers 1,000
Lambert Azimuthal Equal Area

N W E S

Human-Environment Interaction Climate can have a significant effect on the lives of people in a region. Throughout history, people have found ways to adapt to most climates. **Identify** Which countries have tropical wet climates? **Draw Inferences** In what ways do you think people adapt to living in a tropical wet climate?

Go Online
PHSchool.com Use Web Code
lap-5112 for step-by-step map skills practice.

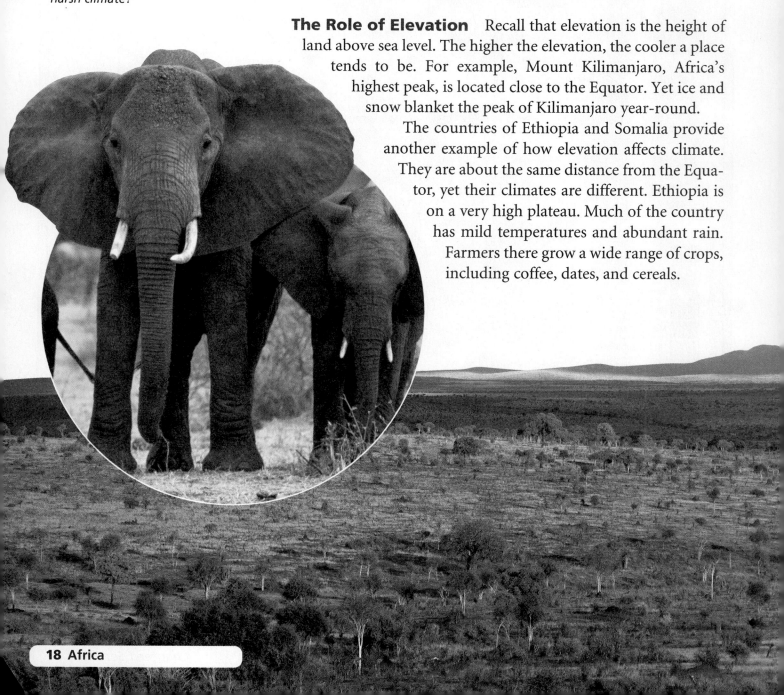

Distance From the Equator   Look at the map on page 17 titled Africa: Climate Regions. Notice that the Equator runs through the midsection of the continent. Regions near the Equator are usually hot. Now find the Tropic of Cancer and the Tropic of Capricorn, which are equal distances north and south of the Equator. As you can see, much of Africa lies in the region between these two lines of latitude. This region has a tropical climate. Therefore, much of Africa lies in a tropical climate region.

The location of a place in relation to the Equator influences more than the place's climate—it also influences the place's seasons. North of the Equator, winter and summer occur at the same time as they do in the United States and the rest of the Northern Hemisphere. South of the Equator, the seasons are reversed. For example, July in South Africa is the middle of winter.

The Role of Elevation   Recall that elevation is the height of land above sea level. The higher the elevation, the cooler a place tends to be. For example, Mount Kilimanjaro, Africa's highest peak, is located close to the Equator. Yet ice and snow blanket the peak of Kilimanjaro year-round.

The countries of Ethiopia and Somalia provide another example of how elevation affects climate. They are about the same distance from the Equator, yet their climates are different. Ethiopia is on a very high plateau. Much of the country has mild temperatures and abundant rain. Farmers there grow a wide range of crops, including coffee, dates, and cereals.

Home to Many Animals
The open grasslands of Tanzania's Tarangire National Park are home to many thousands of large animals. Elephants may be seen in herds of 500 or more at a time. **Infer** *Given that animals thrive in this environment, do you think it has a mild or a harsh climate?*

Because Ethiopia usually gets plenty of rain, many farmers there do not irrigate their crops. To **irrigate** is to supply with water through a ditch, pipe, channel, or sprinkler. Even so, the country sometimes goes through a **drought** (drowt), or a long period of little or no rain. With little water, crops and livestock are harder to raise, and food becomes scarce. Ethiopia has suffered severe droughts several times since the 1980s.

Somalia is at a much lower elevation than Ethiopia is. The Somalian climate is hot and dry. Farming is possible only near a river or in or near an oasis, where crops can be irrigated. An **oasis** is a fertile place in a desert, with water and vegetation. Fresh underground water can support life in a region that gets little rain.

Unpredictable Rainfall Rainfall varies greatly from one region of Africa to another. Along parts of the west coast, winds carry moisture from the warm ocean over the land. Rainfall there averages more than 100 inches (250 centimeters) per year. Compare that with your own height. Forty inches (100 centimeters) of rain might fall during June alone. But in parts of the Sahara in the north and the Namib Desert in the south, rain may not fall at all for several years in a row.

Farmers who live in dry regions can never be sure whether there will be enough rain for their crops. Some farmers choose to plant a variety of crops, each needing a different amount of rainfall. These farmers hope they will have at least one successful crop.

✔ **Reading Check** **How does elevation affect the climate of regions in Africa?**

Graph Skills

The city of Kimberley is located in a desert region, while the city of Kisangani is located in a tropical region. **Identify** Which city has higher temperatures throughout the year? Which city gets more total rainfall in a year? **Synthesize Information** How does location help explain the differences in temperature and in rainfall?

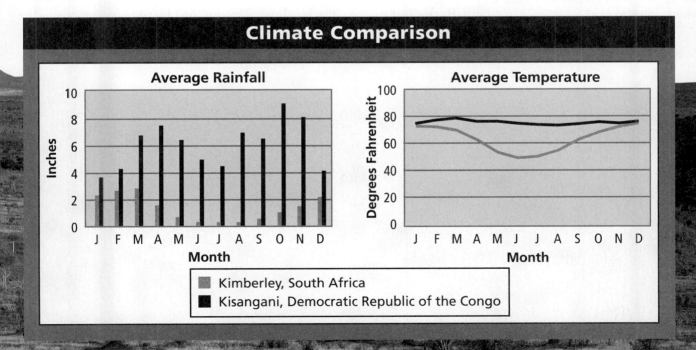

Climate Comparison

Average Rainfall

Average Temperature

■ Kimberley, South Africa
■ Kisangani, Democratic Republic of the Congo

Vegetation Regions of Africa

Africa's vegetation varies across the land. Near the Equator, there are rain forests. North and south of the rain forests lie **savanna,** a region of tall grasses with scattered trees. Beyond the savanna, many parts of northern Africa, as well as the southwestern coast of the continent, are covered in desert.

Tropical Rain Forests Tropical rain forests are regions where rain falls often throughout the year. Rain forests exist in parts of West and Central Africa, covering close to 20 percent of the continent. Rain forests are well known for supporting a great number and variety of life forms. Forest moisture provides a rich environment of trees and plants that supports animals such as gorillas and chimpanzees.

People in rain forest regions live in towns, cities, or on farms built on cleared land. Cacao (kuh KAY oh), the plant from which chocolate is made, and cassava grow well in these regions. People also fish, hunt, and harvest timber in the rain forests. However, logging threatens these forests and the many species that live in them.

Tropical Savannas The most common vegetation in Africa is tropical savanna. Tall grasses, thorny bushes, and scattered trees grow in the savanna region. It is also home to large herd animals such as lions, elephants, and zebras. Tropical savannas cover more of Africa than any other type of vegetation.

The savanna has two seasons: dry and wet. During the dry season, farming is impossible. Trees lose their leaves and rivers run dry. Farmers use this time to trade, build houses, and visit friends. In the wet season, the land turns green and farmers plant crops.

World's Largest Desert
The Sahara is famous for sand dunes like the ones shown below. However, most of the Sahara is rock plateau or gravel. Mountains exist there as well.
Apply Information *Do you think the Sahara is an easy place for people and animals to live?*

Deserts in Africa Beyond the savanna lie the deserts. The immense Sahara extends across most of North Africa. This desert covers almost as much land as the entire United States. A journalist traveling in the Sahara described what she saw:

> **[H]orizon-to-horizon vistas [views] of sand in a palette of colors, luxurious arches of palm trees swaying in the wind . . . heaving mountains of rough stone unbroken by the slightest sign of vegetation, vast expanses of sand obscured [hidden] by a veil of dust.**
>
> —*Christine Negroni,* The New York Times

The southern edge of the Sahara meets the savanna in a region called the Sahel (sah HEL), which is the Arabic word for "shore" or "border." The Sahel is very hot and dry. Each year it receives only 4 to 8 inches (10 to 20 centimeters) of rain. Small shrubs, grass, and some trees grow there.

The Namib and Kalahari deserts reach across Namibia and Botswana in Southern Africa. Large parts of the Kalahari are covered in scrub and small bushes, while the smaller Namib has more sand dunes.

The fennec fox, the world's smallest fox, lives in the Sahara.

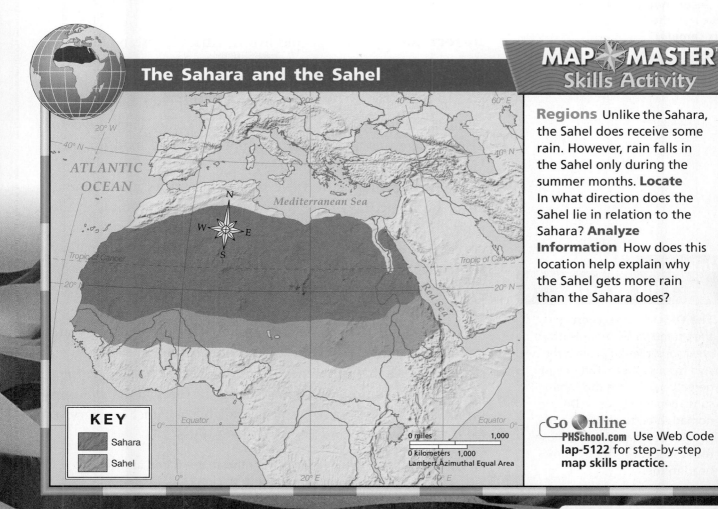

The Sahara and the Sahel

ATLANTIC OCEAN

Mediterranean Sea

Tropic of Cancer

Red Sea

Equator

KEY

Sahara

Sahel

0 miles 1,000
0 kilometers 1,000
Lambert Azimuthal Equal Area

MAP★MASTER™ Skills Activity

Regions Unlike the Sahara, the Sahel does receive some rain. However, rain falls in the Sahel only during the summer months. **Locate** In what direction does the Sahel lie in relation to the Sahara? **Analyze Information** How does this location help explain why the Sahel gets more rain than the Sahara does?

Go Online
PHSchool.com Use Web Code lap-5122 for step-by-step map skills practice.

A desert nomad traveling through the Sahara with his camel

Desert Living Few people live in Africa's deserts. Most of those who do are nomads, or people who have no permanent, settled home. Nomads move around to various places, often following the same route each year, to make their living. Most nomads are herders who also take part in trade. They travel to places where they know they can find water and food for their herds of goats, camels, or sheep.

Some nomadic herders live mainly in Africa's mountainous areas. In spring, they leave their winter grazing grounds in the foothills and head up into the mountains. Other nomadic herders live mainly in the flat desert areas. During the dry season, they set up tents near oases (oh AY seez). When the rainy season comes, they move their goats and camels to pastures that are better for grazing.

Desert nomads have herded camels for hundreds of years because the animals are well suited to desert life. They are large, strong animals that can transport goods on their backs over long distances. In addition, when a camel eats, it stores fat in the hump on its back. If no food or water is available, a camel can survive for several days by using the stored fat as food.

✓ **Reading Check** What kinds of vegetation are found in Africa's savanna regions?

Climate and Health

The climate people live in can affect their health. Throughout Africa, there are regions that present health risks to livestock and people. In rain forest regions, the moist environment is home to many disease-carrying insects. Even in the drier grasslands, disease and illness take their toll.

Sleeping Sickness   Nearly one fifth of Africa is home to the tsetse (TSET see) fly, a pest that makes raising cattle almost impossible. A tsetse bite can kill cattle and can cause a disease called sleeping sickness in humans. African researchers, together with cattle herders, have worked to find ways to control the spread of the tsetse fly. Cattle herders in Kenya are setting traps for flies. Herders in the country of Uganda catch flies by sewing into tents netting that contains poison.

Malaria   Another disease, malaria (muh LEHR ee uh), is spread to humans by the bite of an infected mosquito. Mosquitoes thrive in warm, moist climates and breed in swamps, ponds, and pools of standing water. These conditions make malaria a particular problem in parts of Africa south of the Sahara. Researchers continue to look for ways of fighting the spread of malaria. Protective clothing and insecticide can help prevent infection.

 Reading Check What is being done to control the spread of the tsetse fly?

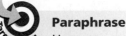 **Paraphrase**
Use your own words to paraphrase the paragraph at the left. What would be a good way to restate *take their toll*? In your own words, you might say "disease and illness cause serious problems."

 Section 2 Assessment

Key Terms
Review the key terms at the beginning of this section. Use each term in a sentence that explains its meaning.

Target Reading Skill
Read the paragraphs under Desert Living on page 22. Then, paraphrase the paragraphs in 25 words or fewer.

Comprehension and Critical Thinking
1. (a) Identify Name three factors that influence climate.

(b) Summarize Give an example of how one of these factors can influence the climate of an area.

2. (a) Name Identify the types of vegetation found in each of Africa's four regions.

(b) Identify Effects How do climate and vegetation affect the ways Africans make a living?

3. (a) Recall What health risks do people and animals in different climate regions of Africa face?

(b) Draw Conclusions In which of Africa's climate regions do you think you would be least likely to contract malaria?

Writing Activity
Choose a region of Africa that you would like to live in or visit. Write a short essay about the climate and vegetation. Include several reasons why the region is of interest to you.

 **Go Online PHSchool.com**

For: An activity on vegetation in Africa
Visit: PHSchool.com
Web Code: lad-5102

Interpreting Diagrams

Africa makes up about one fifth of all the land on Earth. It is a plateau continent with sloping coastal plains, a broad central basin, towering mountains, and a deep rift, or crack, in Earth's surface. If you could drive across the widest stretch of Africa, going 65 miles (105 kilometers) per hour and not stopping for gas or sleep, the trip would take about three full days.

An effective way to learn about Africa's landforms is by looking at a cross-sectional diagram. A cross section is what you would see if you sliced through the continent from its highest point to its lowest point and looked at it from the side.

Learn the Skill

To interpret information in any type of diagram, including a cross-sectional diagram, follow the steps below.

1 **Study the diagram.** Notice the various parts of the diagram. What can you learn from the title? What details are shown?

2 **Read the labels.** Notice the lines that lead from each label to the cross section. Make sure you understand what all the labels refer to.

3 **Summarize the information in the diagram.** Describe what you learned from studying the diagram and its labels.

Cross-Sectional Diagram of Africa South of the Sahara

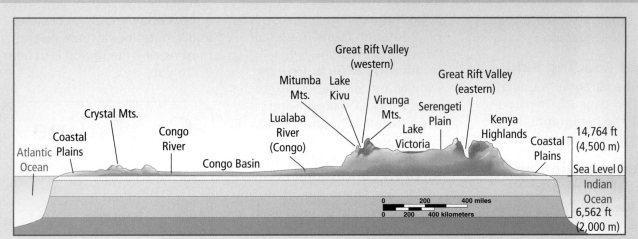

Practice the Skill

Study the cross section of Africa on page 24. Use the steps below to interpret the diagram and learn about Africa's landforms.

1 Look at the diagram. What information can you learn from the title? What kinds of landforms are shown?

2 Examine the labels. Name the mountain ranges and bodies of water shown in the diagram. Identify the elevation of at least three features in the diagram.

3 Write a sentence or two describing the ways in which the elevation of Africa changes as you travel from the Atlantic Ocean to the Indian Ocean.

Apply the Skill

Study the diagram of Earth's movements on pages M2–M3 of the MapMaster Skills Handbook. In a sentence or two, summarize the information given in the diagram.

The Virunga Mountains of East Africa

Resources and Land Use

Prepare to Read

Objectives

In this section you will

1. Discover the ways in which Africans make use of their agricultural resources.
2. Learn about the mineral and energy resources found in Africa.
3. Find out what African countries are doing to improve their economic health.

Taking Notes

As you read, look for details about Africa's natural resources. Copy the chart below, and use it to record your findings.

Land Use and Economy

Agriculture	Minerals and Energy	Economic Health
•	•	•
•	•	•

Target Reading Skill

Summarize When you summarize, you review what you have read so far. Then you state the main points in the correct order. Summarizing what you read is a good technique to help you comprehend and study. As you read, pause occasionally to summarize what you have read.

Key Terms

- **subsistence farming** (sub SIS tuns FAHR ming) *n.* raising just enough crops to support one's family
- **cash crop** (kash krahp) *n.* a crop that is raised for sale
- **economy** (ih KAHN uh mee) *n.* a system for producing, distributing, consuming, and owning goods and services
- **diversify** (duh VUR suh fy) *v.* to add variety to; to expand a country's economy by increasing the variety of goods produced

Cacao beans (inset photo) grow on trees as shown below.

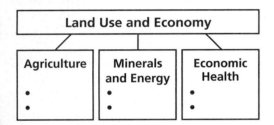

❝Here, in this load, I bear the seeds of a wonderful tree which, if cultivated in this land, will bless its sons ever-lastingly with wealth, and people far and near with health. These are the seeds of the cacao tree which I have brought with me from across the sea. . . . Would you, therefore, be kind enough to grant me a mere acre of land in this neighborhood to try my luck, and yours, and that of this country as a whole?❞

—from the play Cocoa Comes to Mampong
by Michael Francis Dei-Anang

In the excerpt above, the character Tete Quarshie (TEH tay KWAWR shee) asks for land on which to plant cacao trees in Ghana. These trees, from which cocoa and chocolate are made, originally grew only in Central and South America. As Americans, Europeans, and Africans began to trade with one another, they found that cacao trees could grow in West Africa. In the play, the people grant Tete Quarshie the land, who then raises the first crop of cacao beans in Ghana. Cacao is now one of Africa's many agricultural resources.

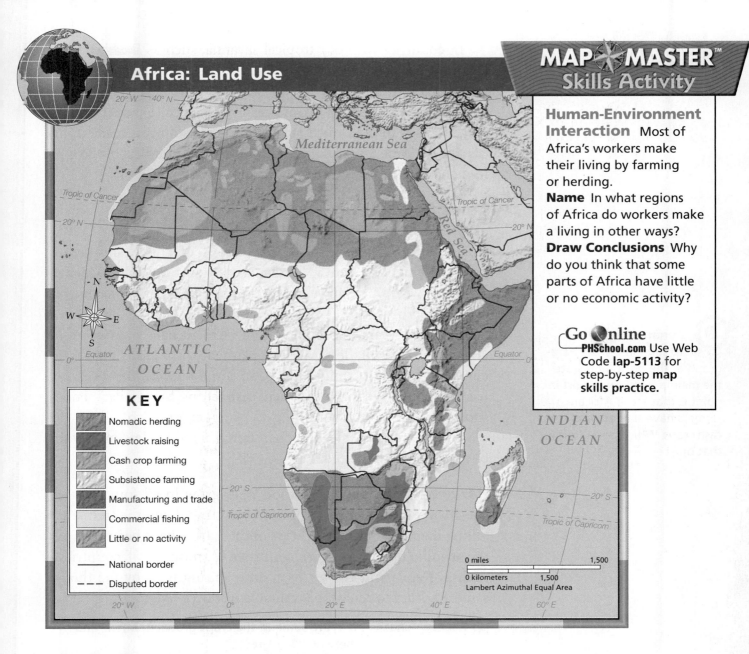

MAP★MASTER™
Skills Activity

Human-Environment Interaction Most of Africa's workers make their living by farming or herding.

Name In what regions of Africa do workers make a living in other ways?

Draw Conclusions Why do you think that some parts of Africa have little or no economic activity?

Go Online
PHSchool.com Use Web Code lap-5113 for step-by-step **map skills practice.**

KEY

- Nomadic herding
- Livestock raising
- Cash crop farming
- Subsistence farming
- Manufacturing and trade
- Commercial fishing
- Little or no activity

—— National border
--- Disputed border

0 miles 1,500
0 kilometers 1,500
Lambert Azimuthal Equal Area

Agricultural Resources

Most Africans are farmers. Some of these farmers live in areas with fertile soil and much rain. But most live on land that is difficult to farm because of poor soil or too little rain. Others lack enough land or tools to make a good living.

Farming to Live On the map above, you can see how much of Africa's land is used for subsistence farming, or raising just enough crops to support one's family. Subsistence farmers may sell or trade a few crops for other items they need.

In North African countries such as Morocco, subsistence farmers raise barley and wheat. They also irrigate fields to grow fruits and vegetables. Farms at Saharan oases in Egypt produce dates and small crops of barley and wheat.

In countries with dry tropical savanna, such as Burkina Faso (bur KEE nuh FAH soh) and Niger, subsistence farmers grow grains. In regions with more rainfall, farmers also grow vegetables, fruits, and root crops such as yams and cassava. Tapioca (tap ee OH kuh), which is used in the United States to make pudding, is made from cassava. In West Africa, corn and rice are important crops. People in many of Africa's cultures fish or raise goats or poultry.

Crops for Sale In all regions of Africa, farmers grow **cash crops,** or crops that are raised for sale. Farmers in Ivory Coast, Ghana, and Cameroon grow cash crops of coffee and cacao beans. Farmers in Kenya, Tanzania (tan zuh NEE uh), Malawi (MAH lah wee), Zimbabwe, and Mozambique grow tea as one of their cash crops.

In recent years, more and more farmers have planted cash crops. As a result, less land is planted with crops that can completely meet a family's needs. In some regions, this practice has led to food shortages when cash crops have failed. Food shortages can also occur when the market prices of coffee or other cash crops fall steeply. Then families receive less money to buy the things they need.

Harvesting Trees Hardwood trees grow in all four regions of Africa. People can earn money by cutting down the trees and selling them. Thousands of acres of these trees have been cut and the wood shipped to other countries. A number of countries, such as Kenya and Ivory Coast, are planting trees by the thousands in order to renew this valuable resource.

✓ **Reading Check** What are some of the crops grown in Africa, and where are they grown?

Summarize
To summarize the paragraph at the right, first state the main points. An important point is that more African farmers have started to plant cash crops. Which point follows that one?

Target Skill

Replanting the Forest
Thousands of Kenyan women have responded to the cutting down of trees in their country. Like the women shown here, they have prepared millions of young trees for local families to plant. **Predict** *How easy do you think it will be for people in Kenya to replace all the cut trees?*

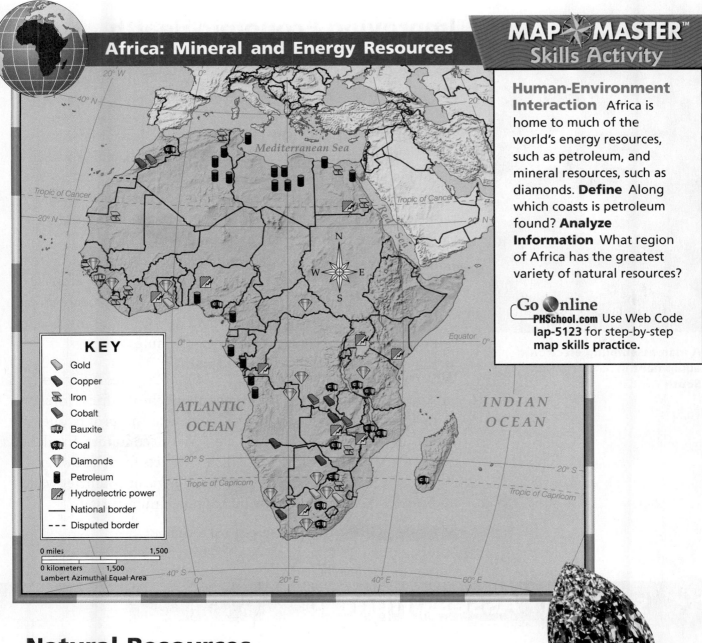

Africa: Mineral and Energy Resources

MAP★MASTER™ Skills Activity

Human-Environment Interaction Africa is home to much of the world's energy resources, such as petroleum, and mineral resources, such as diamonds. **Define** Along which coasts is petroleum found? **Analyze Information** What region of Africa has the greatest variety of natural resources?

Go Online
PHSchool.com Use Web Code lap-5123 for step-by-step map skills practice.

KEY

- Gold
- Copper
- Iron
- Cobalt
- Bauxite
- Coal
- Diamonds
- Petroleum
- Hydroelectric power
- — National border
- - - - Disputed border

0 miles 1,500
0 kilometers 1,500
Lambert Azimuthal Equal Area

Natural Resources

Each African country has its own economy. An **economy** is a system for producing, distributing, consuming, and owning goods and services. You have read that farming is an important part of many African economies. The same is true of mining. Look at the map above. Notice how many countries conduct mining operations.

Parts of Africa are rich in mineral resources. Some African countries have large amounts of petroleum, which is used to make oil and gasoline. Major oil producers include Libya and Algeria in North Africa, and Nigeria, Cameroon, Gabon, and Angola along the west coast of Africa. Ghana is a leading exporter of gold. Other mineral resources from Africa include copper, silver, uranium, titanium, and diamonds.

Diamonds that have just been mined (bottom photo) are not nearly as dazzling as ones that have been cut (top photo).

✓ **Reading Check** How is petroleum used?

A man assembling electronic equipment in Johannesburg, South Africa

Improving Economic Health

As you have read, most of Africa's workers are farmers. When an economy of a nation is dependent on one kind of industry, such as farming, it is called a specialized economy.

Strengthening Economies In Africa, economic success relies on farming regions receiving enough rainfall, and crops selling at high enough prices. For that reason, African countries are trying to diversify (duh VUR suh fy) their economies. To **diversify** means to add variety. These countries are working to produce a variety of crops, raw materials, and manufactured goods.

In general, a diverse economy is more flexible than a specialized economy is. For example, suppose a country's major cash crop fails or world prices for one of its major mineral exports suddenly drop. A country with a diverse economy would not be hurt as much as a country that depends only on farming or mining.

Where Does the Money Go? Mining requires many workers and costly equipment. Throughout much of Africa, foreign companies mine African resources and take the profits out of Africa. This system does little to help African economies. In addition, Africa has few factories in which products from its own raw materials can be made. Therefore, many African countries want to diversify their economies by including manufacturing.

✓ **Reading Check** What is a specialized economy?

Section 3 Assessment

Key Terms

Review the key terms at the beginning of this section. Use each term in a sentence that explains its meaning.

Target Reading Skill

Reread the paragraphs under Improving Economic Health. Then write a summary of them. Include at least two main points.

Comprehension and Critical Thinking

1. (a) Recall What makes most land Africans live on hard to farm?

(b) Compare and Contrast Compare subsistence farming with farming to raise cash crops. How are they similar? How are they different?

2. (a) Identify What are some of the important natural resources found in Africa?

(b) Draw Conclusions What do you think happens to most of Africa's mineral resources after they are mined?

3. (a) Recall What kind of work is done by most Africans?

(b) Predict In what ways could African countries benefit from diversifying their economies?

Writing Activity

List some of Africa's natural resources that you and your family use. Which resource would you miss most if you did not have it? Write a paragraph explaining why.

For: An activity on natural resources in Africa
Visit: PHSchool.com
Web Code: lad-5103

Review and Assessment

◆ Chapter Summary

Section 1: Land and Water

- Africa can be divided into four regions: North, West, East, and Central and Southern. Africa's major landforms include plateaus, mountains, coastal plains, and a rift valley.
- Africa's four major rivers are the Nile, the Congo, the Zambezi, and the Niger.

Section 2: Climate and Vegetation

- Distance from the Equator and elevation are both factors that influence climate.
- Africa's vegetation regions include tropical rain forests, tropical savannas, and deserts.
- Disease-carrying insects thrive in some of Africa's climate regions, threatening the health of the people who live there.

Section 3: Resources and Land Use

- Africa's agricultural resources are used for subsistence farming and cash crops.
- Natural resources, such as minerals, are an important part of African economies.
- African countries are working to improve their economic health by diversifying their specialized economies.

Taka Mountains, Sudan

◆ Key Terms

Choose the key term from the list that best completes each sentence.

1. _____ is the height of land above or below sea level.

2. A(n) _____ is a deep crack in the surface of Earth.

3. A(n) _____ flows into a river.

4. People who practice _____ raise just enough crops to support their families.

5. A(n) _____ is a region of tall grasses with scattered trees.

6. In areas that receive plenty of rain, many farmers do not need to _____ their crops.

7. A nomad traveling through the Sahara would probably visit a(n) _____ for water.

8. A(n) _____ is a system for producing, distributing, consuming, and owning goods and services.

9. To _____ is to add variety.

10. A period of little or no rainfall is a(n) _____.

Key Terms
plateau
elevation
drought
rift
fertile
tributary
irrigate
oasis
savanna
nomad
subsistence farming
cash crop
economy
diversify

Review and Assessment (continued)

◆ Comprehension and Critical Thinking

11. (a) Describe Describe the physical features of each of the major rivers in Africa.
(b) Identify Cause and Effect How did the regular flooding of the Nile in the past affect farmers in the Nile Valley? How did the building of the Aswan High Dam change life for farmers?

12. (a) Recall What do elevation and distance from the Equator have to do with climate?
(b) Explain Why are some parts of Africa cold even though they are near the Equator?
(c) Compare and Contrast Compare the climates of Ethiopia and Somalia. Explain why their climates are similar or different.

13. (a) Locate Where in Africa can you find tropical savannas? Tropical rain forests? Deserts?
(b) Describe What characterizes the climate and plant life of each vegetation region?
(c) Apply Information Choose one of these regions and describe how the people who live there adapt to their environment. Give examples.

14. (a) Name List three cash crops raised in Africa.
(b) Identify Causes Why is there little or no farming in much of North Africa and parts of Southern Africa?
(c) Summarize Why and in what ways are many African nations trying to strengthen and diversify their economies?

◆ Skills Practice

Interpreting Diagrams You have learned how to interpret diagrams in this chapter's Skills for Life activity. You have also learned how to summarize information found in diagrams.

Review the steps you followed to learn this skill. Then turn to the diagram of Earth's longitude on page M5 of the MapMaster Skills Handbook. Identify and summarize the main ideas in the diagram.

◆ Writing Activity: Math

Make a bar graph that shows the lengths of rivers in Africa. Include the four rivers mentioned in the chapter as well as at least three others that you research on your own. Then write a short paragraph comparing the lengths of the various rivers.

MAP MASTER™ Skills Activity

Africa

Place Location For each place listed, write the letter from the map that shows its location.

1. Nile River
2. Congo River
3. Sahara
4. Namib Desert
5. Zambezi River
6. Kalahari Desert
7. Niger River
8. Great Rift Valley

Go Online
PHSchool.com Use Web Code lap-5120 for an interactive map.

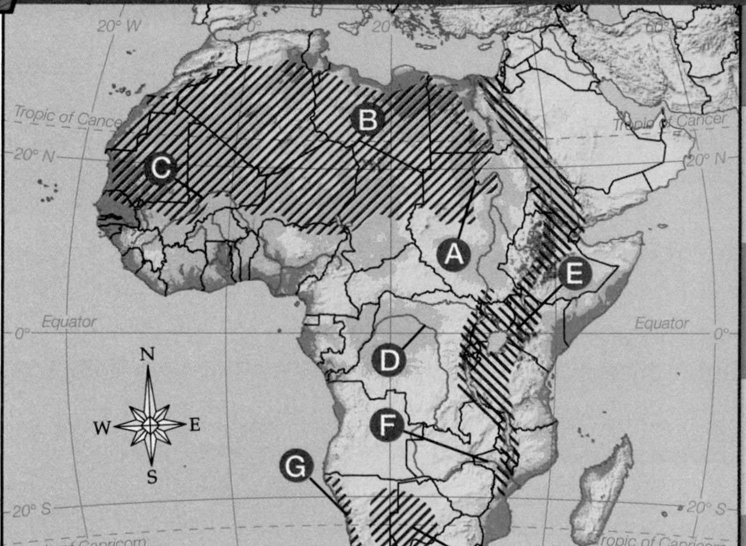

Standardized Test Prep

Test-Taking Tips

Some questions on standardized tests ask you to analyze parts of maps. Study the map key below. Then follow the tips to answer the sample question.

KEY

- Nomadic herding
- Livestock raising
- Commercial farming
- Subsistence farming
- Manufacturing and trade
- Little or no activity

TIP On a map key, the color column lines up with the data in the information column. To find the information you need, move from a given color to the data on the right.

Pick the letter that best answers the question.

On a land-use map, Angola is colored mostly yellow with a small amount of light green. Using the key at the left, you can determine that the people of Angola

A make a great deal of money.

B use the land mainly to support themselves.

C export many products.

D use their land in many different ways.

TIP Restate the question in your own words to make sure you understand it: *What conclusion can you draw from the map key about the people of Angola and their land?*

Think It Through Yellow on the map stands for subsistence farming. Light green stands for commercial farming. Subsistence farmers grow just enough food to feed and support their families. Since most of Angola is colored yellow, you can rule out A and D. Commercial farmers may raise their crops for export. However, since most of Angola is yellow, you can rule out C also. The correct answer is B.

Practice Questions

Use the tips above and other tips in this book to help you answer the following questions.

1. Most of North Africa is along the border of the
   - **A** Mediterranean Sea.
   - **B** Indian Ocean.
   - **C** Atlantic Ocean.
   - **D** Red Sea.

2. Areas that are higher in elevation
   - **A** tend to be closer to the Equator.
   - **B** tend to be cooler than places lower in elevation.
   - **C** have very mild climates.
   - **D** have little or no rainfall.

3. African economies
   - **A** are based largely on manufacturing.
   - **B** could benefit from increased diversification.
   - **C** rely solely on exports.
   - **D** are usually dependent on a wide variety of industries.

Study the map key below, and then answer the question that follows.

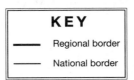

KEY

—— Regional border

—— National border

4. The boundaries of Egypt are marked by black and red lines. Using the key, you can conclude that
   - **A** Egypt is part of two regions of Africa.
   - **B** Egypt borders other nations of Africa but not other regions.
   - **C** Egypt borders other regions of Africa but not other nations.
   - **D** Egypt borders other regions and nations.

Go Online
PHSchool.com

Use Web Code **laa-5100** for **Chapter 1** self-test.

Chapter 2

Africa: Shaped by Its History

Chapter Preview

This chapter will introduce you to the history of Africa and help you understand how historical events have affected people throughout the region.

Target Reading Skill

Reading Process   In this chapter you will focus on processes that help you understand and remember what you read. Setting a purpose, predicting, asking questions, and using prior knowledge are all processes that will help you learn as you read.

▶ This ancient Egyptian mural, painted on an interior wall of a tomb, is more than 3,000 years old.

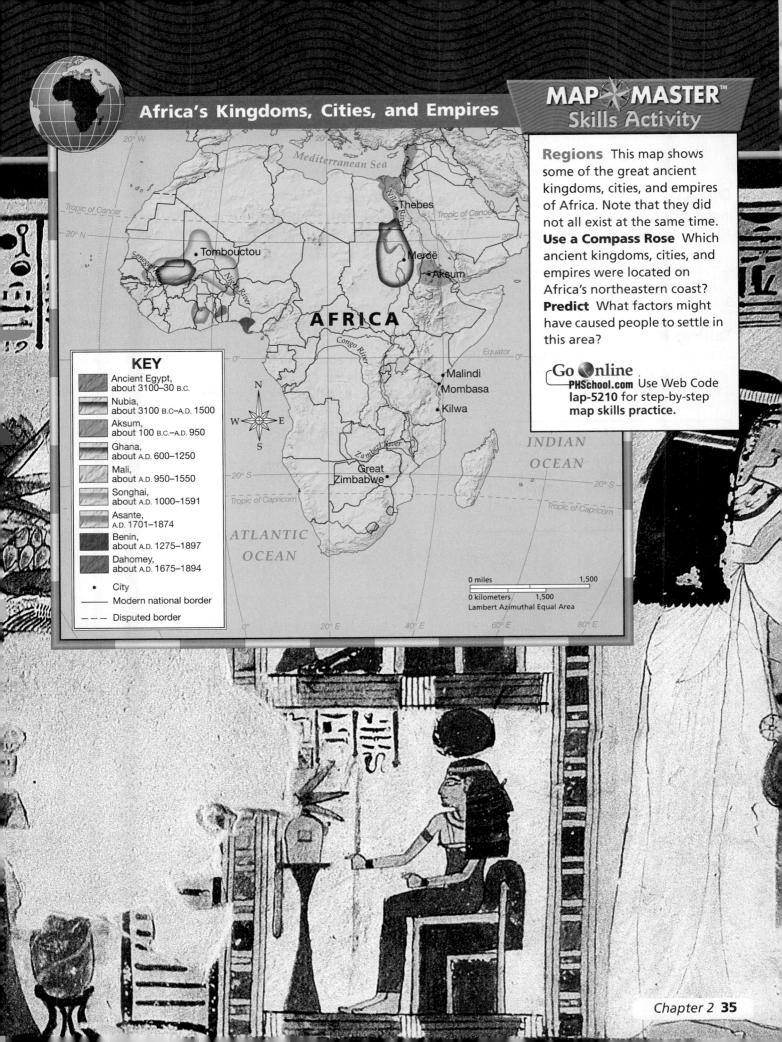

Africa's Kingdoms, Cities, and Empires

MAP MASTER™
Skills Activity

Mediterranean Sea

Thebes
Meroë
Aksum

Tombouctou

AFRICA

Congo River

Equator

Malindi
Mombasa
Kilwa

Great
Zimbabwe

INDIAN
OCEAN

ATLANTIC
OCEAN

KEY

- Ancient Egypt, about 3100–30 B.C.
- Nubia, about 3100 B.C.–A.D. 1500
- Aksum, about 100 B.C.–A.D. 950
- Ghana, about A.D. 600–1250
- Mali, about A.D. 950–1550
- Songhai, about A.D. 1000–1591
- Asante, A.D. 1701–1874
- Benin, about A.D. 1275–1897
- Dahomey, about A.D. 1675–1894
- • City
- — Modern national border
- – – – Disputed border

0 miles 1,500
0 kilometers 1,500
Lambert Azimuthal Equal Area

Regions This map shows some of the great ancient kingdoms, cities, and empires of Africa. Note that they did not all exist at the same time. **Use a Compass Rose** Which ancient kingdoms, cities, and empires were located on Africa's northeastern coast? **Predict** What factors might have caused people to settle in this area?

Go Online
PHSchool.com Use Web Code lap-5210 for step-by-step map skills practice.

African Beginnings

Prepare to Read

Objectives

In this section you will

1. Examine the ways in which the survival skills of early Africans changed over time.
2. Find out about early civilizations that arose along the Nile River.
3. Learn about the Bantu migrations.

Taking Notes

As you read, look for details about Africa's first people. Copy the chart below, and use it to record your findings.

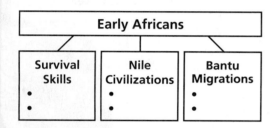

Target Reading Skill

Set a Purpose for Reading
When you set a purpose for reading, you give yourself a focus. Before you read this section, look at the headings and illustrations to see what the section is about. Then set a purpose for reading this section. Your purpose might be to learn about the people who lived in Africa long ago. Finally, read to meet your purpose.

Key Terms

- **domesticate** (duh MES tih kayt) *v.* to adapt wild plants or animals and breed them for human use
- **civilization** (sih vuh luh ZAY shun) *n.* a society that has cities, a central government, and social classes and that usually has writing, art, and architecture
- **migrate** (MY grayt) *v.* to move from one place to settle in another
- **ethnic group** (ETH nik groop) *n.* a group of people who share the same ancestors, culture, language, or religion

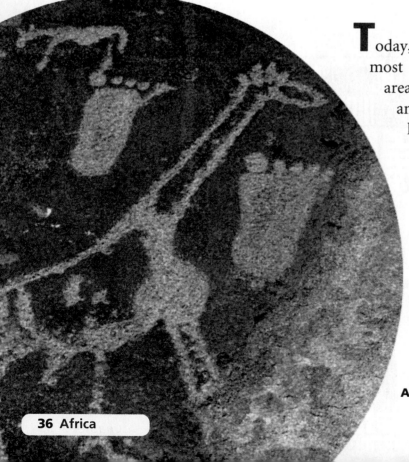

Today, the dry sands and rocks of the Sahara cover most of North Africa. But 10,000 years ago, this area was wet enough to support many people and animals. Scientists think Africa's first farmers lived in what is now the Sahara. Ancient rock paintings tell their story.

The history of humans in Africa goes back even further in time than the history of those early farmers. Scientists believe that our early human ancestors lived in East Africa at least 2 million years ago. Today, scientists study the stone tools and bones that these ancestors left behind. By doing so, they learn about the ways our early human ancestors found to survive.

Ancient cave painting from Namibia

Changing Survival Skills

What skills did our early human ancestors need to survive? Like people today, they needed to find food, water, and shelter to live. Survival skills changed and developed over the course of many thousands of years.

Hunting and Gathering Our early human ancestors were hunter-gatherers. A hunter-gatherer is someone who hunts animals and gathers food in the wild to survive. Hunter-gatherers hunted animals to use the meat for food and the hides and fur for clothing and shelter. They ate foods such as fruits, nuts, and roots. They made tools out of wood, animal bones, and eventually stone. The first use of stone tools marks the beginning of a time period scientists call the Stone Age.

The stone tools made by our early human ancestors worked very well. The scientist Louis Leakey found some of the first evidence of human ancestors in East Africa. He also taught himself how to make and use their tools. Using a two-inch, 25,000-year-old stone knife, Leakey could skin and cut up a gazelle in just 20 minutes.

Studying Early Human Ancestors
This stone tool (above) was made by one of our early human ancestors. For more than 30 years, Louis Leakey studied finds like this one at Olduvai Gorge (left) in Tanzania. His family (below) also studied them. **Analyze Images** *Do you find it easy or hard to tell this stone tool from an ordinary stone?*

Set a Purpose
What purpose did you set for the section? Has the text you have read so far helped you toward achieving this purpose? If not, set a new purpose for the rest of the section.

African Farmers Today
In African communities that practice agriculture today, women play a variety of roles. Here, Central African women carry firewood to their homes. **Predict** *What activities are essential to a successful agricultural community?*

Farming and Herding Between 10,000 and 6,000 years ago, some hunter-gatherers began to farm and to herd animals. As you read earlier, farming in Africa probably began in North Africa, when the area that is now the Sahara offered more water than is available there today. The first farmers probably planted wild grains such as barley. At first, gatherers just protected the areas where these grains grew best. Then they began to save some seeds to plant for the next year's crop.

Later, people began to **domesticate** plants, or adapt them for their own use. They threw away seeds from weaker plants and saved seeds from stronger ones. People also domesticated certain wild animals by taming and breeding them.

Early Settlements Domesticating plants and animals meant people could have better control over their food supply. They did not have to travel to places where grains were already growing. Instead, they planted the crops they wanted. As a result, they could settle in one place. Most early farmers settled on fertile land near a water supply. Some communities produced a food surplus, or more than what was needed. Surpluses allowed some people in the community to do work other than farming.

✓ **Reading Check** What was the Stone Age?

Civilizations on the Nile

Over a period of hundreds of thousands of years, some Stone Age groups became civilizations. A **civilization** is a society with cities, a government, and social classes. A social class is a group that is made up of people with similar backgrounds, wealth, and ways of living. Social classes form when people do different jobs. The types of jobs people do determine whether they are rich, poor, or in the middle. Civilizations also usually have architecture, writing, and art. A few thousand years ago, two important African civilizations—Egypt and Nubia—arose along the Nile River.

Egypt Each summer, the Nile River used to flood its banks. The flooding waters would cover the ground with a layer of fertile silt that was ideal for farming because it enriched the soil. Around 5000 B.C., people began farming along the river's banks. They settled in scattered villages. Over many years, these villages grew into the civilization of ancient Egypt.

Ancient Egypt was ruled by kings and queens. The kings of Egypt were called pharaohs (FEHR ohz). The people believed that their pharaohs were also gods. When kings and queens died, they were buried in tombs. Some of the tombs were built as large pyramids. People painted murals and picture-writing symbols called hieroglyphs (HY ur oh glifs) on the inner walls of the tombs. The ancient Egyptians became skilled in papermaking, architecture, medicine, and astronomy.

Nubia In about 6000 B.C., settled hunting and fishing communities began to arise along the Nile south of Egypt. About 1,000 years later, these communities began farming. This area was called Nubia. Scientists believe the formation of Nubian kingdoms may have started around 3100 B.C.

One of the greatest Nubian kingdoms was centered in the city of Napata. Around 724 B.C., the Nubians of Napata conquered Egypt. Nubians ruled Egypt for about 60 years. A later Nubian kingdom was based farther south, in the city of Meroë (MEHR oh ee). Meroë began to weaken in the A.D. 200s. It was finally conquered in A.D. 350 by invading forces from the Ethiopian kingdom of Aksum (AHK soom).

Leftover From Ancient Times
The Nubian mural (top) was painted inside a tomb more than 3,000 years ago. The pair of Egyptian leather sandals (above), which are similar to the ones shown in the mural, are more than 5,000 years old. **Infer** *What kind of information can objects like these teach us about ancient civilizations?*

✓ **Reading Check** What are social classes, and how are they formed?

Kingdoms, City-States, and Empires

Prepare to Read

Objectives

In this section you will
1. Learn how trade affected the development of early East African civilizations.
2. Examine the forces that shaped the history of the North African trading powers.
3. Find out how West African kingdoms gained wealth and power.

Taking Notes

As you read, look for details about important African kingdoms and city-states. Copy the table below, and use it to record your notes.

Early African Civilizations		
Kingdom or City-State	Location	Historical Events

Target Reading Skill

Predict Making predictions before you read helps you set a purpose for reading and remember what you read. First, preview the section by looking at the headings. Then note illustrations or anything else that stands out. Finally, predict what might be discussed in the text. For example, after previewing this section, you might predict that the text will explain the history of trade in Africa. As you read, compare what you read to your prediction.

Key Terms

- **Swahili** (swah HEE lee) n. a Bantu language spoken in much of East Africa; also an ethnic group
- **city-state** (SIH tee stayt) n. a city that is also an independent state, with its own traditions, government, and laws
- **pilgrimage** (PIL gruh mij) n. a religious journey
- **Tombouctou** (tohm book TOO) n. a city in Mali near the Niger River; also spelled *Timbuktu*

Aksum was the first African kingdom to make coins for trade.

In the decades before A.D. 100, a Greek writer made a list of goods for sale in the markets of Adulis, East Africa. The list included the following:

> **❝Cloth made in Egypt . . . many articles of flint glass . . . and brass, which is used for ornament and in cut pieces instead of coin; sheets of soft copper, used for cooking utensils and cut up for bracelets and anklets for the women; iron, which is made into spears used against the elephants and other wild beasts, and in their wars.❞**
>
> —*anonymous Greek trader*

Adulis was a bustling trade center along the Red Sea. It was also the main port of the wealthy and powerful kingdom of Aksum.

East African Trading Civilizations

Early East African civilizations grew strong from trade. Turn to the map titled Africa: Regions on page 9. Notice that the boundaries of East Africa include the Red Sea and the Indian Ocean. East Africa's early trading civilizations developed on or near a coastline, providing access to important markets in Arabia, India, and East Asia.

Aksum The kingdom of Aksum was located in East Africa, where the present-day countries of Ethiopia and Eritrea lie. Around 1000 B.C., African and Arab traders began settling along the west coast of the Red Sea. They were the ancestors of the people of Aksum. Over time, Aksum came to control trade in the Red Sea area. By the A.D. 200s, the kingdom controlled a trade network that stretched from the Mediterranean Sea to India.

Ideas, as well as goods, traveled along trade routes. In the A.D. 300s, many people in Aksum became Christian as news about the religion spread. Aksum became a center of the early Ethiopian Christian Church. During the A.D. 600s, Aksum began to decline as Arabs took control of much of the region's trade.

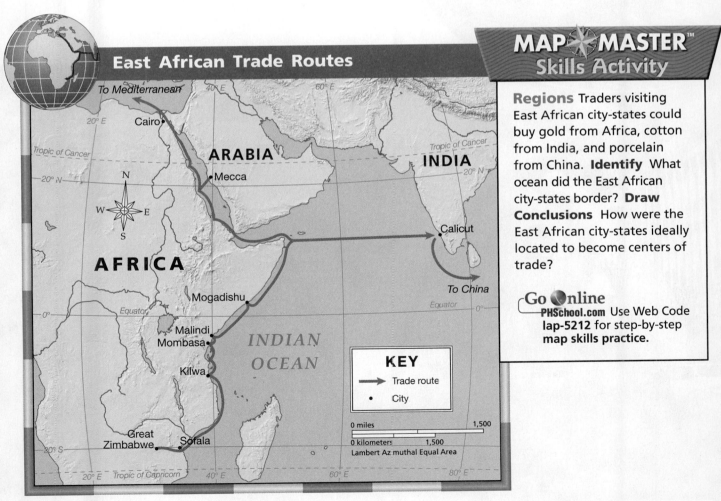

East African Trade Routes

KEY
→ Trade route
• City

0 miles — 1,500
0 kilometers — 1,500
Lambert Az muthal Equal Area

MAP MASTER™ Skills Activity

Regions Traders visiting East African city-states could buy gold from Africa, cotton from India, and porcelain from China. **Identify** What ocean did the East African city-states border? **Draw Conclusions** How were the East African city-states ideally located to become centers of trade?

Go Online
PHSchool.com Use Web Code lap-5212 for step-by-step map skills practice.

Cities of Trade Around the time that Aksum declined, trading cities arose along East Africa's coast. Traders from these cities used seasonal winds to sail northeast to India and China. The traders carried animal skins, ivory, and gold and other metals. When the winds changed direction, the traders sailed back. They brought many goods, including cotton, silk, and porcelain.

Trade affected the culture of coastal East Africa. Some of the traders who visited the area or settled in it were Muslim. They introduced the religion of Islam to East Africa. As well, a new language, called Swahili (swah HEE lee), developed in the area. Swahili is a Bantu language that includes some Arab words. Today, it is the most widely spoken Bantu language in Africa.

Rise of City-States Some East African trading cities grew into powerful city-states. A **city-state** is a city that has its own traditions, government, and laws. It is both a city and an independent state. City-states often control much of the surrounding land. Among the greatest of the East African city-states were Malindi (muh LIN dee), Mombasa (mahm BAH suh), Great Zimbabwe (grayt zim BAHB way), and Kilwa (KEEL wah).

Kilwa Ibn Battutah (IB un bat TOO tah) was a Muslim from North Africa who became famous for traveling to and writing about many countries. He visited Kilwa in 1331. He had seen great cities in China, India, and West Africa. Ibn Battutah wrote that Kilwa was "one of the most beautiful and best-constructed towns in the world." In Kilwa, people lived in three- and four-story houses made of stone and sea coral.

Kilwa and other East African city-states grew rich from trade and taxes. Traders had to pay huge taxes on goods they brought into the city. "Any merchant who wished to enter the city paid for every five hundred pieces of cloth, no matter what the quality, one gold [piece] as entrance duty," reported one visitor. "After this, the king took two thirds of all the merchandise, leaving the trader one third."

In the early 1500s, Kilwa and the other East African city-states were conquered and destroyed by the European country of Portugal. The Portuguese wanted to build their own trading empire.

Southern and East African Trade Ties Inland and south from the East African city-states, another great trading civilization developed. Great Zimbabwe was located near the bend of the Limpopo (lim POH poh) River in Southern Africa. It was connected to the trade civilizations of East Africa through a trade network that extended to the coast of the Indian Ocean. Great Zimbabwe reached the peak of its power in about the year 1300. At one time, thousands of people lived in the gigantic stone buildings that covered the area. Today, ruins of Great Zimbabwe remain, including city walls, a fortress, and homes.

Many tall walls of Great Zimbabwe still stand today.

✓ **Reading Check** What kinds of goods traveled to and from East Africa's trading cities?

Predict Is the text saying what you predicted it would? If not, look over the headings and illustrations again, and then revise your prediction.

North African Trading Powers

North Africa's history was shaped in part by its location. The region's major boundaries are the Sahara and the Mediterranean Sea. Its long Mediterranean coastline attracted sea traders. As early as 1000 B.C., ships from Phoenicia (fuh NISH uh) began searching the North African coast for ports that would connect them to Africa's riches. Phoenicia included present-day Lebanon and parts of Syria and Israel.

The Rise and Fall of Carthage By 800 B.C., the Phoenicians had established the city of Carthage (KAHR thij) as a trading post in present-day Tunisia. In time, Carthage became a powerful city-state that controlled the coast of North Africa. Carthage grew rich from the trade of textiles, metals, slaves, and food products. Possibly the wealthiest city in the world at the time, Carthage maintained control over Mediterranean trade from the late 500s B.C. through the 200s B.C. However, wars with the Roman Republic weakened the Carthaginians. In 146 B.C., Carthage fell to the Roman Empire, and the city was destroyed.

Roman and Islamic Influences Under Roman rule, cities grew up in areas that are parts of present-day Morocco, northern Algeria, and Tunisia. Christianity also spread to North African cities. The Romans built thousands of miles of roads throughout the territory, and North Africa's ports flourished.

After the Roman Empire fell in A.D. 476, invading forces competed for control of parts of North Africa. During the A.D. 600s, Arabs took control of Egypt and began to invade areas to the west of it. Thus began a long period of Arab control of North Africa. With Arab rule came the spread of Islam, the major religion of the Arabs. Soon many North Africans became Muslim. Then through trade, North Africa's Muslims helped spread Islam to people in West Africa, many of whom also accepted the religion.

Islam and Art
As Islam spread into North Africa, so did Islamic art styles. The gate shown above, which leads into the city of Fès, Morocco, is Islamic in design.
Analyze Images *How would you describe Islamic art from looking at this gate?*

✓ **Reading Check** Why did the Phoenicians establish Carthage?

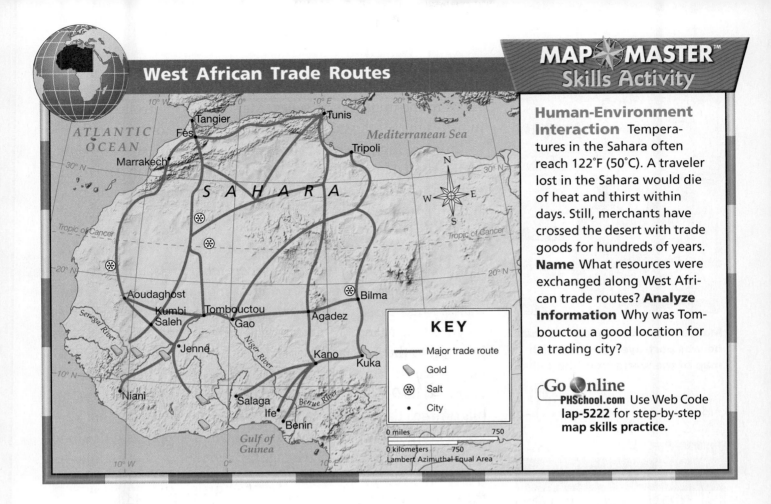

West African Trade Routes (map)

ATLANTIC OCEAN

Tangier
Fès
Tunis
Tripoli
Marrakech
Mediterranean Sea

SAHARA

Tropic of Cancer

Aoudaghost
Kumbi Saleh
Tombouctou
Gao
Bilma
Agadez
Jenné
Niger River
Senegal River
Kano
Kuka
Niani
Salaga
Ife
Benin
Benue River
Gulf of Guinea

KEY
——— Major trade route
◇ Gold
✳ Salt
• City

0 miles 750
0 kilometers 750
Lambert Azimuthal Equal Area

Human-Environment Interaction Temperatures in the Sahara often reach 122°F (50°C). A traveler lost in the Sahara would die of heat and thirst within days. Still, merchants have crossed the desert with trade goods for hundreds of years. **Name** What resources were exchanged along West African trade routes? **Analyze Information** Why was Tombouctou a good location for a trading city?

Go Online
PHSchool.com Use Web Code lap-5222 for step-by-step map skills practice.

West African Kingdoms

Around the time that East and North African city-states were developing, great trading kingdoms arose on the west side of the continent. The power of the West African kingdoms was based on the trade of salt and gold. People need salt to survive, especially in areas with hot climates such as West Africa. But there were no local sources of salt in the region. However, West Africa had plenty of gold. In North Africa, the opposite was true. There was salt, but no gold.

A brisk trade between North Africa and West Africa quickly grew. Control of this trade brought power and riches to three West African kingdoms: Ghana (GAH nuh), Mali (MAH lee), and Songhai (SAWNG hy). Forest kingdoms such as Benin (beh NEEN) also grew wealthy from trade.

Ghana You can see on the map titled Africa's Kingdoms, Cities, and Empires on page 35 that the kingdom of Ghana was located between the Senegal and Niger rivers. From that location Ghana controlled much of the trade across West Africa. Ghana's kings grew rich from the taxes they charged on the salt, gold, and other goods that flowed through their land. The flow of gold was so great that Arab writers called Ghana "land of gold."

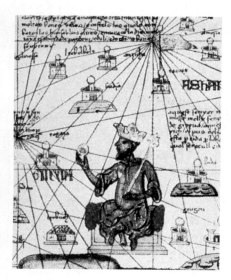

Mansa Musa was so famous that he was portrayed on a Spanish map of the world from the 1300s.

Mali In time, Ghana lost control of its trade routes to a new power, the kingdom of Mali. This kingdom arose in the mid-1200s in the upper Niger valley. Mali's kings controlled the gold mines of the south and the salt supplies of the north.

In Mali, the king was called *Mansa*, which means "emperor." Mali's most famous king, Mansa Musa (MAHN sah MOO sah), gained the throne in about 1312. His 20-year reign brought peace and order to the kingdom.

Mansa Musa and the Spread of Islam Over hundreds of years, Muslim traders had spread their religion, Islam, into much of Africa. Mansa Musa and many of his subjects were Muslim. Mansa Musa based his laws on the teachings of Islam.

In 1324, Mansa Musa made a **pilgrimage,** or a religious journey, to the Arabian city of Mecca. Muslims consider Mecca a holy place. It is the birthplace of Muhammad, the founder of Islam. Mansa Musa brought 60,000 people with him on his pilgrimage. Each of 80 camels carried 300 pounds (136 kilograms) of gold, which Mansa Musa gave to people as gifts along the way. Mansa Musa's pilgrimage brought about new trading ties with other Muslim states. It also displayed Mali's wealth. Hearing the reports, Europe's rulers eagerly sought Mali's gold.

Songhai After Mansa Musa's death in about 1332, the Songhai empire became West Africa's most powerful kingdom. Songhai's rulers controlled important trade routes and wealthy cities. The wealthiest Songhai trading city was **Tombouctou** (tohm book TOO), an important caravan stop located along the Niger River. People considered Tombouctou a great Muslim learning center.

Links Across The World

The Spread of Islam In the A.D. 600s, Islam began to spread west from Arabia through Southwest Asia and North Africa. Later, it reached West Africa. Islam also spread east—to Central Asia, India, Pakistan, Bangladesh, and Indonesia. About one billion people around the world practice Islam today. On some days, millions of Muslims visit the holy site of Mecca, as shown below.

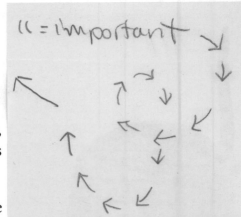

❝Salt comes from the north, gold from the south, and silver from the city of white men. But the word of God and the treasures of wisdom are only to be found in Tombouctou.**❞**

—*West African proverb*

Invaders from North Africa defeated Songhai in 1591. However, Songhai people still live near the Niger River, and Islam remains important in the region.

Forest Kingdoms Songhai traded with kingdoms located to the south in the forested region of West Africa. One such kingdom, Benin, arose in the late 1200s. Trade in ivory, palm oil, and pepper made the kingdom of Benin wealthy. Benin's artisans worked in ivory, bronze, brass, and wood in a distinctive style. They created some of the finest sculptures and carvings of the time.

Because it was located on the coast, Benin also traded with other African kingdoms as well as with Europeans arriving by sea. In the 1500s, Europeans began to trade guns for slaves from coastal forest kingdoms such as Benin, Asante (uh SAHN tee), and Dahomey (duh HOH mee). Many African Americans are descendants of enslaved people from those kingdoms.

✓ **Reading Check** Who was Mansa Musa?

Bronze sculpture from the forest kingdom of Owo

Section 2 Assessment

Key Terms

Review the key terms at the beginning of this section. U... each term in a sentence th... explains its meaning.

Target Reading Skil...

What did you predict abo... section? Did your predic... you remember what you...

Comprehension a... Critical Thinking

1. (a) Name Identify... states that were impo... African trade.
(b) Identify Effects... trade affect the coa... East Africa?

(c) Analyze Information Why do you think East African traders... to pay taxes for the right to ... goods into Kilwa?

... ify Sequence What... ... and North Africa ... throughout its history?

(b) ... information ... become a ... ... Africa?

... Describe How did trade ... the various kingdoms ... Africa?

... Conclusions How did ... Mali, and Songhai become ... from gold and salt ...

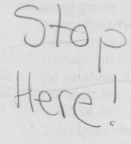

Writing Activity

Suppose you are a traveler visiting one of Africa's ancient kingdoms or city-states during the time that it thrived. Write a short letter home about some of the things that you see and the people that you meet. Explain what your favorite part of the visit has been.

For: An activity on the empire of Ghana
Visit: PHSchool.com
Web Code: lad-5202

European Conquest of Africa

Prepare to Read

Objectives

In this section you will

1. Discover what motivated Europeans to explore the African coast.
2. Find out how the Atlantic slave trade developed in the 1500s.
3. Learn how Europeans colonized regions of Africa.

Taking Notes

As you read, find important details about the European conquest of Africa. Copy the flow-chart below, and use it to record your findings.

```
┌─────────────────────────────────────┐
│ The Portuguese explore West Africa's │
│ coast, looking for better access to  │
│ African gold.                        │
└─────────────────────────────────────┘
    ↓          ↓          ↓
┌─────────────────────────────────────┐
│                                     │
└─────────────────────────────────────┘
    ↓          ↓          ↓
┌─────────────────────────────────────┐
│                                     │
└─────────────────────────────────────┘
```

Target Reading Skill

Ask Questions Before you read this section, preview the headings and illustrations to see what the section is about. Write one question that will help you understand or remember something important in the section. For example, you could write this question: "Why did Europeans originally go to Africa?" Then read to answer your question.

Key Terms

- **Cape of Good Hope** (kayp uv good hohp) *n.* a former province of the Republic of South Africa; the point of land at the southern end of Cape Peninsula, South Africa
- **plantation** (plan TAY shun) *n.* a large farm where cash crops are grown
- **Olaudah Equiano** (oh LOW duh ek wee AHN oh) *n.* an antislavery activist who wrote an account of his enslavement
- **colonize** (KAHL uh nyz) *v.* to settle in an area and take control of its government

Many Africans stayed in cells like this one at Gorée.

On the island of Gorée (goh RAY), off the coast of the West African country of Senegal, stands a museum called the House of Slaves. It honors the millions of Africans who were enslaved and then shipped across the Atlantic Ocean. Many Africans passed through the building that now houses the museum. Their last view of Africa was an opening called "The Door of No Return." Beyond it lay the ocean and the slave ships bound for the Americas.

The Atlantic slave trade began in the 1500s and continued through the late 1800s. But contact between Europeans and Africans began long before that. In North Africa, Europeans traded for gold from the empires of Ghana and Mali. Why do you think Europeans' first contacts with Africans took place in North Africa?

Europeans on the Coast

After 1500, Europe's relationship with Africa changed. It had begun as trade between equals. But it turned into the enslavement and forced migration of millions of Africans. The African slave trade eventually ended in the 1800s. Afterward, Europeans became more interested in Africa's natural resources. By 1900, European countries had divided Africa among themselves.

Portuguese Exploration In the mid-1400s, the Portuguese began sailing along the West African coast in search of gold. For centuries, gold from West Africa had been transported across the Sahara to North African ports. It was then shipped across the Mediterranean to arrive at European markets. But the Portuguese and other Europeans wanted to trade directly for West African gold and ivory, instead of dealing with North African merchants. They also wanted to trade with Asia.

Many inventions helped the Portuguese explore Africa's coast. The Portuguese used a lateen sail, a triangle-shaped sail designed in North Africa. The lateen sail allowed ships to sail against the wind as well as with it. And better instruments, such as the astrolabe (AS troh layb), helped sailors navigate at sea. With these improvements, Portuguese sailors became the first Europeans to travel south along Africa's coasts.

A Change in Trade Relations At first, Africans and Europeans traded with one another as equals. Africans traded gold, cotton, ivory, skins, metal objects, and pepper. In return, Europeans traded copper, brass, and clothing. Europeans also introduced corn, cassava, and yams from the Americas. These plants became food crops in Africa. Africans in turn introduced Europeans to okra, watermelon, and the best type of rice for growing in the Americas.

Over time, however, the trade relationship changed. In 1498, three Portuguese ships rounded the tip of Southern Africa and sailed north along Africa's east coast. The wealth of the East African city-states amazed the Portuguese. More Portuguese ships followed—not to trade but to seize the riches of the city-states. Portugal controlled the wealth of East Africa's coast until well into the 1600s.

Portuguese Ship, African Sails
This illustration shows a typical Portuguese sailing ship of the 1400s, called a caravel. It used lateen sails.
Synthesize *How does this ship show that Europeans adopted elements of African culture?*

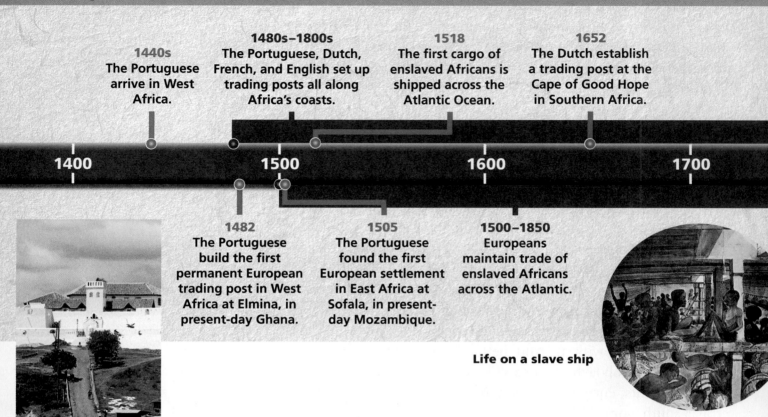

1440s
The Portuguese arrive in West Africa.

1480s–1800s
The Portuguese, Dutch, French, and English set up trading posts all along Africa's coasts.

1518
The first cargo of enslaved Africans is shipped across the Atlantic Ocean.

1652
The Dutch establish a trading post at the Cape of Good Hope in Southern Africa.

1400   1500   1600   1700

1482
The Portuguese build the first permanent European trading post in West Africa at Elmina, in present-day Ghana.

1505
The Portuguese found the first European settlement in East Africa at Sofala, in present-day Mozambique.

1500–1850
Europeans maintain trade of enslaved Africans across the Atlantic.

Life on a slave ship

Trading post at Elmina

European Trade Spreads The Dutch, French, and English soon followed the Portuguese. They set up trading posts along Africa's coasts, where sailors could get supplies. The Dutch built a trading post on the **Cape of Good Hope,** a point of land at Africa's southern tip. Soon, settlers arrived. They moved inland, building homes and farms.

As Europeans spread out, sometimes by force, their relations with Africans worsened. But it was the growing trade in enslaved Africans that poisoned future relations between Africans and Europeans the most.

✓ Reading Check What advantages allowed the Portuguese to be the first Europeans to trade directly with West Africans?

The Atlantic Slave Trade

Before the 1500s, slavery was common in some parts of Africa. There, enslaved people became the property of their owners and were forced to work for them. Slaves could win their freedom after a few years. Some became important citizens among the people who had enslaved them. Slaves could even be bought out of slavery by their own people.

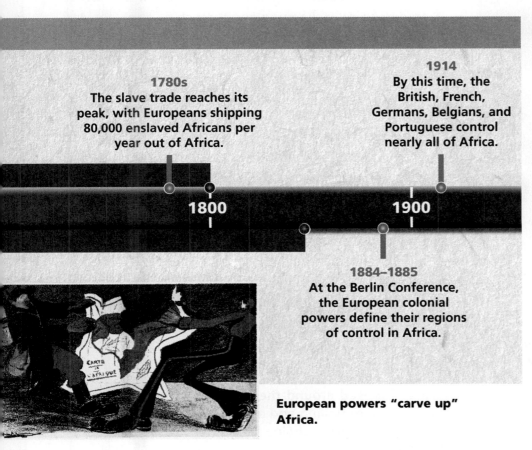

1780s
The slave trade reaches its peak, with Europeans shipping 80,000 enslaved Africans per year out of Africa.

1914
By this time, the British, French, Germans, Belgians, and Portuguese control nearly all of Africa.

1800

1900

1884–1885
At the Berlin Conference, the European colonial powers define their regions of control in Africa.

European powers "carve up" Africa.

■ Timeline Skills

Over the course of 500 years, Europeans had a strong influence on Africa. **Note** When did Europeans establish their first trading post in Africa? **Identify Effects** What were the effects of European trade interests on Africa?

Then the European powers began to establish colonies in North, South, and Central America, as well as the Caribbean. The Europeans practiced a different type of slavery in the Americas. They treated the enslaved Africans as property that they shipped across the Atlantic to the Americas. The Europeans rarely freed their slaves. When the African slave trade ended in the mid-1800s, millions of Africans had been taken from their homelands, most never to return.

The Demand for Slaves European settlers in the Americas needed workers for their mines and plantations. A **plantation** is a large farm where cash crops are grown. Instead of paying plantation workers, the settlers preferred to use enslaved laborers. At first the settlers enslaved Native Americans. But many Native Americans became sick and died from diseases or brutal working conditions. Others ran away.

Therefore the European settlers decided to enslave Africans instead. The settlers knew Africans were skilled farmers, miners, and metal workers. They also thought Africans would easily adapt to the climate of the American tropics, which is similar to that of Africa. And since Africans would be in unfamiliar territory, they would not be able to escape easily.

The Slave Trade Begins By the 1600s, Portuguese traders were exchanging goods, such as guns, for African slaves. Some African nations refused to take part. But others sold people they captured during battles. By 1780, about 80,000 African slaves were being shipped across the Atlantic each year.

The Horrors of Slavery Captured Africans were often branded with hot irons to identify them as slaves. On the journey across the Atlantic, captives lay side by side on filthy shelves stacked from floor to ceiling. They received little food or water. As many as 20 percent of the slaves died during each crossing. To make up for these losses, ships' captains packed in even more people.

Olaudah Equiano (oh LOW duh ek wee AHN oh) was a slave who bought his own freedom and then fought against slavery. Equiano had been captured and sold at a slave auction in 1756, at about age 11. He felt sure he would die. In a book he later wrote about his experience, Equiano explained,

> **❝[W]hen I looked around the ship and saw a large furnace of copper boiling and a multitude of black people of every description chained together . . . I no longer doubted of my fate. ❞**
>
> —*The Interesting Narrative of the Life of Olaudah Equiano, or Gustavus Vassa, the African*, by Olaudah Equiano

Equiano proved luckier than most African slaves. In time, he was able to buy his freedom. For most enslaved people, freedom was little more than a distant dream.

The Effects of Slavery on Africa Some Africans grew wealthy from the slave trade. Overall, however, the slave trade was a disaster for Africa. West Africa lost much of its population. Robbed of skilled workers, and with many families torn apart, many African societies broke down.

✔ Reading Check **What fueled the European demand for slaves?**

The Trials of Slavery
Olaudah Equiano (top right) was a slave who bought his own freedom. He traveled to America in cramped quarters on a slave ship similar to this model (above). **Analyze Images** *Do you think it would have been bearable to live on a ship like this one?*

Europeans Colonize Africa

In the mid-1800s, the African slave trade ended. Europeans then began to raid Africa's interior for its natural resources. They wanted the resources in order to run factories all across Europe. They also viewed Africa as a place to build empires. Many Africans fiercely resisted European conquest. But their old guns proved no match for modern European weapons.

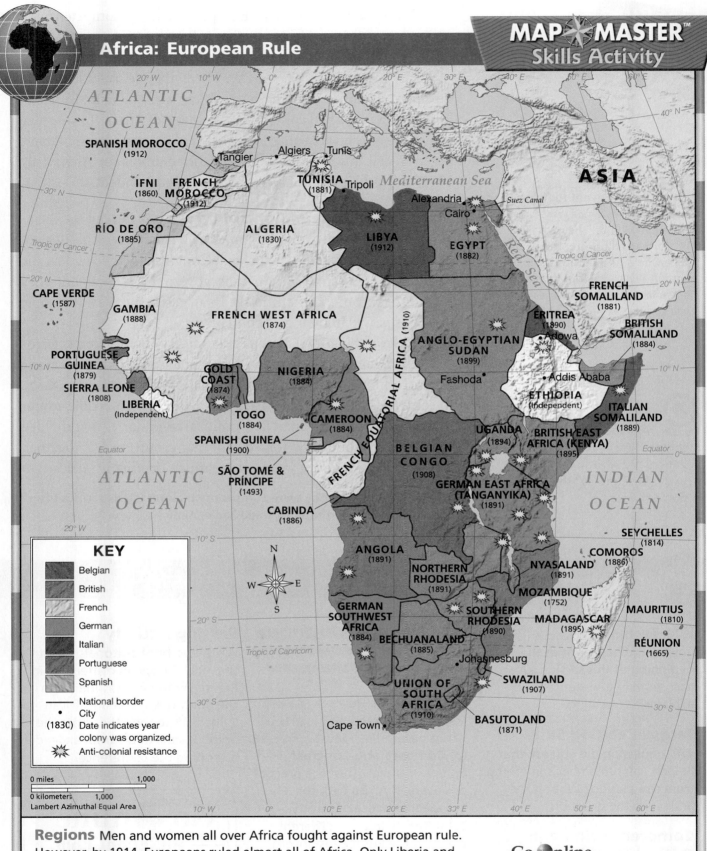

Africa: European Rule

ATLANTIC OCEAN

SPANISH MOROCCO (1912)
•Tangier
Algiers •Tunis
ASIA

IFNI (1860)
FRENCH MOROCCO (1912)
TUNISIA (1881)
•Tripoli
Mediterranean Sea

RÍO DE ORO (1885)
ALGERIA (1830)
LIBYA (1912)
Alexandria
Cairo•
Suez Canal

Tropic of Cancer
EGYPT (1882)
Red Sea
Tropic of Cancer

CAPE VERDE (1587)
GAMBIA (1888)
FRENCH WEST AFRICA (1874)
FRENCH SOMALILAND (1881)

ERITREA (1890)
•Adowa
BRITISH SOMALILAND (1884)

ANGLO-EGYPTIAN SUDAN (1899)

PORTUGUESE GUINEA (1879)
SIERRA LEONE (1808)
LIBERIA (Independent)
GOLD COAST (1874)
NIGERIA (1884)
FRENCH EQUATORIAL AFRICA (1910)
Fashoda•
•Addis Ababa
ETHIOPIA (Independent)
ITALIAN SOMALILAND (1889)

TOGO (1884)
SPANISH GUINEA (1900)
CAMEROON (1884)
UGANDA (1894)
BRITISH EAST AFRICA (KENYA) (1895)

SÃO TOMÉ & PRÍNCIPE (1493)
Equator
BELGIAN CONGO (1908)
Equator
INDIAN OCEAN

ATLANTIC OCEAN
CABINDA (1886)
GERMAN EAST AFRICA (TANGANYIKA) (1891)

ANGOLA (1891)
NORTHERN RHODESIA (1891)
NYASALAND (1891)
SEYCHELLES (1814)
COMOROS (1886)

MOZAMBIQUE (1752)
MAURITIUS (1810)

GERMAN SOUTHWEST AFRICA (1884)
BECHUANALAND (1885)
SOUTHERN RHODESIA (1890)
MADAGASCAR (1895)
RÉUNION (1665)

Tropic of Capricorn

•Johannesburg
SWAZILAND (1907)

UNION OF SOUTH AFRICA (1910)
BASUTOLAND (1871)
Cape Town•

KEY

- Belgian
- British
- French
- German
- Italian
- Portuguese
- Spanish
- —— National border
- • City
- (1830) Date indicates year colony was organized.
- ✸ Anti-colonial resistance

N W E S

0 miles 1,000
0 kilometers 1,000
Lambert Azimuthal Equal Area

Regions Men and women all over Africa fought against European rule. However, by 1914, Europeans ruled almost all of Africa. Only Liberia and Ethiopia remained independent. **Identify** Name two African countries that were not yet ruled by Europeans in 1900. **Draw Conclusions** Why do you think most of the regions that resisted colonization were near the coasts?

Go Online
PHSchool.com Use Web Code lap-5213 for step-by-step map skills practice.

How Stamps Reveal History
These postage stamps were printed in the early 1900s. They are from the German colony in present-day Cameroon and the British colony in present-day Kenya, Uganda, and Tanzania. **Infer** *Did Europeans view their colonies as African or European?*

Ask Questions
Ask yourself why the competition among European nations for African territory was referred to as "the scramble for Africa."

The Scramble for Africa European nations competed with one another to gain African territory. But they did not want this competition to lead to war. In 1884, leaders of several European countries met in Berlin, Germany. There, they set rules for which European countries could claim which African land. By 1900, European nations had colonized many parts of Africa. To **colonize** means to settle an area and take control of its government. People began to call this rush for territory "the scramble for Africa." By 1914, only Ethiopia and Liberia remained independent.

Effects of European Control on Africa Not all the European countries ruled their colonies the same way. The Belgian government directly ran the Belgian Congo (now the Democratic Republic of the Congo). Africans governed Nigeria, but they took orders from British officials. In all cases, the African people had little power in their governments.

The scramble for Africa caused long-lasting problems. Europeans had gained power in part by encouraging rivalries among African ethnic groups. Europeans also took the best land to farm. In some areas, they forced Africans to labor under terrible conditions. Europeans also drew new political boundaries that divided some ethnic groups and forced differing groups to live together. Later, these boundaries would cause much conflict in Africa.

✓ **Reading Check** Why were Europeans still interested in Africa after the slave trade had ended?

Section 3 Assessment

Key Terms
Review the key terms at the beginning of this section. Use each term in a sentence that explains its meaning.

Target Reading Skill
What question did you ask that helped you remember something from this section? What is the answer to the question?

Comprehension and Critical Thinking
1. (a) Recall What region of Africa did most Europeans trade with before the mid-1400s?

(b) Identify Causes How did the trade relationship between Europe and Africa change after the late 1400s?
2. (a) Describe How was slavery traditionally practiced in parts of Africa before the 1500s?
(b) Compare and Contrast Compare and contrast the practice of slavery in Africa with the European practice of slavery.
3. (a) Recall In what different ways did the Europeans govern their African colonies?
(b) Identify Sequence How did relations between Africa and Europe change over time?

Writing Activity
Write two brief editorials about the 1884 European conference in Berlin. Write one editorial from the point of view of an African leader. Write the other from the point of view of a European leader attending the conference.

For: An activity on the Boers
Visit: PHSchool.com
Web Code: lad-5203

Section 4 Independence and Its Challenges

Prepare to Read

Objectives

In this section you will

1. Learn about the growth of nationalism in Africa.
2. Find out about the effects of World War II on Africa and on the growing independence movement.
3. Examine the different challenges faced by African nations on their paths to independence.

Taking Notes

As you read, find details on the causes and effects of the African movement for independence. Copy the flowchart below, and use it to record your findings.

Causes	Event	Effects
• • •	African independence movement	• • •

Target Reading Skill

Use Prior Knowledge Prior knowledge is what you already know about a topic before you begin to read. Building on what you already know can give you a head start on learning new information.

Before you begin to read, page through your reading assignment, looking at the headings and illustrations to spark your memory. Write down what you know about a certain topic, such as World War II. As you read, connect what you learn to what you already know.

Key Terms

- **nationalism** (NASH uh nul iz um) *n.* a feeling of pride in one's homeland; a group's identity as members of a nation
- **Pan-Africanism** (pan AF rih kun iz um) *n.* the belief that all Africans should work together for their rights and freedoms
- **boycott** (BOY kaht) *n.* a refusal to buy or use certain products or services
- **democracy** (dih MAHK ruh see) *n.* a government over which citizens exercise power

On April 18, 1980, the people of Rhodesia took to the streets. They had recently elected Robert Mugabe (muh GAH bee) prime minister in Rhodesia's first free election. People waited excitedly through the evening. Then, at midnight, the British flag came down for the last time. At that moment, the British colony of Rhodesia became the independent country of Zimbabwe.

The fight for independence had been difficult and sometimes violent. Now, Prime Minister Mugabe asked all the people to work together. They would have to build a new nation. Zimbabwe was one of the last African countries to win independence. But the movement for freedom there had begun many years before.

People in Zimbabwe celebrate the country's independence.

The Growth of Nationalism

After "the scramble for Africa," many Africans dreamed of independence. In 1897, Mankayi Sontanga (mun KY ee sun TAHN guh) put this dream to music. His song, called "Bless, O Lord, Our Land of Africa," expressed the growing nationalism of Africans. **Nationalism** is a feeling of pride in one's homeland.

Political Parties and Nationalism Most European colonial rulers did not view Africans as their equals. For that reason, many African leaders knew they would have to work hard at developing pride in being African. The colonial powers had drawn political borders that combined many nations and ethnic groups. Some of these groups were old rivals. African leaders saw that to end colonial rule, they would have to build a spirit of unity.

Nationalism grew during the early 1900s. In 1912, Africans in South Africa formed a political party called the South African Native National Congress. (Today this party is the African National Congress, or the ANC.) Party members protested laws that limited the rights of black South Africans. In 1920, African lawyers in British West Africa formed the National Congress of British West Africa. This group also worked to gain rights for Africans, including the right to vote.

A better life for all

ANC

Pan-Africanism In the 1920s, Africans formed a movement based on **Pan-Africanism,** the belief that all Africans should work together for their rights and freedoms. This movement stressed unity and cooperation among all Africans, whether they lived in Africa or not. Their slogan was "Africa for Africans." The movement won many supporters.

One of the greatest leaders of the Pan-African movement was Léopold Senghor (lay oh POHLD sahn GAWR) of Senegal. Senghor was a poet and a political leader. He encouraged Africans to study their traditions and be proud of their culture. Senegal became independent in 1960, with Senghor as its first president.

✓ **Reading Check** **Name two African political parties. What work did these parties do?**

Africa and World War II

A major boost to African independence came unexpectedly in the 1930s and 1940s, when World War II unfolded. The war would inspire many people throughout Africa to seek freedom for their own nations.

The Invasion of North Africa During World War II, Great Britain, France, and the United States formed a group called the Allies. Together, the Allies fought the armies of Germany, Italy, and Japan, which were invading much of the world. German and Italian forces invaded North Africa, much of which was under British or French colonial control. Italian forces also invaded Ethiopia.

These men from Ghana fought in the British Army during World War II.

Some African nations played a major role in supporting the Allies. Countries such as Liberia and the Belgian Congo supplied the Allies with rubber and other needed resources. Allied planes were allowed to use African airfields to move supplies into Asia. Many thousands of African soldiers fought and died to help free Europe from conquest. About 170,000 soldiers from West Africa and 280,000 soldiers from East Africa and Southern Africa served in the British Army.

An Inspirational Victory Africans came home victorious. After the sacrifices they made, however, they wanted their own freedom. One soldier said, "We have been told what we fought for. That is 'freedom.' We want freedom, nothing but freedom."

✓ **Reading Check** **What parts of Africa were invaded during World War II?**

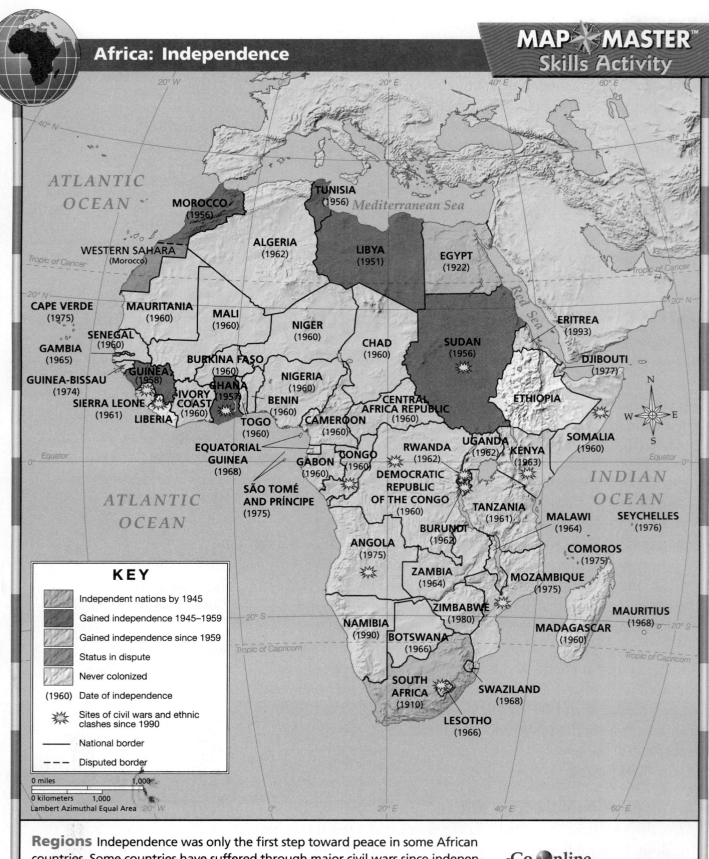

ATLANTIC OCEAN

MOROCCO
(1956)

TUNISIA
(1956)   *Mediterranean Sea*

WESTERN SAHARA
(Morocco)

ALGERIA
(1962)

LIBYA
(1951)

EGYPT
(1922)

Red Sea

Tropic of Cancer

CAPE VERDE
(1975)

MAURITANIA
(1960)

MALI
(1960)

NIGER
(1960)

CHAD
(1960)

SUDAN
(1956)

ERITREA
(1993)

DJIBOUTI
(1977)

SENEGAL
(1960)

GAMBIA
(1965)

GUINEA-BISSAU
(1974)

GUINEA
(1958)

BURKINA FASO
(1960)

NIGERIA
(1960)

GHANA
(1957)

IVORY
COAST
(1960)

BENIN
(1960)

SIERRA LEONE
(1961)

LIBERIA

TOGO
(1960)

CAMEROON
(1960)

CENTRAL
AFRICA REPUBLIC
(1960)

ETHIOPIA

EQUATORIAL
GUINEA
(1968)

GABON
(1960)

CONGO
(1960)

RWANDA
(1962)

UGANDA
(1962)

KENYA
(1963)

SOMALIA
(1960)

SÃO TOMÉ
AND PRÍNCIPE
(1975)

DEMOCRATIC
REPUBLIC
OF THE CONGO
(1960)

BURUNDI
(1962)

TANZANIA
(1961)

MALAWI
(1964)

SEYCHELLES
(1976)

ATLANTIC OCEAN

INDIAN OCEAN

ANGOLA
(1975)

ZAMBIA
(1964)

MOZAMBIQUE
(1975)

COMOROS
(1975)

ZIMBABWE
(1980)

MAURITIUS
(1968)

NAMIBIA
(1990)

BOTSWANA
(1966)

MADAGASCAR
(1960)

Tropic of Capricorn

SOUTH
AFRICA
(1910)

SWAZILAND
(1968)

LESOTHO
(1966)

KEY

	Independent nations by 1945
	Gained independence 1945–1959
	Gained independence since 1959
	Status in dispute
	Never colonized
(1960)	Date of independence
✺	Sites of civil wars and ethnic clashes since 1990
——	National border
– – –	Disputed border

0 miles   1,000
0 kilometers   1,000
Lambert Azimuthal Equal Area

Regions Independence was only the first step toward peace in some African countries. Some countries have suffered through major civil wars since independence. **Identify** During what period of time did the most African countries gain independence? **Analyze Information** Why do you think there was an increase in the number of countries that became independent after a certain time?

Go Online
PHSchool.com Use Web Code
lap-5214 for step-by-step
map skills practice.

Different Paths to Independence

World War II did not only inspire Africans to win their freedom. The war also weakened the economies of colonial powers such as France and Great Britain. Colonialism was about to come to an end in Africa.

Winds of Change Public opinion began to turn against the practice of colonialism as well. Many people in Britain felt they could no longer afford a colonial empire. Even the United States and the Soviet Union—Britain's allies during the war—began to speak out against colonialism.

British leader Harold Macmillan realized that Britain would not be able to keep its African colonies. "The winds of change are blowing across Africa," he said. As more and more Africans demanded freedom, European countries began to give up their African colonies. Some colonial powers gave up their colonies peacefully, while others fought to maintain control. Ghana was granted its independence from Britain. But Algeria, a French colony, had to fight for its freedom.

Independence Across Africa
Women in Mauritius in 1965 hold up signs asking for independence from Britain (bottom). Prince Philip of Britain and Prime Minister Jomo Kenyatta of Kenya shake hands at an independence ceremony in 1963 (below). **Predict** *Do you think Mauritius and Kenya gained independence peacefully or through fighting?*

From Gold Coast to Ghana In the Gold Coast colony, Kwame Nkrumah (KWAH mee un KROO muh) organized protests against British rule in the early 1950s. The protests were peaceful strikes and boycotts. In a **boycott,** people refuse to buy or use certain products or services. The British jailed Nkrumah several times for his actions, but the protests continued. In 1957, the people achieved their goal: independence. The new country took on the name Ghana, and Nkrumah became its president.

War in Algeria The French people who had settled in Algeria thought of it as more than a colony. To them, it was part of France. Algerians disagreed. They were willing to fight for the right to govern themselves. A bloody war began in Algeria in 1954. The eight-year struggle cost the lives of 100,000 Algerians and 10,000 French. But by 1962, the Algerians had won.

Challenges of Independence The new leaders of Africa had spent many years working for independence. But the colonial powers had rarely allowed Africans to gain experience in government. After agreeing to independence, the colonial powers did little to prepare the new leaders to govern. As a result, many new governments in Africa were unstable.

The Right to Vote
A key part of democracy is allowing all citizens to vote. An elderly woman casts her vote in an election in Mali (below). Voters line up for miles to cast votes in South Africa's first democratic elections in 1994 (bottom).
Apply Information *Why do you think South Africans were willing to walk miles in order to cast a vote?*

In some African countries, African military leaders took control of the government by force. Military governments do not always govern fairly. The people often have few rights. Further, citizens may be jailed if they protest. But military governments have held together some African countries that otherwise might have been torn apart by war.

Building Democracy In many parts of Africa, there is a long history of democracy. A **democracy** is a government over which citizens exercise power. In a democracy, citizens influence governmental decisions. Some countries have made traditional ways a part of governing. For example, in Botswana, lively political debates take place in "freedom squares." These outdoor meetings are like the traditional kgotla (GOHT lah), in which people talk with their leaders.

Most African countries are less than 50 years old. In contrast, the stable, democratic country of the United States is more than 200 years old. Many Africans feel that building stable countries will take time. As one leader said, "Let Africa be given the time to develop its own system of democracy."

✓ **Reading Check** How did Algeria gain independence?

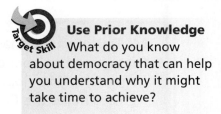

Use Prior Knowledge What do you know about democracy that can help you understand why it might take time to achieve?

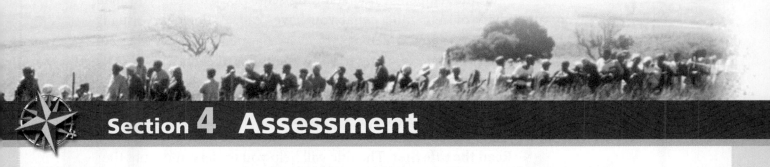

Section 4 Assessment

Key Terms
Review the key terms at the beginning of this section. Use each term in a sentence that explains its meaning.

Target Reading Skill
Look back at what you wrote down about what you already knew. How did what you learned relate to what you already knew?

Comprehension and Critical Thinking
1. (a) Recall How did Africans respond to years of colonial rule?

(b) Infer Why did African leaders encourage people to feel pride about being African?

2. (a) Describe What was Africa's role in World War II?

(b) Identify Effects How did World War II boost the independence movement in Africa?

3. (a) Identify Causes What pressures forced European countries to give up their colonies?

(b) Compare and Contrast How was Ghana's road to independence similar to that of Algeria? How was it different?

Writing Activity
Use a book, an encyclopedia, or the Internet to research an African country that won its independence after 1950. Write a headline and a short newspaper article that might have appeared on the day that country became independent.

Writing Tip Be sure to write a good headline for your newspaper article. The headline should identify the main point of the article. It should also be catchy so that the reader wants to read on.

Mr. DeNoto's class had just finished reading about the ways African countries gained independence. Then the class formed groups. Each group was going to build a float to celebrate the independence of an African country.

"Let's make the flag first," said Tamika.

"No, no, we need to build the float frame first," cried Ari.

"Well, I don't see how we can do anything until we buy the materials we need!" complained Sarah.

Mr. DeNoto held up a hand to quiet the class. "Building a float is complicated. The first thing you have to do is make a plan," he said. "Otherwise, you might cover the same ground more than once. You might even forget an important step. Adam, why don't you come up to the board and be our scribe? We're going to make a flowchart to help us plan."

A flowchart shows sequence, or the order in which actions or events happen. Understanding sequence can help you plan an activity or remember what you have read. A flowchart usually uses arrows to show which step or event happens when. A diagram such as a timeline uses dates to show the order of events.

Learn the Skill

Use these steps when you read a diagram for sequence.

1 **Read the title first.** The title will help you understand what the diagram is about. Mr. DeNoto's class titled its flowchart Building a Float. From the title, you know that the flowchart shows how the class plans to build a float.

2 **Find clues that show the order of events.** On a flowchart, the arrows tell you the order in which you should read the chart. Find the beginning and start there. Mr. DeNoto's class decided that their first step would be "Choose a country."

3 **Read the diagram carefully for connections.** Think about how one step leads to the next step. What are the connections? If there are no illustrations, try imagining each step in your head to help you understand the sequence.

Practice the Skill

Follow the steps below to read the flowchart about Ghana.

1 Read the title. What does it tell you the flowchart will be about?

2 Find the beginning of the chart and identify the first step. Start there and follow the arrows through each step.

3 Now reread the flowchart and answer these questions: (a) What is the first step on the flowchart? (b) What step leads to Nkrumah being jailed? (c) What step comes after Nkrumah being jailed? (d) What is the final result of the Gold Coast colony's struggle for independence?

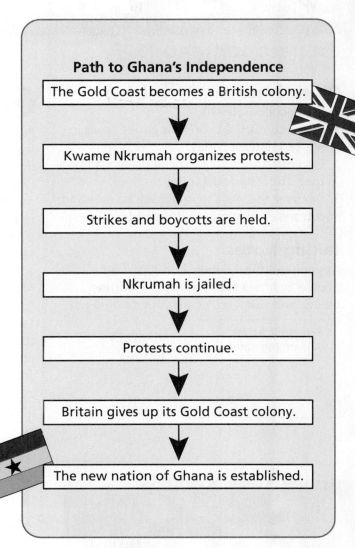

Path to Ghana's Independence

The Gold Coast becomes a British colony.

↓

Kwame Nkrumah organizes protests.

↓

Strikes and boycotts are held.

↓

Nkrumah is jailed.

↓

Protests continue.

↓

Britain gives up its Gold Coast colony.

↓

The new nation of Ghana is established.

After Ghana was established, its government created this coat of arms to represent the nation.

Apply the Skill

Turn to pages 52–53 and study the timeline. Use the steps in this skill to understand what events are shown on the timeline as well as what the sequence of events was.

Issues for Africa Today

Prepare to Read

Objectives

In this section you will

1. Learn about the economic issues faced by African nations today.
2. Find out about major social issues and how they affect Africans today.
3. Discover the ways in which Africa is facing current environmental challenges.

Taking Notes

As you read, find details about issues faced by people in Africa today. Copy the outline below, and use it to record your findings.

> I. Economic issues
>   A. Farming and mining
>   1.
>   2.
>   B.
> II.

Target Reading Skill

Predict As you have learned, making predictions before you read helps you set a purpose for reading and helps you remember what you read.

Before you read this section, think about what you know about Africa's history. Then predict some issues the region might face today. As you read, connect what you read to your prediction. If what you learn doesn't support your prediction, revise the prediction.

Key Terms

- **commercial farming** (kuh MUR shul FAHR ming) *n.* the large-scale production of crops for sale
- **hybrid** (HY brid) *n.* a plant that is created by breeding different types of the same plant
- **literate** (LIT ur it) *adj.* able to read and write
- **life expectancy** (lyf ek SPEK tun see) *n.* the average length of time a person can expect to live

A young man digs an irrigation ditch in Niger.

In the past, nothing grew during the dry season in the Sahel. Farmers had to travel to cities to find work. Now, the West African country of Niger has a new irrigation program for its part of the Sahel. Irrigation allows farmers to grow a second crop during the dry season, in addition to their usual crop in the wet season. One farmer says that raising two crops a year means he can stay on village land.

> **❝Dry-season crops are such a normal practice now that everyone grows them. Before, each year after the harvest, I went to the city to look for work. But today, with the dry-season crops, I have work in the village. Truly it is a good thing.❞**
>
> —*Adamou Sani, farmer*

Niger's irrigation program is one way Africans are improving their lives. Africans are also finding ways to meet economic, social, and environmental challenges.

Economic Issues

The colonial powers saw Africa as a source of raw materials and a market for their own manufactured goods. They did little to build factories in Africa. Today, African countries still have little manufacturing. Most economies are based on farming and mining.

Farming Farming is the most important economic activity in Africa. About 60 percent of workers are farmers. And more than half of the goods that African countries sell overseas are farm goods. Africans practice two kinds of farming—subsistence farming and commercial farming. Recall that subsistence farmers work small plots of land. They try to raise as much food as their families need. **Commercial farming** is the large-scale production of cash crops for sale. In Africa, commercial farmers grow cash crops such as coffee, cacao, and bananas.

Mining Many African nations have rich mineral resources. They export minerals to other countries. Nigeria has oil and coal. The Democratic Republic of the Congo and Zambia have copper, while South Africa has gold and diamonds.

Farming for Food or for Profit?
A man bicycles through a banana farm in Ivory Coast (bottom). A woman picks coffee in Zambia (below). **Analyze Information** *Do you think the farms shown are commercial or subsistence farms? Explain why.*

South African Gold Mine

In South Africa's deep-level gold mines, miners work as far down as two miles (3.2 kilometers) underground. The mines run 24 hours a day. Because it is so hot at that depth, deep-level mining requires ventilation and cooling. In addition to tunnels, there are shafts, elevators to lift the ore to the surface, and surface processing plants. South Africa produces almost half of the world's gold.

Working in the Mines
Miners like this man train for their jobs by stepping up and down on blocks for hours in a very hot room.

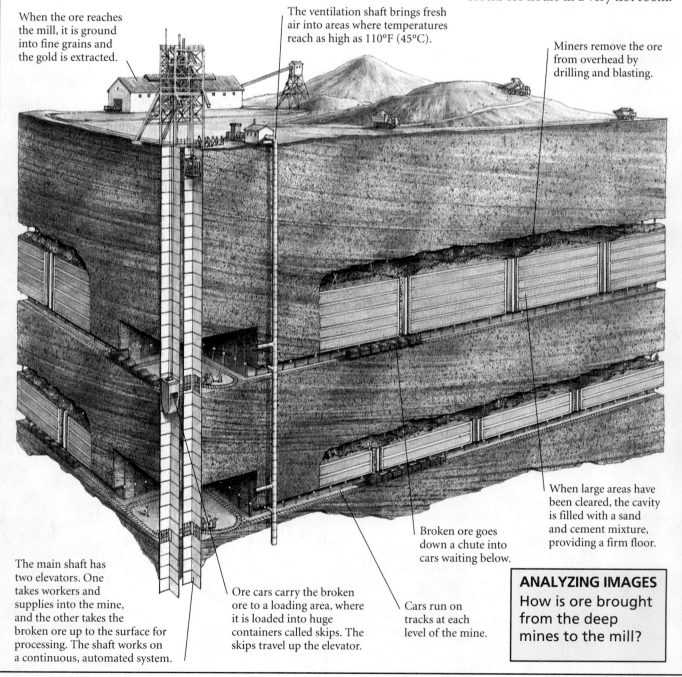

When the ore reaches the mill, it is ground into fine grains and the gold is extracted.

The ventilation shaft brings fresh air into areas where temperatures reach as high as 110°F (45°C).

Miners remove the ore from overhead by drilling and blasting.

When large areas have been cleared, the cavity is filled with a sand and cement mixture, providing a firm floor.

Broken ore goes down a chute into cars waiting below.

The main shaft has two elevators. One takes workers and supplies into the mine, and the other takes the broken ore up to the surface for processing. The shaft works on a continuous, automated system.

Ore cars carry the broken ore to a loading area, where it is loaded into huge containers called skips. The skips travel up the elevator.

Cars run on tracks at each level of the mine.

ANALYZING IMAGES
How is ore brought from the deep mines to the mill?

Economic Challenges About 75 percent of African countries have specialized economies—they depend on exporting one or two products. Gambia depends on peanuts, while Zambia relies on the export of copper. As a result, African economies are especially sensitive to the rise and fall of world prices. A fall in prices hurts economies that depend on the sale of one crop or mineral.

African countries are now trying to reduce their dependence on one export by diversifying their economies. For example, Senegal became independent in 1960. At that time, more than 70 percent of Senegal's people worked in the peanut industry. Today, Senegal has other major export industries, such as fishing, fish processing, and mining. Peanuts now account for only a small percent of the money Senegal earns from exports.

Farming Improvements African nations face another economic problem—how to feed a growing population. Several governments are trying to help farmers increase the size of their crops. One method they use is to develop hybrid plants. A **hybrid** is a plant created by breeding different types of the same plant. The goal is that the best qualities of each type of plant will show up in the hybrid. Since the late 1990s, West Africans have been planting hybrid rice that combines the best aspects of African and Asian rices. As a result, these farmers have been able to produce more rice.

✓ **Reading Check** **Which two activities do most African economies depend upon?**

Predict
Based on what you know about specialized economies, predict whether more African countries are likely to change their economies.

Expanding Economies
Today, fish markets like the ones below are helping Senegal's economy succeed. Fish products have become Senegal's major export. **Generalize** *What advantages do you think the fishing industry offers to a country with a specialized economy?*

A South African girl focuses on her schoolwork.

Social Issues

In addition to making economic improvements, African nations also must provide social services to their growing populations. Many Africans need better access to education and health care.

Education African children must often contribute to their family's income by working on family farms or by selling goods in the market. When girls and boys go to school, families sacrifice. But most Africans are willing to make this sacrifice because they know education can improve their children's lives.

It has long been a tradition in Africa for communities to actively support their schools. If needed, people will construct new schools. For example, parents in South Africa have often helped to build new schools when the government could not do it alone. Even so, many of the schools are overcrowded, so students must take turns attending classes. The headmaster at one such school said that students "who couldn't cram into the desks knelt on the floor or stood on their toes so as not to miss a word the teacher was saying." African students are often expected to help keep their school and its grounds clean. The students might do this by sweeping the floors or disposing of the trash.

Reading and Writing The number of Africans who are literate varies from country to country. Being **literate** means being able to read and write. In all African countries, more people have learned to read and write since independence. When Mozambique gained independence from Portugal in 1975, less than 7 percent of its people were literate. Today, about 48 percent of the people in Mozambique are literate. In Tanzania, progress with literacy has been even more dramatic. When the country gained independence from Britain in 1961, only 15 percent of Tanzania's people were literate. Today, about 78 percent of Tanzanians can read and write.

Health Another social issue that differs from country to country in Africa is life expectancy—the average length of time a person can expect to live. In Morocco, life expectancy is between 67 and 72 years. In Southern Africa, however, the average life expectancy is less than 50 years. In the Southern African country of Botswana, people only live an average of 32 years.

The main reason for low life expectancy in Africa is childhood disease. There are many diseases for which children have low resistance. For example, insects spread diseases such as malaria. Unclean drinking water and living conditions help spread other diseases. The virus called HIV causes AIDS. Millions of African children have been born with HIV, and millions more adults have died of AIDS before age 50.

Preventing Disease Although the problem of AIDS exists around the world, it is worst in Southern Africa. One reason is that many Southern Africans who are poor cannot afford drugs that might help them. Also, many people have not had access to education, so they have not learned how to prevent the disease. African governments are working with groups such as the World Health Organization to prevent and treat health problems. Some progress has been made. For example, individuals and organizations in Uganda have worked hard to reduce the number of HIV infections there. Because of its success, Uganda may serve as a model for preventing and controlling HIV in other countries.

✓ **Reading Check** **What is the main reason for low life expectancy in Africa?**

Health Concerns in Africa
Children surround a health worker at a clinic in Gambia as she writes down information about their health.
Predict *In what ways do you think the health worker can help this community?*

The Environment

Like other countries around the world, the countries of Africa face a number of environmental challenges. About two thirds of Africa is desert or dry land. High-quality farmland is scarce, and rainfall may vary greatly over the year. These environmental factors make farming especially challenging in parts of Africa.

Soil Problems People in Africa's rural areas often struggle to make a living. Much of the land in Africa is poor for farming. People thus need great areas of land to raise enough crops to support their families. They may cut down trees to use or sell the wood and to clear land for farming. With no cover from trees, soil is exposed to wind and rain. The soil then erodes, or wears away. Soil erosion reduces the amount of land on which food can grow. Without enough farmland, many Africans face starvation.

Solutions From Science Improvements in science can help feed Africans and protect Africa's environment. Irrigation projects, hybrids, and plants that hold water in the ground have all increased crop harvests. To fight soil erosion, Nigerian farmers now plant traditional crops like yams in long rows. Between the rows they plant trees that hold the soil in place. African nations still face many challenges, but they are trying to meet these challenges by using their resources and improving education.

Men plant trees in Madagascar to help prevent erosion.

✓ **Reading Check** How have Nigerian farmers fought soil erosion?

Section 5 Assessment

Key Terms
Review the key terms at the beginning of this section. Use each term in a sentence that explains its meaning.

Target Reading Skill
What did you predict about this section? How did your prediction guide your reading?

Comprehension and Critical Thinking
1. (a) Recall Do many African nations today have specialized economies?

(b) Draw Conclusions Why are African nations trying to diversify their economies?

2. (a) Identify What social issues are people facing in Africa today?

(b) Infer Literacy rates in most African countries have increased since independence. Education has also improved. From these facts, what can you infer that people value in Africa?

3. (a) Name Give an example of an environmental challenge African nations face today.

(b) Analyze How is that challenge being addressed?

Writing Activity
Suppose you are the economic advisor to the president of an African country. Write a brief report on some steps the president might take to improve the economy.

For: An activity on environmental issues in Africa
Visit: PHSchool.com
Web Code: lad-5205

Review and Assessment

◆ Chapter Summary

Section 1: African Beginnings

- Our ancestors were originally hunters and gatherers and became herders and farmers.
- The early African civilizations of Egypt and Nubia arose along the Nile River.
- When Bantu-speaking farmers migrated, Bantu languages spread throughout much of Africa.

Section 2: Kingdoms, City-States, and Empires

- Along East Africa's coast, civilizations grew strong from trade.
- North Africa was shaped by the Carthaginians, the Romans, and the Arabs.
- West African kingdoms grew rich from trade with North Africa.

Bronze head

Section 3: European Conquest of Africa

- Europeans explored Africa's coast to expand their trade ties beyond North Africa.
- Europeans expanded their trade with Africa to include slaves, whom they sent to work on plantations in the Americas.
- European countries claimed African lands for themselves, which had lasting effects on Africa.

Section 4: Independence and Its Challenges

- Fueled by increased feelings of African nationalism, African political parties and leaders worked for the rights of Africans.
- Africans who fought in World War II returned home seeking freedom and independence for their own countries.
- After World War II, African nations gradually gained independence from colonial powers.

Section 5: Issues for Africa Today

- To increase economic stability, African countries are trying to diversify their economies.
- Africans today are working to increase literacy rates and life expectancy.
- Africans are trying to address environmental issues, such as soil erosion, through the help of science, education, and the sensible use of land and other resources.

South Africa

◆ Reviewing Key Terms

Use each key term below in a sentence that shows the meaning of the term.

1. domesticate
2. civilization
3. migrate
4. ethnic group
5. city-state
6. pilgrimage
7. plantation
8. colonize
9. nationalism
10. Pan-Africanism
11. boycott
12. democracy
13. commercial farming
14. hybrid
15. literate
16. life expectancy

Review and Assessment (continued)

◆ Comprehension and Critical Thinking

17. (a) List Identify some of the skills early Africans used to survive.
(b) Draw Conclusions How did the onset of farming affect early civilizations in Africa?

18. (a) Name Identify an ancient trading civilization from each of the following areas: East Africa, North Africa, and West Africa.
(b) Explain Why was trade important to ancient African civilizations?
(c) Analyze Information What was the relationship between trade and the spread of Islam in Africa?

19. (a) Recall How did the relationship between Europeans and Africans begin?
(b) Identify Sequence How did the relationship between Europeans and Africans change over time?
(c) Identify Effects Describe the effects of the Atlantic slave trade on Africa.

20. (a) Define What is meant by the phrase "the scramble for Africa"?

(b) Describe What challenges have African nations faced since independence?
(c) Make Inferences In what ways did colonial rule cause problems for African countries after independence?

21. (a) Identify What economic, social, and environmental issues challenge Africans today?
(b) Explain How are Africans working to improve their economies and social conditions?

◆ Skills Practice

Sequencing In the Skills for Life activity in this chapter, you learned how to show sequence. Review the steps you followed to learn this skill. Then make a timeline of key events in this chapter.

◆ Writing Activity: Language Arts

In the 1800s, many people in the United States spoke out against slavery. They were called abolitionists because they wanted to abolish, or put an end to, slavery. Using what you have learned about the slave trade, write a speech that could be used by an abolitionist to help end slavery.

MAP★MASTER™
Skills Activity

Africa

Place Location For each place listed below, write the letter from the map that shows its location.

1. Original homeland of Bantu speakers
2. Great Zimbabwe
3. Tombouctou
4. Ancient Egypt
5. Kilwa
6. Kingdom of Mali
7. Nubia
8. Aksum

Go Online
PHSchool.com Use Web Code lap-5220 for an interactive map.

Standardized Test Prep

Test-Taking Tips

Some questions on standardized tests ask you to analyze a reading selection. Study the passage below. Then follow the tips to answer the sample question.

> In A.D. 1312, Mansa Musa became emperor of Mali. As emperor, he controlled huge supplies of gold and salt. Mansa Musa brought laws based on Islam to his land. Mali became a safe place to live and travel. The emperor also promoted trade with North Africa. His fame spread to Europe.

TIP Try to identify the main idea, or most important point, in the paragraph. Every sentence in a paragraph helps to support this idea.

Pick the letter that best answers the question.

From this paragraph, it is clear that Mansa Musa

A ~~became too powerful for the good of his people~~.

B ~~was the most powerful ruler in the world at that time~~.

C brought order and prosperity to his land.

D traveled to Europe to promote trade.

TIP Cross out answer choices that don't make sense. Then choose the BEST answer from the remaining choices.

Think It Through You can rule out A and B. Mansa Musa was powerful, but the paragraph doesn't suggest that he was too powerful or that he was the world's most powerful ruler. That leaves C and D. It is true that Mansa Musa's travels promoted trade, but the paragraph doesn't mention a trip to Europe. The correct answer is C.

Practice Questions

Use the tips above and other tips in this book to help you answer the following questions.

1. An early civilization formed in which area along the Nile River?

   A Mali   B Ghana

   C Nubia   D Great Zimbabwe

2. During the time of the Atlantic slave trade,

   A Europeans traded weapons for African slaves.

   B slaves in the European colonies usually won their freedom after a few years.

   C almost all slaves survived the voyage across the Atlantic.

   D Africans did not profit from slavery.

3. What was the goal of the Pan-African movement?

   A bringing all Africans together in one nation

   B bringing all Africans living around the world together to work for their rights and freedoms

   C bringing only Africans living in Africa together to work for their rights and freedoms

   D bringing all Africans living outside of Africa back to Africa

Read the passage below, and then answer the question that follows.

> European countries competed with one another to gain African territory. Instead of going to war over territory, they set rules for how they could claim African land. By 1900, European nations had colonized many parts of Africa.

4. What can you conclude from this passage about the colonization of Africa?

   A Africans did not resist colonization.

   B Africa was colonized sometime after 1900.

   C European nations believed they could benefit from controlling Africa's resources.

   D European nations were not good at fighting wars with one another.

Use Web Code **laa-5200** for **Chapter 2 self-test.**

Chapter Preview

This chapter will introduce you to the cultures of Africa and help you understand what the lives of the people in the region are like.

Section 1
The Cultures of North Africa

Section 2
The Cultures of West Africa

Section 3
The Cultures of East Africa

Section 4
The Cultures of Southern and Central Africa

Target Reading Skill

Comparison and Contrast In this chapter you will focus on comparing and contrasting ideas to help you understand the text that you read. Making comparisons, identifying contrasts, and using signal words are all ways for you to learn as you read.

▶ A dancer leaps through the air to the rhythm of the drums at a performance in Burundi.

KEY

Afroasiatic languages
Nilo-Saharan languages
Niger-Congo languages
Khoisan languages
Austronesian languages
Other languages
Uninhabited

——— National border
--- Disputed border

Arabic

Mediterranean Sea

Arabic

Tamasheq
(Tuareg)
Songhai

Poular
(Fulani)

Hausa

Arabic

Amharic

Yoruba
Igbo

Akan
(Asante)

Somali

Kikuyu

Lingala

Swahili

ATLANTIC
OCEAN

INDIAN
OCEAN

Shona

Zulu

Afrikaans
Xhosa

Tropic of Cancer
20° N
Equator
0°
20° S
Tropic of Capricorn

0 miles   1,500
0 kilometers   1,500
Lambert Azimuthal Equal Area

Place This map shows the major language groups in Africa. Many individual languages exist within each group. In all, more than 1,500 languages are spoken in Africa. **Identify** Name the two African language groups that are the largest. **Draw Conclusions** Why do you think large numbers of people who live near one another tend to speak languages from the same language group?

Go Online
PHSchool.com Use Web Code
lap-5310 for step-by-step
map skills practice.

Section 1

The Cultures of North Africa

Prepare to Read

Objectives

In this section you will
1. Learn about the elements of culture.
2. Discover how Islam influences life in North Africa.
3. Find out about cultural change in North Africa.

Taking Notes

As you read, find details about the cultures of North Africa. Copy the outline below, and use it to record your findings.

> I. The elements of culture
>   A.
>   1.
>   2.
>   B.
> II. Islamic influence

Target Reading Skill

Make Comparisons
Making comparisons between groups or situations can help you see what they have in common. As you read this section, compare the ways of life of different peoples in North Africa. Look for similarities among ethnic groups, among people who live in different locations, or among other groups that are logical to compare.

Key Terms

- **culture** (KUL chur) *n.* the way of life of people who share similar customs and beliefs
- **Quran** (koo RAHN) *n.* the sacred book of Islam; also spelled *Koran*
- **cultural diffusion** (KUL chur ul dih FYOO zhun) *n.* the spread of customs and ideas from one culture to another

A carpet salesman in Marrakech

In the North African country of Morocco, carpets are an export. But they are also part of everyday life. In some Moroccan homes, carpets serve as more than just floor coverings. People may use them as places to sit and to sleep. People also use special carpets as prayer mats.

Suppose your family lives in the Moroccan city of Marrakech (ma ruh KESH). A typical day might unfold in the following way. After breakfast, your mother spends the day weaving carpets. She learned this skill from her mother, who learned it from her mother. Her workday ends at sunset, when she hears the crier who calls out from the nearby mosque (mahsk), the Muslim house of worship. When she hears the call, your mother joins many others in reciting this prayer in Arabic: "There is no god but God, and Muhammad is His messenger."

The Elements of Culture

The way of life you just read about is different in some ways from yours. In other words, Morocco's culture is somewhat different from yours. **Culture** is the way of life of a group of people who share similar customs and beliefs.

What Defines Culture? Culture has many elements. Culture includes food, clothing, homes, jobs, and language. It also includes things that are not so easy to see, such as how people view their world and what their beliefs are. These views and beliefs shape the way people behave. In Morocco, for example, many people take time from their activities to pray several times each day.

Shared Elements Different cultures may have elements in common. People in different places sometimes share the same language, although they may speak different dialects, or versions of that language. Similarly, cultures sometimes share the same religion, although people may practice it in different ways.

Some shared elements of culture are easy to notice. People of different cultures might wear similar clothing or live in similar housing. In many rural villages in Morocco, for example, houses are made of thick adobe (uh DOH bee), a type of brick made from sun-dried clay. Far from Morocco, in Mexico and in the southwestern United States, many people in rural areas also live in adobe houses.

✓ **Reading Check** **Name some cultural elements that are easy to see.**

Links to
Science

Building With Adobe
Adobe bricks are made of clay and plant fibers. The fibers strengthen the bricks and keep them from crumbling. People have built with adobe since ancient times in many parts of the world. Native Americans have built with adobe for hundreds of years in the southwestern United States, where it is still used today.

Adobe is a good building material because it acts as an insulator, a material that helps keep outside heat from traveling inside. This insulating quality is especially important in hot climates, such as Morocco's (below).

Religion and Culture in North Africa

The peoples of North Africa are spread out over a large area that includes the following countries: Egypt, Libya, Tunisia, Algeria, and Morocco. North Africans have many different backgrounds and ways of life. The Arabic language helps unify the different peoples of North Africa. So does Islam.

Muslim Beliefs Religion is an important part of North African culture. More than 95 percent of North Africans are Muslims. Muslims believe in God, whom they call by the Arabic word *Allah* (AL uh). The founder of Islam was a man named Muhammad. Muslims believe that Muhammad was a prophet, or a religious teacher who speaks for God or a god. In Islam, Jesus and the prophets of the Hebrew Bible, or Christian Old Testament, are also believed to be God's messengers. However, Muhammad is considered God's final messenger.

The sacred book of Islam is called the **Quran** (koo RAHN). Muslims consider the Quran to be the word of God. They believe that God revealed the verses of the Quran to the prophet Muhammad. Like the Hebrew and Christian Bibles, the Quran contains many kinds of writing, including stories, promises, and instructions. The Quran teaches about God, and it also provides a guide to living. The Quran forbids lying, stealing, and murder. It also prohibits gambling, eating pork, and drinking alcohol.

■ Chart Skills

Muslims call Muhammad's most essential teachings the Five Pillars of Islam. These pillars are duties that all Muslims are expected to follow, such as praying daily, as shown above. **Define** What are alms? **Infer** Why do you think Muhammad wanted Muslims to regularly declare their belief in God?

The Five Pillars of Islam

Pillar	Description
Declaration of Faith	Muslims must regularly declare the belief that there is only one God and Muhammad is God's messenger.
Prayer	Muslims must pray five times each day, facing in the direction of the holy city of Mecca.
Almsgiving	Muslims must give alms, or money that goes to the needy.
Fasting	Muslims must fast during daylight hours in the month of Ramadan.
Pilgrimage	Muslims must make a pilgrimage to Mecca at least one time in their lives if they are able.

Islam and Law The Islamic system of law is based on the Quran. Islamic law governs many aspects of life, including family life, business practices, banking, and government. Because so many North Africans are Muslims, Islamic law influences the cultures of the region.

Ethnic Groups of North Africa Most North Africans are Arabs. Because the Arab influence is so strong, North Africa is sometimes seen as a part (the western end) of the Arab world. But the region has other ethnic groups besides the Arabs. The largest of these groups is the Berbers, who live mainly in Algeria and Morocco. Most Berbers speak both Berber and Arabic, and almost all are Muslim.

Many Berbers live in cities, while others live in small villages in rugged mountain areas. They make their living by herding and farming. The Tuareg (TWAH reg) are a group of Berbers who live in the Sahara, the enormous desert that stretches across the southern part of North Africa. The Tuareg herd camels, goats, and other livestock and also engage in long-distance trade.

Mixing Old and New
As is traditional for Muslim women, these Moroccan girls are wearing head scarves. At the same time, one is using a cell phone. **Analyze Images** *Do you think these girls would say it is easy or difficult to blend old and new ways?*

Traditional and Modern Lifestyles In parts of rural North Africa, some people live traditionally, or in ways similar to those of their parents and grandparents. But traditional and modern ways of life mix in towns and large cities such as Cairo (KY roh), in Egypt, and Tunis (TOO nis), in Tunisia.

Some city people work at traditional crafts such as carpet weaving. Others work as architects, scientists, bus drivers, or bankers. Some sell baskets in outdoor markets. Others sell television sets, books, and other items in modern stores. The peoples of North Africa may live vastly different lives, yet Islam helps form a common bond of culture among them.

Make Comparisons The people who live in North Africa's cities practice a variety of lifestyles. What element of culture do they have in common?

✓ **Reading Check** **What are the two largest ethnic groups of North Africa?**

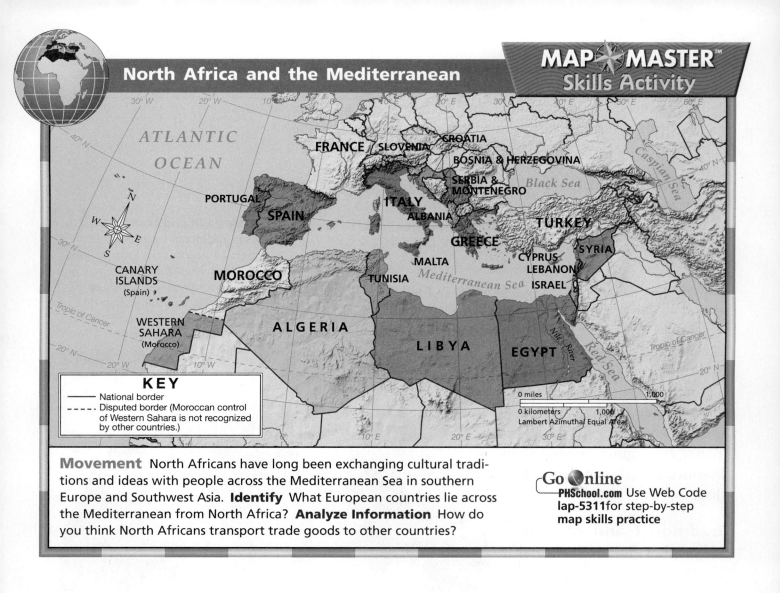

ATLANTIC OCEAN

FRANCE
SLOVENIA
CROATIA
BOSNIA & HERZEGOVINA
SERBIA & MONTENEGRO
Black Sea
Caspian Sea
PORTUGAL
SPAIN
ITALY
ALBANIA
TURKEY
GREECE
CYPRUS
SYRIA
LEBANON
CANARY ISLANDS (Spain)
MOROCCO
MALTA
TUNISIA
Mediterranean Sea
ISRAEL
WESTERN SAHARA (Morocco)
ALGERIA
LIBYA
EGYPT
Nile River
Red Sea
Tropic of Cancer

KEY
— National border
----- Disputed border (Moroccan control of Western Sahara is not recognized by other countries.)

0 miles 1,000
0 kilometers 1,000
Lambert Azimuthal Equal Area

Movement North Africans have long been exchanging cultural traditions and ideas with people across the Mediterranean Sea in southern Europe and Southwest Asia. **Identify** What European countries lie across the Mediterranean from North Africa? **Analyze Information** How do you think North Africans transport trade goods to other countries?

Go Online
PHSchool.com Use Web Code lap-5311for step-by-step map skills practice

Cultural Change in North Africa

North Africa's mix of traditional and modern ways of life shows that culture does not stay the same forever. It changes all the time. Cultural changes often occur when people move from one place to another. As they travel, people share their customs and ideas with others. They also learn about new ideas and customs. The result is **cultural diffusion,** or the spread of customs and ideas to new places. *Diffusion* means "spreading out."

A Hub of Trade Study the map above. An important factor in the diffusion of culture in North Africa is location. Because of its location, North Africa has been a hub, or center, of trade for people from Europe, Asia, North Africa, and other parts of Africa. Thus, the peoples of these regions have come into contact with one another's cultures. Many customs and ideas have spread into and out of North Africa.

Tunisian pottery

Conquering Empires The mixing of cultures in North Africa did not occur only through trade. It also occurred through conquest. North Africa was home to the ancient Egyptians, one of the world's oldest civilizations. Once the ancient Egyptians had developed trade links with ancient civilizations in both Europe and Southwest Asia, these civilizations competed with one another for power. The ancient Egyptians both conquered and were conquered by other empires. Through these conquests, more cultural diffusion occurred.

In Algeria, women in traditional Muslim clothes walk alongside women and men in Western dress.

Western and Muslim Cultures One of the more recent influences on North Africa is Western culture, meaning the cultures of Europe and North America. Some Muslims are concerned that their countries are becoming too Westernized. More people are wearing Western clothes, buying Western products, seeing films produced by the West, and adopting Western ideas. Some Muslims fear that these influences will lead to the loss of Muslim values and traditions. They want to preserve their way of life. All over Africa, people face the challenge of how to preserve the traditions they value as their countries change.

✔ **Reading Check** With what regions have North Africans traditionally traded?

 Section 1 Assessment

Key Terms
Review the key terms at the beginning of this section. Use each term in a sentence that explains its meaning.

 Target Reading Skill
Other than religion, what is an element of culture that most North Africans have in common?

Comprehension and Critical Thinking
1. **(a) Name** What are some elements of culture?

(b) Draw Conclusions How do you think cultural beliefs shape the way people behave?
2. **(a) Recall** What are the beliefs of the followers of Islam?
(b) Analyze Information How has Islam influenced the cultures of North Africa?
3. **(a) Locate** Describe North Africa's location.
(b) Cause and Effect How has North Africa's location contributed to cultural diffusion?
(c) Analyze Information Do you think that adding new elements to a culture has to lead to the loss of old ones?

Writing Activity
What is your culture? What traditions in your culture do you think are the most important ones to preserve? Write an essay describing these customs and explaining why you value them.

Writing Tip To help you get started, write a list of traditions and customs you practice throughout the year.

The Cultures of West Africa

Prepare to Read

Objectives

In this section you will
1. Learn about West Africa's ethnic diversity.
2. Find out about the importance of family ties in West African culture.
3. Examine the West African tradition of storytelling.

Taking Notes

As you read, look for details about the cultures of West Africa. Copy the flowchart below, and use it to record your findings.

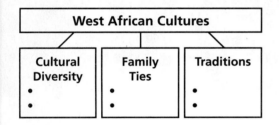

West African Cultures

Cultural Diversity	Family Ties	Traditions
•	•	•
•	•	•

Target Reading Skill

Identify Contrasts
Identifying contrasts between two groups or situations can help you see what is unique about each one. As you read this section, contrast the cultures in West Africa with the cultures in the United States. List the differences that relate to language and to family life.

Key Terms

- **cultural diversity** (KUL chur ul duh VUR suh tee) *n.* a wide variety of cultures
- **kinship** (KIN ship) *n.* a family relationship
- **nuclear family** (NOO klee ur FAM uh lee) *n.* the part of a family that includes parents and children
- **extended family** (ek STEN did FAM uh lee) *n.* the part of a family that includes parents, children, and other relatives
- **lineage** (LIN ee ij) *n.* a group of families descended from a common ancestor
- **clan** (klan) *n.* a group of lineages

Mauritanian students in school

In Mauritania (mawr uh TAY nee uh), North Africa meets West Africa. There, the Sahara merges into the tree-dotted grasslands of the savanna. But geography is not the only part of Mauritanian life that reveals major contrasts. Culture does, too. If you were to attend school in one of the small villages in southern Mauritania, you could see this firsthand. You would hear teachers speaking in French, even though they probably also know the country's official language, Arabic. Outside the classroom, students would speak the local language of their ethnic group, which might differ from town to town.

Cultural Diversity of West Africa

Being able to speak more than one language is useful in West Africa, which is home to hundreds of ethnic groups. The region is famous for its **cultural diversity,** or wide variety of cultures. Unlike the ethnic groups of North Africa, those of West Africa are not united by a single religion or a common language.

A Region of Many Languages Think about your community. Imagine that the people who live nearby speak a different language. How could you communicate with them? Suppose you want to shop in a store, eat in a restaurant, or attend a sports event taking place in the next town. It might seem like visiting another country.

This situation is exactly what many West Africans experience. The hundreds of ethnic groups in West Africa speak different languages. Sometimes groups in neighboring villages speak different languages. In order to communicate, most West Africans speak more than one language. Some speak four or five languages. This practice helps unify countries with many ethnic groups. People use these various languages when they travel or conduct business. They often use French, English, Portuguese, or a local language called Hausa to communicate among various ethnic groups.

Rural and Urban Workers The ethnic groups in West Africa differ in more than just the languages they speak. Like North Africans, West Africans make a living in various ways. Many West Africans live in rural areas. A typical village consists of a group of homes surrounded by farmland. The villagers grow food for themselves as well as cash crops to sell. In the Sahara and the dry Sahel just south of it, many people herd cattle, goats, sheep, or camels. Along the coast, most West Africans make a living by fishing. Some West Africans live in large cities where they may work in hospitals, hotels, or office buildings.

✔ **Reading Check** How does cultural diversity affect the people of West Africa?

Many Languages in One Place
If you were shopping at this market in West Africa, you might hear a number of languages being spoken. **Draw Conclusions** *How do you think people communicate in situations like this?*

West African Families

Like North Africans, West Africans see themselves as members of a number of groups. Just as you belong to a family, one or more ethnic groups, and a country, so do West Africans.

Kinship and Customs One of the strongest bonds that West Africans have is the bond of **kinship,** or family relationship. The first level of kinship is the **nuclear family,** which consists of parents and their children. The next level is the **extended family,** a group consisting of the nuclear family plus other relatives. It may include grandparents, aunts, uncles, and cousins. Often, members of a West African extended family all live together. They also work together and make decisions together. Family members care for the elderly, the sick, and the less well-off. They also watch over the children of other families in the village and willingly help neighbors.

Larger Kinship Groups In many rural areas, kinship reaches beyond extended families to larger groups. One such group is a **lineage,** or a group of families that can trace their descent back to a common ancestor. Some people also recognize larger kinship groups called clans. A **clan** is a group of lineages. As with a lineage, the people in a clan can all trace their roots back to a common ancestor. Members of a clan may be more distantly related to one another than members of a lineage because the group of members is larger in a clan.

West African Family Ties
Members of an extended family in Nigeria gather in front of their home (bottom). A woman in Ivory Coast cares for her granddaughter (below). **Identify Effects** *What effects do you think the strong kinship ties of West Africa have on communities?*

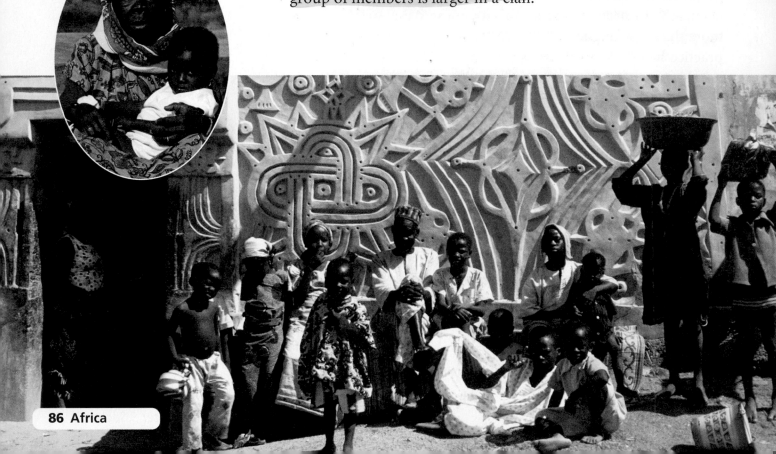

Kinship

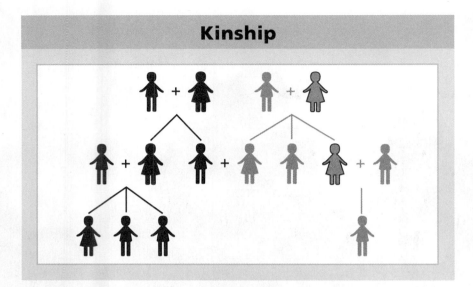

■ **Diagram Skills**

The diagram shows the extended family of the married couple at the center. The husband's lineage is in purple, and the wife's is in orange. In a matrilineal society, this family would trace descent through the women who are outlined in red.

Identify How many nuclear families exist in the extended lineage?

Synthesize What is the relationship of the woman at the top of the purple lineage to the three siblings at the bottom of it?

Tracing Lineage Different traditions govern the ways West African groups trace their ancestry. Some groups are matrilineal (mat ruh LIN ee ul), meaning that they trace their descent through female ancestors. In matrilineal societies, a person's father is not considered part of the person's lineage. Within the lineage, children consider their mother's brother their closest adult male relative. Their father is a member of another lineage. Most groups, however, are patrilineal (pat ruh LIN ee ul)—they trace their descent through the male side of the family.

Families live close together in West African villages such as this one in Mali.

Changes in Family Life Although traditional family ties are still strong in West Africa, family life is changing. More and more people are moving from rural villages to urban areas. This trend, known as urbanization, is occurring not only in Africa but throughout the world.

Many young men are looking for work to support themselves and their families. They travel long distances to West Africa's cities to find jobs. The women often stay in the rural homes. They raise the children and farm the land. The men come home from time to time to visit their families and to share what they have earned.

✔ **Reading Check** What responsibilities do extended family members have toward one another?

Master of Storytelling
Boys from an Ivory Coast village listen intently as a griot tells them a legend about their ethnic group's history. **Synthesize** *How does oral storytelling help preserve a culture's history?*

Keeping Traditions Alive

Cultural changes, such as urbanization, affect different families in different ways. As they adapt to these changes, most West Africans try to maintain strong family ties. They pass their history, values, and traditions on to the young.

Storytelling Traditions One important way in which West African traditions are being preserved is through the art of vivid and exciting storytelling. Traditional West African stories are spoken aloud rather than written down. A storyteller called a griot (GREE oh) passes a group's oral traditions on from one generation to another.

Stories of tricksters, animal fables, proverbs, riddles, and songs are all part of West Africa's oral tradition. The details in the stories tell about the histories of ethnic groups and kinships. At the same time, they teach children cultural values. An African proverb reflects the value that West Africans place on handing down traditions from generation to generation: "The young can't teach traditions to the old."

African musicians perform around the world, from Massachusetts (left) to Ivory Coast (right).

Cultural Influence The traditions of West Africa have greatly influenced other cultures, especially American culture. Many of the enslaved Africans who were brought to the United States came from West Africa. They brought with them the only things they could: their ideas, stories, dances, music, and customs. The trickster tales of Br'er Rabbit, as well as blues and jazz music, have their roots in West Africa.

Today, West African culture—its stories, music, dances, art, cooking, and clothing—is popular in many countries outside of Africa. Griot guitarists and other musicians from West Africa have international followings. In recent years, four Africans have won the Nobel Prize for literature. One of them is West African—the Nigerian writer Wole Soyinka (WOH lay shaw YING kuh).

✓ **Reading Check** What does a griot do?

 ## Section 2 Assessment

Key Terms
Review the key terms at the beginning of this section. Use each term in a sentence that explains its meaning.

 Target Reading Skill
Identify one contrast between the way West Africans use language and the way Americans do.

Comprehension and Critical Thinking
1. (a) Recall In what ways is West Africa culturally diverse?

(b) Identify Effects How does cultural diversity create communication challenges for West Africans?
2. (a) Describe What kinds of kinship ties are found in West African societies?
(b) Draw Conclusions How do you think living together with members of one's extended family helps build a sense of community?
3. (a) Explain What purpose does storytelling serve in West African culture?
(b) Analyze What is the meaning of the proverb "The young can't teach traditions to the old"?

Writing Activity
Suppose you live with your extended family in a small village in West Africa. Make a list of the advantages and disadvantages of your way of life. Indicate which are most important to you.

For: An activity on the cultures of West Africa
Visit: PHSchool.com
Web Code: lad-5302

Skills for Life

Comparing and Contrasting

Nathan and Antonio went to the mall to buy CDs. When Antonio saw the CD Nathan had chosen, he commented, "I like that CD. But I think the band's new CD is better. They use more drums on the new CD."

Nathan argued. "I disagree. I like the way the band sounded on the old CD. They had two singers, and the two voices together sounded better than this one singer's voice alone." The girl working at the register smiled. She couldn't hear any differences in the CDs. She thought they were both great.

When you look for differences between two or more items, you *contrast* them. To *compare*, you do one of two things: you look for similarities between two or more items, or you look for similarities *and* differences between two or more items. If you are asked to compare, ask if you should find similarities only, or similarities and differences.

Learn the Skill

Follow these steps to learn how to compare and contrast.

1 **Identify a topic and purpose.** What do you want to compare or contrast, and why? Some purposes for comparing and contrasting are to make a choice, to understand a topic, or to discover patterns.

2 **Select some categories for comparison and contrast.** For example, if you wanted to choose between two bikes, your categories might be color, cost, and types of tires.

3 **Make notes—or a chart—about the categories you are comparing or contrasting.** Some categories call for a yes or no answer. Other categories, such as color or cost, require that you note specific details.

4 **Notice the similarities and differences.** Are the details the same or different for each item?

5 **Draw conclusions.** Write a few sentences explaining whether the items are more similar or more different.

Practice the Skill

Use the steps below, plus your own knowledge, to compare and contrast the two scenes from Africa that are shown in the photographs on this page. Use what you find to determine a pattern in the photographs.

1 What is your topic? What is the purpose?

2 Study the photographs. Then write down at least three categories for comparison and contrast.

3 For each category, take notes on what the photographs show.

4 Now study your notes to see what is similar and what is different about the two photographs.

5 Write a conclusion that explains whether the scenes in the photographs are mostly similar or mostly different. Include a description of one pattern you see in the photographs. Can you describe a third photograph that would fit the pattern?

Chimpanzees in Tanzania

Giraffes in Kenya

Apply the Skill

Reread Sections 1 and 2 of this chapter. Use the steps you learned in this skill to compare and contrast the cultures of North Africa and West Africa.

The Cultures of East Africa

Prepare to Read

Objectives
In this section you will
1. Find out how geography has affected the development of East African cultures.
2. Learn how and why ideas about land ownership are changing in East Africa.

Taking Notes
As you read, find details about the cultures of East Africa. Copy the concept web below, and use it to record your findings.

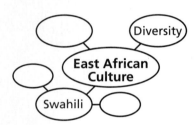

Target Reading Skill

Use Signal Words
Signal words point out relationships among ideas or events. Certain words or phrases, such as *like* and *as with*, can signal a comparison or a contrast. As you read this section, notice the comparisons between East Africa and other parts of Africa.

Key Terms
- **Swahili** (swah HEE lee) *n.* an ethnic group in East Africa that resulted from the mixing of African and Arab ways more than 1,000 years ago; also a language
- **heritage** (HEHR uh tij) *n.* the values, traditions, and customs handed down from one's ancestors

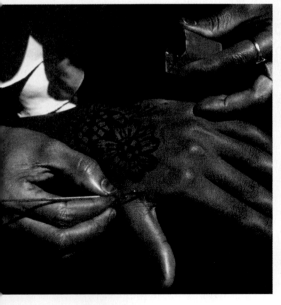

A woman in Lamu gets her hand decorated with henna.

In the neighborhood square, old friends often sit together playing dominoes. A man on a donkey may wander past amidst the occasional roar of motorcycles. Down the street, there is a store that sells spices next to a shop that offers fax services and Internet connections. Nearby, behind shuttered windows that filter the hot sun, women take turns making intricate designs on one another's hands using a natural dye called henna. In former East African city-states such as Lamu (LAH moo), in Kenya, and Zanzibar (ZAN zuh bahr), in Tanzania, such traditional and modern ways are interwoven.

Geography and Cultural Diversity
Like West Africa, East Africa is a region of great cultural diversity. In some parts of the region, such as Lamu and Zanzibar, the diversity reveals itself in the contrast between old and new ways. In other parts, it is reflected in the diversity of languages spoken or religions practiced.

Indian Ocean Connections Much of the cultural diversity of East Africa comes from contact among people from many cultures. Like other Africans, the people of East Africa have often been exposed to other cultures through trade. Turn to the political map of Africa on page 3 of the Regional Overview. Notice how much of East Africa's long coastline borders the Indian Ocean. This ocean provides a trade and travel route for East Africans as well as for the people living across the ocean to the east. These people include Arabs, Indians, and other Asians, even those from countries as far away from Africa as China and Malaysia.

Swahili Culture The connection across the Indian Ocean dates back to early times. Nearly 2,000 years ago, Arab traders began to settle in the coastal villages of East Africa. Members of various African cultures took on elements of Arab culture from the newcomers. The Arabs took on elements of African culture as well. The **Swahili** are an ethnic group that resulted from this mixing of African and Arab ways.

Most people who live in Lamu or Zanzibar are Swahili. A professor in Zanzibar described the history of the Swahili to a reporter in this way:

> **We have always been middlemen—between the land and the sea, the producers and the buyers, the African and the Arabian. That is not a concern; it is our strength. We will survive. Swahili culture may not be quite the same tomorrow as today, but then nothing living is.**
>
> —Professor Abdul Sheriff

Swahili Arts and Crafts
Swahili craftsmen are known for carving front doors with detailed decoration on their frames. This one is in Zanzibar, Tanzania. **Analyze Images** *Why do you think people would choose a front door as a place to show their craft?*

One important strength of the Swahili people is their ability to adapt to other cultures. To adapt is to adjust to new things or circumstances. At the same time, the Swahilis try to preserve their **heritage**, or the values, traditions, and customs handed down from their ancestors.

Widespread Swahili Language Swahilis live along East Africa's coast from Somalia to Tanzania. Recall from Chapter 2 that the Swahili language is a Bantu language that contains many Arabic words. Although the Swahili are just one of hundreds of ethnic groups in East Africa, their language is used among ethnic groups throughout the region for business and communication. In Tanzania, children are educated in Swahili through the primary grades. Later, they learn English as well. By promoting the use of Swahili, East African nations are helping to preserve their African heritage and to establish unity among different peoples.

Signal Words
What signal words are used to compare the number of languages spoken in East Africa and West Africa?

Other Languages As is true of West Africa, East Africa is home to many ethnic groups who speak different languages. It is not unusual for people in the region to know three languages or more. For example, in Ethiopia more than 80 languages are spoken, and in Kenya about 40 are spoken. About 1,000 languages can be heard in Sudan alone. The variety of languages spoken in the region is largely due to the long history of migrations of ethnic groups from other parts of the continent. For example, the Bantu migration that you read about earlier brought many Bantu-speaking peoples from West Africa to East Africa.

Religion As with languages, religious beliefs in East Africa reflect the cultural diversity of the region. Both Islam and Christianity have large followings there. Islam was introduced to East Africa by Arab traders. Christianity spread into Ethiopia in the A.D. 300s after being introduced to North Africa when the area was a part of the Roman Empire. During the 1800s, Europeans pushed into Africa and spread Christianity even farther. In addition, traditional religions are still practiced in East Africa.

✓ **Reading Check** **What religions are practiced by East Africans?**

Changing Ideas About Land

In East Africa, as in the rest of Africa, most people live in rural areas, where they farm and tend livestock. The ways in which they work the land and view land ownership are part of the culture of East Africans.

Before Land Was Owned Before Europeans took over parts of Africa in the 1800s, individual Africans did not buy or sell land. The very idea of owning land did not exist. Families had the right to farm plots of land, but the size and location of the plots might change over time.

Traditionally in Africa, extended families farmed the land to produce food for the whole group. Men cleared the land and broke up the soil. Women then planted the seeds, tended the fields, and harvested the crops. Meanwhile, the men herded livestock or traded goods.

The Rise and Fall of Plantations The practice of owning land privately was introduced into much of Africa by European settlers. In parts of East Africa, the British set up plantations. When many African countries became independent, their governments broke up the colonial plantations and sold the land to individual Africans.

Some land in East Africa is still available to buy. But much of it is poor farmland in areas where few people live. In fertile areas such as the Ethiopian Highlands and the Great Rift Valley, most of the land good for farming is already taken. Many people live in these fertile areas. In densely populated countries such as Rwanda (roo AHN duh) and Burundi (boo ROON dee), conflicts have developed over land.

The Legacy of Land
Agriculture is part of life all over East Africa. Farmers work fields of a large plantation (bottom). An Ethiopian farmer tends his fields (inset).
Synthesize Information *Why has farmland caused conflicts in some East African countries?*

Julius Nyerere, Tanzania's first president

Where Is Home? Traditionally, Africans feel a strong bond to the land where they grew up. Like the rest of Africa, East Africa is becoming increasingly urban. Yet even people who spend most of their time in a city often do not call it home. If asked where home is, an East African will usually name the village of his or her family or clan. Most people consider their life in the city temporary. They expect to return to their villages at some point.

Tanzania's former president Julius Nyerere (JOOL yus nyuh REHR uh) is one example. After he stepped down as president in 1985, Nyerere moved back to his home village. Although he was far from Dar es Salaam (DAHR es suh LAHM), one of Tanzania's two capital cities, Nyerere continued to be involved in world affairs. Until his death in 1999, he spent his mornings working in the fields, where he grew corn and millet on his farm.

In an interview in 1996, Nyerere said: "In a sense I am a very rural person. I grew up here, and [working in] Dar es Salaam was a duty. I did my duty and after retiring in 1985, I came back here and said, 'Ah, it's good to be back.' " Many other East Africans feel the same. They do their duty by earning money in the city, but they never forget their rural roots.

✓ **Reading Check** How did East Africans farm before Europeans arrived?

 Section 3 Assessment

Key Terms

Review the key terms at the beginning of this section. Use each term in a sentence that explains its meaning.

Target Reading Skill

Make a list of all the signal words you found as you read this section. Describe the comparison that each signal word indicates.

Comprehension and Critical Thinking

1. (a) Locate Where in East Africa do the Swahilis live?

(b) Summarize How did East Africa become a region with great diversity of language and religion?

(c) Make Inferences What is the importance of the Swahili language in East Africa?

2. (a) Recall When was private land ownership introduced to East Africa?

(b) Summarize How have ideas about land ownership changed over time in East Africa?

(c) Identify Point of View How did traditional East African ideas about land differ from those of Europeans who took over parts of Africa?

Writing Activity

Write a description of the place that you consider home. Tell what home means to you and explain why. How does your meaning of home compare to Julius Nyerere's feelings about his homeland?

> **Writing Tip** Before you begin, think of important details about your home that you can use in your description. Use vivid language to make your description come to life.

The Cultures of Southern and Central Africa

Prepare to Read

Objectives

In this section you will
1. Learn about the cultural diversity of Southern Africa.
2. Examine different ways of life in Central Africa and learn about the diverse cultures of the region.

Taking Notes

As you read, look for details about the cultures of Southern and Central Africa. Copy the table below, and use it to record your findings.

Southern Africa	Central Africa
•	•
•	•
•	•

Target Reading Skill

Compare and Contrast Comparing and contrasting can help you sort out and analyze information. When you compare, you examine the similarities between things. When you contrast, you look at the differences.

As you read this section, compare and contrast the cultures of Southern and Central Africa. Look for similarities and differences in ethnic groups and in economic conditions.

Key Terms

- **migrant worker** (MY grunt WUR kur) *n.* a laborer who travels away from where he or she lives to find work
- **compound** (KAHM pownd) *n.* a fenced-in group of homes

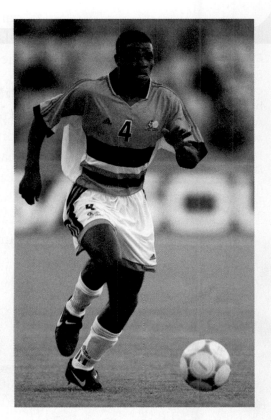

A member of South Africa's national soccer team

Soccer is a popular sport all around the world. It is no surprise, then, that it is a favorite sport of people in the country of South Africa. But the fact that the sport is played there reveals more than just that South Africans love fun and recreation. It is proof of the changing political times in South Africa.

Soccer came to South Africa from Europe. As you will read in Chapter 17, Europeans settled in the region from the mid-1600s through the 1800s. After the country gained independence in 1910, the white minority of the population took charge of the government. As part of their rule, the white population denied other members of society certain basic rights. For example, black South Africans were not allowed to play on many of the nation's sports teams.

In 1994, the South African government was restructured, and equal rights were extended to all. Today, when black and white soccer players run onto the field, all South Africans have reason to cheer.

Diversity in Southern Africa

Like the rest of Africa, Southern Africa has a great deal of cultural diversity. Most of the people of Southern Africa are black Africans. They belong to a variety of ethnic groups, many of which speak separate languages. In addition, there are certain ethnic groups that have greater numbers of members in Southern Africa than in other parts of Africa—for example, people of European descent.

European Influence Southern Africa attracted Europeans for a variety of reasons. The Portuguese arrived in Mozambique in the 1500s and soon began transporting slaves out of Africa. In the 1600s, Dutch and British settlers moved to the Cape of Good Hope at the southern tip of Africa. They grew wheat and herded cattle. Many of the Dutch eventually spread to the north to places such as Malawi, where they started up a mining industry and enlisted local people as laborers. The British also moved north, to Zimbabwe and Zambia.

European Ethnic Groups Southern Africa is home to three main groups of people with European ancestry. One group is descended from the British settlers. These Africans speak English. Another group is Afrikaners (af rih KAHN urz), who are descendants of the Dutch settlers. They speak Afrikaans (af rih KAHNZ), a language related to Dutch. The third group, descended from the Portuguese settlers, speaks Portuguese.

Urbanization The cultural diversity of Southern Africa extends beyond ethnic differences. It is also represented by the contrast between rural and urban lifestyles. For hundreds of years, people in the region lived in villages or small cities. European settlers started a process of urbanization in Southern Africa. The region now includes a number of cities inhabited by more than 1 million people. The largest are Cape Town and Johannesburg in South Africa and Maputo in Mozambique.

Effects of Urbanization
Even though it sits nestled between ocean and mountains, Cape Town has grown to be one of South Africa's largest cities. Its population is about 3 million people. **Infer** *How do you think the presence of numerous large cities changes the culture of a region?*

Industry in South Africa South Africa is the richest, most urban, and most industrialized country in Africa. During the 1900s, South African industries created a great demand for labor. Hundreds of thousands of people came from nearby countries in Southern Africa to work on South African mines. They formed a large force of **migrant workers,** or laborers who travel away from where they live to find work. These migrant workers had to live together in **compounds,** or fenced-in groups of homes. They were far from their families, clans, and ethnic groups. They worked long hours in dangerous conditions for low wages.

A woman in Zimbabwe spreads fertilizer on corn plants.

New Roles for Women The workers who migrated to South Africa for work were mostly men. While they were gone, the women had to take on the men's responsibilities. Traditionally, women had raised the children and farmed the land. Men had cared for the animals, dealt with local matters, and headed the households. Once the men were gone for a year or two at a time, the women began to make the household and community decisions. For most women, this change was a challenge. For example, many of the women had no training for the new tasks. But the change was also rewarding for many women because they gained new rights, responsibilities, and skills.

✓ **Reading Check** **Name two cities in Southern Africa that have a population of more than one million people.**

Life in Central Africa

Like the people of Southern Africa and the rest of Africa, Central Africans went through many cultural changes in the 1900s. But many people in the region still follow old traditions as well.

Economics and Culture In some ways, Central Africa's cultural diversity is a result of sharp economic contrasts that exist in the region. On the Atlantic coast, the countries of Angola, Congo, Gabon, Cameroon, and Equatorial Guinea have large oil reserves. The cities in these coastal areas tend to benefit most from the oil wealth. People living near the coast also gain more exposure to cultures outside of Africa, allowing for the exchange of traditions and customs.

Compare and Contrast Compare and contrast the ways industry affects culture in Southern and Central Africa. Are there more similarities or more differences?

Mbuti Art The lives of the Mbuti (em BOO tee) are very different from the lives of most people in Central Africa. They are hunter-gatherers who live in the rain forests of Congo. The Mbuti live off the land the way their ancestors have for more than 3,000 years.

For example, they make some of their cloth out of tree bark. Men pound the bark with mallets until it is almost as soft as velvet. Then women draw shapes and patterns on the cloth. Many art galleries in the United States and Europe collect Mbuti bark-cloth drawings for their shapes and patterns.

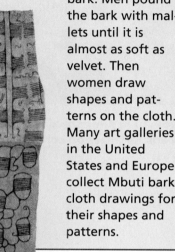

In contrast, living conditions get poorer as you move in from the coast to the interior areas of Angola, Congo, the Democratic Republic of the Congo, and the Central African Republic. There, village societies are organized by kinship groups, and land is owned by clans. In less-populated rural areas, individual families live and work on their own land.

Diverse Ways of Life Like the rest of the continent, Central Africa contains great cultural diversity. The Democratic Republic of the Congo alone has about 200 ethnic groups.

Millions of people live in crowded shantytowns or cinder-block apartments in Kinshasa, the largest city in the Democratic Republic of the Congo. They walk or take buses or trucks to work in factories, offices, and hotels. Millions of others live in rural areas. Some Central African people are Roman Catholic or Protestant. Others practice religions that blend Christian and traditional African beliefs. Still others are Muslim.

What one writer said about North Africa applies to Central and Southern Africa as well. To define the real North African, he said, "you have to define which one you mean: the rich or the poor, the Berber women of the mountains or the college girls on motorbikes. . . ." Old, new, and mixtures of the two live on in all regions of Africa.

✓ **Reading Check** What are some examples of cultural diversity in Central Africa?

Section 4 Assessment

Key Terms
Review the key terms at the beginning of this section. Use each term in a sentence that explains its meaning.

Target Reading Skill
Name two similarities between Southern Africa and Central Africa. Name two differences.

Comprehension and Critical Thinking
1. (a) Identify When did the process of urbanization in Southern Africa begin?

(b) Explain Why did people from all over Southern Africa migrate to South Africa?

(c) Identify Causes How were the lives of many Southern African women affected by South Africa even though the women never moved there?

2. (a) Recall What industry has brought wealth to some of the countries on Central Africa's Atlantic coast?

(b) Contrast How do the economics and culture of Central Africa's Atlantic coast differ from the economics and culture of its interior areas?

Writing Activity
Write a short report summarizing the ways in which economics have affected culture in Southern Africa and Central Africa. Point out any similarities or differences.

For: An activity on the region of Southern Africa
Visit: PHSchool.com
Web Code: lad-5304

Review and Assessment

◆ Chapter Summary

Section 1: The Cultures of North Africa

- Culture has many elements, such as food, language, and beliefs.
- Islam has greatly influenced life in North Africa.
- Because of North Africa's location, the people of the region have been exposed to the cultures of its trading partners, including Europe, Asia, and other parts of Africa.

Morocco

Section 2: The Cultures of West Africa

- West Africa has great ethnic diversity. Most West Africans speak several languages.
- West Africans are bound by strong kinship ties.
- West Africans have kept their cultural values alive by passing them on to younger generations.

Section 3: The Cultures of East Africa

- East Africa's location has contributed to the region's cultural diversity.
- Ideas about land use and ownership have changed over time, but even urban East Africans still feel a bond to their rural villages.

Section 4: The Cultures of Southern and Central Africa

- Southern Africa's diverse culture includes people with three types of European ancestry—Dutch, British, and Portuguese.
- South Africa has had strong economic and cultural influences on Southern Africa.
- Central Africa has great cultural diversity and economic contrasts.

Zimbabwe

◆ Key Terms

Match the definitions in Column I with the key terms in Column II. There are more terms than definitions.

Column I

1. the spread of customs and ideas from one culture to another

2. a group of families descended from a common ancestor

3. the values, traditions, and customs handed down from one's ancestors

4. the part of a family that includes parents and children only

5. an ethnic group in East Africa

6. a laborer who travels away from where he or she lives to find work

Column II

A Quran

B culture

C cultural diffusion

D cultural diversity

E nuclear family

F extended family

G lineage

H heritage

I Swahili

J migrant worker

Review and Assessment (continued)

◆ Comprehension and Critical Thinking

7. **(a) Recall** What is culture?
   (b) Describe What are some elements of North Africa's culture?

8. **(a) Identify** What is the role of kinship in West African cultures?
   (b) Explain How is urbanization changing traditional family life in West Africa?

9. **(a) Locate** Describe East Africa's location.
   (b) Analyze Explain how location has affected East African cultures.
   (c) Summarize How does the Swahili language help unite the people of East Africa?

10. **(a) Recall** What were the traditional African ideas about owning and using land before European rule in the 1800s?
    (b) Make Generalizations How do East Africans view land use and land ownership today?

11. **(a) Recall** In what economic activities did Europeans in Southern Africa take part?
    (b) Identify Causes What economic activity in South Africa caused many Southern Africans to migrate to that country?
    (c) Make Inferences Is the life of a migrant worker an easy one?

12. **(a) Note** Describe the cultures of Central Africa.
    (b) Compare In what ways are the cultures of Central Africa like those in other parts of Africa?

◆ Skills Practice

Comparing and Contrasting In the Skills for Life activity in this chapter, you learned how to compare and contrast. You learned how to note similarities and differences and then draw a conclusion based on your findings.

Review the steps you followed to learn this skill. Then reread the part of Section 1 called Cultural Change in North Africa and the part of Section 3 called Geography and Cultural Diversity. List the similarities and differences between the cultures of these two regions. Draw a conclusion about these cultures based on your findings.

◆ Writing Activity: Language Arts

Suppose an exchange student from an African country has come to stay at your home for six weeks. You and your family are sharing your first dinner with this visitor. Write a dialogue in which you ask your visitor about African culture and the visitor asks you similar questions about your culture. Use what you have learned in this chapter to write your visitor's answers to questions.

MAP★MASTER™
Skills Activity

Africa

Place Location For each place listed, write the letter from the map that shows its location.

1. Mediterranean Sea
2. North Africa
3. West Africa
4. East Africa
5. Southern and Central Africa

Go Online
PHSchool.com Use Web Code **lap-5320** for an **interactive map.**

Standardized Test Prep

Test-Taking Tips

Some questions on standardized tests ask you to analyze a graphic organizer. Study the concept web below. Then follow the tips to answer the sample question.

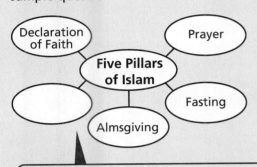

TIP When you study a concept web, notice the kind of information that goes in each oval. The main idea is in the center oval, and the supporting details are in the outer ovals.

Pick the letter that best answers the question.

What is the fifth Pillar of Islam that belongs on this concept web?

A The Quran

B Pilgrimage

C Duties of a Muslim

D The influence of Islam

TIP Use logic, or good reasoning, to be sure you choose an answer that makes sense.

Think It Through The center of the web says "Five Pillars of Islam"—meaning duties required by the religion—and each of the outer ovals shows one duty. What other pillar, or duty, belongs in an outer oval? You can rule out C and D because both are general ideas rather than specific duties. That leaves A and B. Even if you're not sure of the answer, you can see that the other outer ovals involve actions. Because pilgrimage involves an action, you can guess that B is the correct answer.

Practice Questions

Use the tips above and other tips in this book to help you answer the following questions.

1. Which of the following statements is true?
   A Cultural diffusion only occurs on coasts.
   B In general, Africa has little cultural diversity.
   C Cultural changes often occur during travel.
   D Cultural diffusion and cultural diversity are the same thing.

2. Which of the following best explains the meaning of the proverb "The young can't teach traditions to the old"?
   A Traditions do not interest young people.
   B Only adults know customs and traditions.
   C Young people are not the best teachers.
   D Adults must pass traditions on to young people.

3. A cultural group that lives in Southern Africa is the
   A Swahili.
   B Afrikaners.
   C Berbers.
   D Tuareg.

Use the Venn diagram below to answer Question 4. Choose the letter of the best answer.

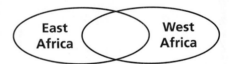

4. Which of the following could be listed in the part of the diagram where *East Africa* and *West Africa* intersect?
   A Cultures affected by coastal trade
   B Indian Ocean location
   C Br'er Rabbit tales
   D Swahili culture

Go Online
PHSchool.com
Use Web Code laa-5300 for Chapter 3 self-test.

Chapter Preview

This chapter will introduce you to some of the countries of North Africa.

Country Databank
The Country Databank provides data and descriptions of each of the countries in the region: Algeria, Egypt, Libya, Morocco, and Tunisia.

Section 1
Egypt
A Nation on the Nile

Section 2
Algeria
Varied Geography, Varied History

Target Reading Skill

Cause and Effect In this chapter you will focus on understanding causes and effects. Identifying causes and effects and recognizing signal words for causes and effects will help you learn as you read.

▶ Some North Africans live in the Sahara in oasis towns, such as Ghardaia, Algeria, shown here.

MAP MASTER™
Skills Activity

Location This map shows the countries of North Africa. Notice that all these countries lie on or north of the Tropic of Cancer. **Name** What bodies of water are most of the major cities of North Africa near? **Make Generalizations** How do you think nearness to the sea might have affected North African cultures?

Go Online
PHSchool.com Use Web Code lap-5410 for step-by-step map skills practice.

Guide for Reading

This section provides an introduction to the five countries that make up the region of North Africa.

- Look at the map on the previous page and then read the paragraphs below to learn about each nation.
- Analyze the data to compare the countries.
- What are the characteristics that most of the countries share?
- What are some key differences among the countries?

Algeria

Capital	Algiers
Land Area	919,590 sq mi; 2,381,740 sq km
Population	32.3 million
Ethnic Group(s)	Arab, Berber, white
Religion(s)	Muslim, Christian, Jewish
Government	republic
Currency	Algerian dinar
Leading Exports	petroleum, natural gas, petroleum products
Language(s)	Arabic (official), Tamazight (official), Kabyle, Shawia, Tamashek, French

Algeria (al JIHR ee uh) is Africa's second-largest country. It is bordered on the west by Mauritania and Morocco, on the north by the Mediterranean Sea, on the east by Tunisia and Libya, and on the south by Niger and Mali. Algeria has long acted as a bridge between Europe and other African lands to the south. Much of Algeria is covered by the Sahara. Most Algerians live in the north, where summers are hot and dry and winters are warm and wet. Following independence from France in 1962, Algeria made improvements in education and literacy. Since the 1990s, Algeria has struggled with economic troubles and civil war.

Algerian girl preparing food

Egypt

Capital	Cairo
Land Area	384,343 sq mi; 995,450 sq km
Population	70.7 million
Ethnic Group(s)	Eastern Hamitic, Nubian, white
Religion(s)	Muslim, Christian
Government	republic
Currency	Egyptian pound
Leading Exports	crude oil and petroleum products, cotton, textiles, metal products, chemicals
Language(s)	Arabic (official), French, English, Berber

Egypt (EE jipt) is bordered on the west by Libya, on the north by the Mediterranean Sea, Israel, and the Gaza Strip, on the east by the Red Sea, and on the south by Sudan. Most of the people live in the fertile valley and delta regions of the Nile River. The rest of Egypt is hot desert. Egypt is famous for the ancient civilization that developed there along the Nile. The ancient Egyptians built pyramids and monuments that today draw tourists and scholars from around the world. Egypt's capital, Cairo, is an important cultural center for the Arabic world.

The Great Pyramids (left) and the Sphinx (below) at Giza, Egypt

Introducing **North Africa** (continued)

Libya

Capital	Tripoli
Land Area	679,358 sq mi; 1,759,540 sq km
Population	5.4 million
Ethnic Group(s)	Arab, Berber, white, Southwest Asian, South Asian
Religion(s)	Muslim
Government	local councils in theory; military dictatorship in practice
Currency	Libyan dinar
Leading Exports	crude oil, refined petroleum products
Language(s)	Arabic (official), Tuareg

Libya (LIB ee uh) is bordered on the west by Algeria and Tunisia, on the north by the Mediterranean Sea, on the east by Egypt and Sudan, and on the south by Chad and Niger. Each year, an average of four inches (10 centimeters) of rain falls in Libya. The country has no rivers that flow year-round. Instead, it relies on groundwater from desert oases and man-made wells. Most Libyans live in urban areas. Large oil and natural gas reserves are important to Libya's economy. Libya gained independence from Italy in 1951. Revolution followed in 1969, leading to the establishment of a military dictatorship.

Morocco

Capital	Rabat
Land Area	172,316 sq mi; 446,300 sq km
Population	31.2 million
Ethnic Group(s)	Arab, Berber
Religion(s)	Muslim, Christian, Jewish
Government	constitutional monarchy
Currency	Moroccan dirham
Leading Exports	phosphates and fertilizers, food and beverages, minerals
Language(s)	Arabic (official), Tamazight, French, Spanish

Morocco (muh RAH koh) is a mountainous country in which earthquakes are common. It is bordered on the west by the Atlantic Ocean, on the north by the Strait of Gibraltar and the Mediterranean Sea, on the east by Algeria, and on the south by Western Sahara. In 1956, Morocco gained independence from France. A year later, Morocco claimed the Spanish colony of Western Sahara as its territory. Today, Morocco occupies Western Sahara, but most countries do not recognize the region as Morocco's possession. Morocco's largest city, Casablanca, lies in the west, along the Atlantic.

Moroccan pottery

Tunisia

Capital	Tunis
Land Area	59,984 sq mi; 155,360 sq km
Population	9.8 million
Ethnic Group(s)	Arab, Berber, white
Religion(s)	Muslim, Christian, Jewish
Government	republic
Currency	Tunisian dinar
Leading Exports	textiles, mechanical goods, phosphates and chemicals, agricultural products, hydrocarbons
Language(s)	Arabic (official), French

SOURCES: DK World Desk Reference Online; CIA World Factbook Online, 2002; *The World Almanac*, 2003

The famed ancient port city of Carthage was founded on the Gulf of Tunis, in the land of present-day Tunisia (too NEE zhuh). In A.D. 698, Carthage fell to the Arabs, who then established Tunis. Tunisia is North Africa's smallest country. It is wedged between Algeria on the west and Libya on the east. It is bordered on the north and east by the Mediterranean Sea. Tunisia is one of the Arab world's most liberal countries, where women make up about one third of the workforce. The importance of education is stressed in Tunisia. Since 1995, enrollment in colleges has doubled.

Berber drummers in Tunisia

Assessment

Comprehension and Critical Thinking

1. Compare and Contrast Compare and contrast the physical characteristics of the countries that make up North Africa.

2. Draw Conclusions What are some characteristics that most of the countries share?

3. Analyze Information What are some key differences among the countries?

4. Categorize What kinds of products are the major exports of North Africa?

5. Infer What part of North Africa's history can you infer from reading the list of languages that are spoken in each country?

6. Make a Bar Graph Create a bar graph showing the population of the countries in the region.

Keeping Current

Access the **DK World Desk Reference Online** at **PHSchool.com** for up-to-date information about all five countries in this chapter.

Web Code: lae-5400

Section

1

Egypt
A Nation on the Nile

Prepare to Read

Objectives
In this section you will
1. Find out how Islam influences Egyptian culture.
2. Learn about daily life in Egypt.

Taking Notes
As you read this section, look for details about life in Egypt. Copy the table below, and use it to record your findings.

Islam in Egypt	• •
Everyday Life in Egypt	• •

Target Reading Skill
Identify Causes and Effects Determining causes and effects can help you understand the relationships among situations or events. A cause makes something happen. An effect is what happens. As you read this section, note the effects Islam and the Nile River have had on life in Egypt.

Key Terms
- **Cairo** (KY roh) *n.* the capital of Egypt
- **Sharia** (shah REE ah) *n.* Islamic law, based on the words and deeds of Muhammad and on comments written by Muslim scholars and lawmakers
- **bazaar** (buh ZAHR) *n.* a traditional open-air market with shops or rows of stalls
- **fellaheen** (fel uh HEEN) *n.* peasants or agricultural workers in Egypt and other Arab countries

Egyptian boy at Ramadan evening meal

For one month of the year, the restaurants in **Cairo,** Egypt's capital, stand empty at noon. Egyptian teenagers try not to think about foods such as pita bread or sweet dates. Only certain people, such as the very young or those who are sick, eat regular meals. It is the Muslim holy month of Ramadan (ram uh DAHN). During this month, followers of Islam fast from dawn to dusk. To fast is to go without food for a period of time. During Ramadan, Muslims eat only after the sun has set.

But Muslims do more than fast during the month of Ramadan. They also focus on prayer and obedience to God. They try to avoid thinking unkind thoughts. And they help the poor and other people who are less fortunate than themselves.

Islam in Egypt

Egypt is located in North Africa. It lies across the Red Sea from Saudi Arabia, where Muhammad, the founder of Islam, was born. As you have read, Islam spread from Arabia across North Africa. Today, most North Africans are Muslim. This is true in Egypt, where Islam is the religion that most people practice. However, a minority of Egypt's population is Christian. Most Egyptian Christians are members of the Coptic Church, which is one of the oldest branches of Christianity in the world. Coptic Christianity existed in Egypt for a few hundred years before Islam did.

Islamic Practices Recall from Chapter 3 that the Quran is the sacred book of Islam. One of the Quran's requirements is that Muslims pray five times each day. Many Egyptians pray in mosques. While they pray, they face southeast so that they pray in the direction of the Muslim holy city of Mecca, in Saudi Arabia. Egyptians also often send their children to mosques to receive religious training. There, young students learn to read and memorize the Quran.

Islam and the Law The Quran is one of the main sources of **Sharia** (shah REE ah), or Islamic law. Sharia is based on the words and deeds of Muhammad, as well as on comments written by Muslim scholars and lawmakers. Muslims in North Africa and Southwest Asia try to renew their faith by living each day according to Sharia.

Most Muslims in Egypt agree that, in general, the laws of their country should be based on the laws of Islam. In 1980, the Egyptian government adopted a new constitutional amendment. This amendment identified Sharia as the main source of the laws of Egypt. Still, not all of Egypt's laws are based on Sharia. In recent years, some Egyptians have argued that all of Egypt's laws should match Islamic law exactly. On this issue, however, many Egyptian Muslims disagree.

✓ **Reading Check** Why do Egyptian Muslims face southeast when they pray each day?

Muslim men praying in a mosque in Cairo

COUNTRY PROFILE

Focus on Geography

Egypt

The most important body of water in Egypt is the Nile River, which flows from the mountains of East Africa north to the Mediterranean Sea. Nearly all of Egypt's people live on the 4 percent of the land that is closest to the Nile's shores. Irrigation with Nile water allows agriculture to thrive, and one third of Egypt's workforce is employed in agriculture. Each month, however, thousands of Egyptians leave crowded farm communities to begin new lives in the cities. Study the map and charts to learn more about Egypt's changing society.

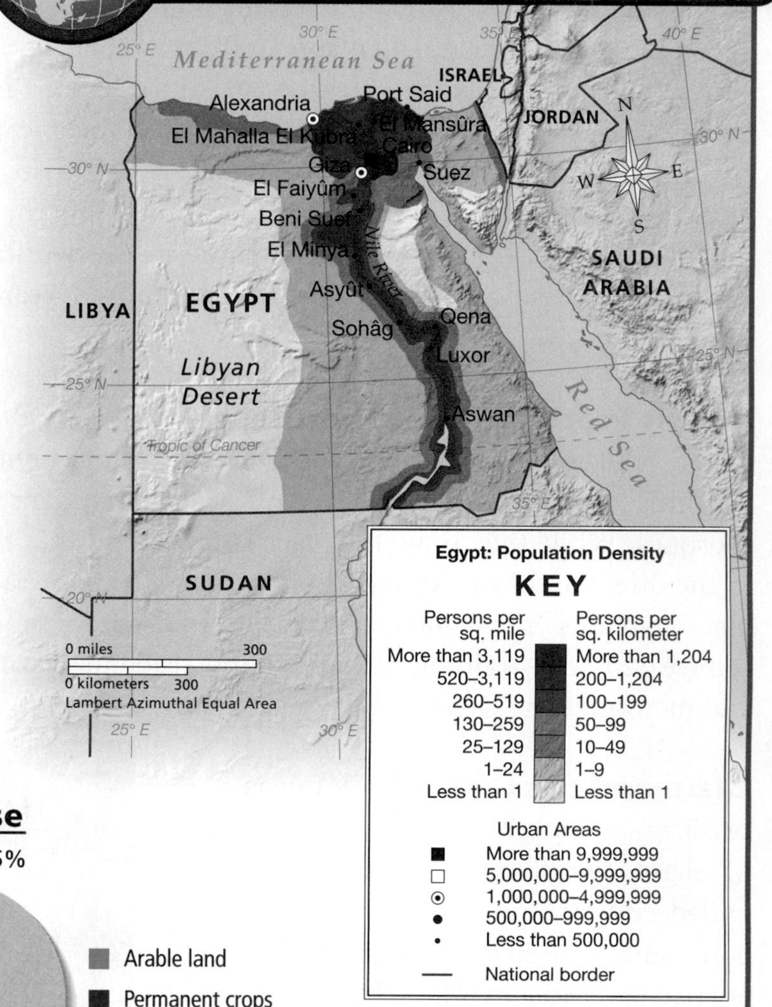

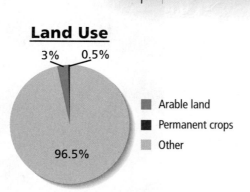

Mediterranean Sea
ISRAEL
JORDAN
Alexandria
Port Said
El Mahalla El Kubra
El Mansûra
Cairo
Giza
Suez
El Faiyûm
Beni Suef
El Minya
Asyût
Nile River
Sohâg
Qena
Luxor
Aswan
LIBYA
EGYPT
Libyan Desert
Tropic of Cancer
SAUDI ARABIA
Red Sea
SUDAN
25° E
30° E
35° E
40° E
30° N
25° N
20° N
N
S
E
W
0 miles 300
0 kilometers 300
Lambert Azimuthal Equal Area
Egypt: Population Density
KEY
Persons per sq. mile
Persons per sq. kilometer
More than 3,119 | More than 1,204
520–3,119 | 200–1,204
260–519 | 100–199
130–259 | 50–99
25–129 | 10–49
1–24 | 1–9
Less than 1 | Less than 1
Urban Areas
More than 9,999,999
5,000,000–9,999,999
1,000,000–4,999,999
500,000–999,999
Less than 500,000
National border

Urban and Rural Population

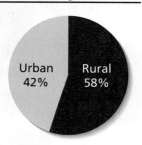

Urban 42%
Rural 58%

SOURCE: *United Nations Population Division*

Land Use

3%
0.5%
96.5%
Arable land
Permanent crops
Other

SOURCE: CIA World Factbook Online, 2003

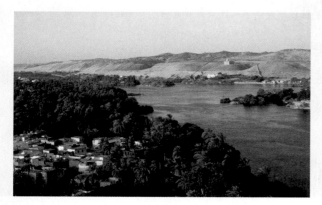

The Nile River

Map and Chart Skills

1. **Locate** In what part of Egypt are most of the major cities located?
2. **Explain** How does Egypt's geography affect where in the country people live?
3. **Predict** What changes could Egyptians make that would allow them to live in areas where currently few people live?

Go Online PHSchool.com — Use Web Code **lae-5401** for **DK World Desk Reference Online.**

Daily Life in Egypt

As you can see from the circle graph in the Country Profile on page 112, Egypt's population is fairly evenly divided between people who live in cities and people who live in villages. City dwellers and villagers live very different lives. One thing they have in common, however, is their dependence on the life-giving waters of the Nile River.

Egypt's Water Source Look at the map of Egypt on page 112 in the Country Profile. You can see that Egypt is most densely populated along the Nile River and in the Nile Delta region. Now turn to page 114 and read about the Aswan High Dam. With the help of this dam, the Nile River allows Egypt's crops to be irrigated year-round. The river supplies water to people in the cities and in rural areas.

But farming practices and population pressures threaten Egypt's water supply. The Aswan High Dam blocks the Nile's rich silt from reaching farmland downstream. Without the silt, the Nile Delta has been shrinking. Farmers have to use more fertilizer to grow their crops. The fertilizers they use, along with waste that comes from urban areas, threaten the safety of Egypt's water supply.

City Life Nearly half of all Egyptians live in cities. Cairo is the nation's capital and also its largest city. It is home to more than 10 million Egyptians. Some parts of Cairo are more than 1,000 years old. Other parts are very modern. Most people live in apartment buildings with electric fans or air conditioning. However, they frequently shop in traditional open-air markets called **bazaars.**

Many people move to the cities from rural areas. They hope to find a better education and jobs. As a result, Cairo is very crowded. There are traffic jams and housing shortages. Some people live in tents that they have set up on boats on the Nile. Others live in homes they have built in the huge cemeteries on the outskirts of Cairo. Overcrowding in Egypt's cities has even affected agriculture. Some farmland has been lost because people have built on it instead of farming on it.

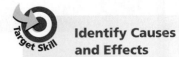

Identify Causes and Effects
What effects of the Aswan High Dam are described in this section?

Outdoor Markets
At a bazaar in Cairo, people buy goods from vendors who set up stands beneath umbrellas along the streets. **Contrast** *How do you think open-air markets are different from indoor shopping centers?*

Aswan High Dam

The Aswan High Dam is one of the modern world's greatest engineering projects. A force of 30,000 workers labored for ten years to build the dam out of layers of rock, clay, and cement. The dam serves three major purposes: it controls flooding, it provides electricity, and it supplies water for crops and drinking year-round.

A View From Above
Located on the Nile River near Aswan, Egypt, the dam created the world's third-largest reservoir–Lake Nasser. The lake is 310 miles (500 kilometers) long.

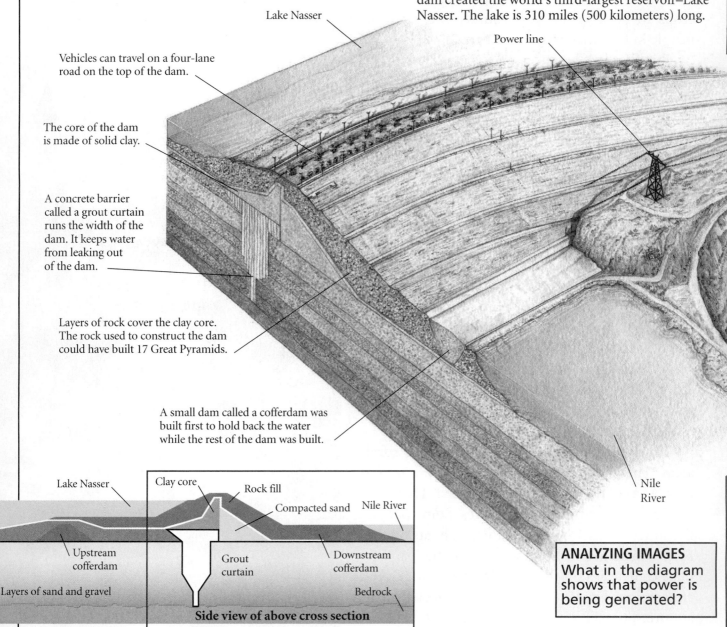

Lake Nasser

Power line

Vehicles can travel on a four-lane road on the top of the dam.

The core of the dam is made of solid clay.

A concrete barrier called a grout curtain runs the width of the dam. It keeps water from leaking out of the dam.

Layers of rock cover the clay core. The rock used to construct the dam could have built 17 Great Pyramids.

A small dam called a cofferdam was built first to hold back the water while the rest of the dam was built.

Nile River

Lake Nasser

Clay core

Rock fill

Compacted sand

Nile River

Upstream cofferdam

Grout curtain

Downstream cofferdam

Layers of sand and gravel

Bedrock

Side view of above cross section

ANALYZING IMAGES
What in the diagram shows that power is being generated?

Rural Life Most of the people in Egypt's rural areas live in villages along the banks of the Nile River or in the Nile Delta region. In Egyptian villages, most of the people make their living by farming. Egypt's rural farmers are called **fellaheen** (fel uh HEEN). Most of the fellaheen do not own the land they farm. Good farmland is scarce because the riverbanks are so narrow. Some fellaheen farm small rented plots of land. Others work in the fields of rich landowners.

Many of the fellaheen live in homes built of mud bricks or of stones. Most of these homes are small. They may have from one to three rooms and a courtyard, which the family often shares with its animals. The roofs of the houses are typically flat. Therefore, the fellaheen can use their roofs as places to store food and firewood, to spread dates or other fruits out to dry, and to dry their laundry after washing it.

Fellaheen working near the Great Pyramids at Giza

 Reading Check What land do the fellaheen farm?

Section 1 Assessment

Key Terms
Review the key terms at the beginning of this section. Use each term in a sentence that explains its meaning.

Target Reading Skill
Many Egyptians are Muslim. What are two effects that Islam has had on life in Egypt?

Comprehension and Critical Thinking
1. (a) Recall Describe Egypt's location.

(b) Identify Cause and Effect How did location affect the spread of Islam into North Africa?
(c) Draw Conclusions In what ways does Islam influence Egyptian culture?
2. (a) Identify Where do most people in Egypt live?
(b) Compare How do the lives of city dwellers compare with the lives of villagers in Egypt?
(c) Analyze What is the importance of the Nile River to the people of Egypt?

Writing Activity
Write a letter from the point of view of a rural Egyptian visiting Cairo for the first time. You may want to include observations of things that a rural person would find unfamiliar or familiar.

For: An activity on Egypt
Visit: PHSchool.com
Web Code: lad-5401

Distinguishing Fact and Opinion

When Aretha got to class, she looked at the chalkboard. Every day, Mr. Copeland began class by writing a discussion topic on the board. On this day, he had written,
Life in Egyptian cities is better than life in rural Egypt.
Aretha wondered how someone decided this and raised her hand. "That statement doesn't tell the whole story! Whose life is it referring to? Are they wealthy or poor? And when did they live?"
Mr. Copeland smiled. "Exactly, Aretha! The statement cannot be proved. It's somebody's opinion."

Distinguishing between fact and opinion is something you need to do almost every day. Doing it helps you reach your own decisions about what you read, see, or hear.

Learn the Skill

To distinguish fact and opinion, use the following steps.

1 **Look for facts by asking what can be proved true or false.** A fact usually tells who, what, when, where, or how much.

2 **Ask how you could check whether each fact is true.** Could you do your own test, such as measuring or counting, or could you find information in a reliable source, such as an encyclopedia?

3 **Look for opinions by identifying personal beliefs or value judgments.** An opinion cannot be proved true *or* false. Look for words that signal personal feelings, such as *I think.* Look for words that judge, such as *better* and *worse* or *should* and *ought to.*

4 **Ask whether each opinion is supported by facts or good reasons.** A well-supported opinion can help you make up your own mind—as long as you recognize it as an opinion and not a fact.

Practice the Skill

Read the letter below from an American student who is traveling in Egypt with her father. Then use the following steps to analyze the letter for facts and opinions.

1 Identify the facts given about the writer's father.

2 Explain how each fact could be proved true or false.

3 Identify statements within the letter that express opinions. Explain whether each opinion signals a personal feeling or a judgment.

4 Which opinion in the letter do you think has the best factual support?

Dear Brenda,

I'm sure my dad will help you with your report on ancient Egypt. He has spent years researching the Valley of Kings, where many ancient Egyptian tombs have been found. Scientists like my dad have learned a lot about ancient Egypt because it had a system of writing, called hieroglyphics. Nobody knows more about hieroglyphics than my dad!

If you could visit while we are here, I know my dad would take you into places that most tourists don't get to see. You would be amazed to see the magnificent tombs. Grave robbers stole many of the mummies and much of the furniture from the tombs. The tomb paintings, which are still there, are unbelievably beautiful. Dad says that the bright colors have faded over time. But I still love looking at them and thinking of how those people lived. You would enjoy it, too, since you like ancient history so much. Please think about coming!

Your friend,
Dominique

Egyptian hieroglyphs

Apply the Skill

Find the editorial page of a daily newspaper. Read through the editorials and select one that interests you. List several facts and several opinions from the editorial. Can the facts be proved? Are the opinions well supported? Explain what you find.

Algeria
Varied Geography, Varied History

Prepare to Read

Objectives

In this section you will

1. Learn about the history and people of Algeria.
2. Find out about life in Algeria's different geographic regions.
3. Examine life in Algeria today.

Taking Notes

As you read, find details about Algeria's past and present. Copy the outline below, and use it to record your findings.

```
I. Algeria's history and people
   A. Algeria's past
      1.
      2.
   B.
II.
```

Target Reading Skill

Use Signal Words Signal words point out the relationships among ideas or events. To help identify the causes and the effects described in this section, look for words like *because, influence,* or *for that reason* that signal a cause or an effect.

Key Terms

- **souq** (sook) *n.* an open-air marketplace in an Arab city
- **casbah** (KAHZ bah) *n.* an old, crowded section of a North African city
- **terrace** (TEHR us) *n.* a flat platform of earth cut into the side of a slope, used for growing crops in steep places

An Algerian desert home

The Sahara covers all of Algeria south of the Atlas Mountains, which cross the northern portion of Algeria from east to west. Water is in short supply in Algeria's desert lands. For that reason, fewer than 3 percent of Algeria's people live there. Because so much of Algeria is desert, more than 90 percent of Algerians live near the coast, where the weather is milder than in the Sahara.

Algeria's Mediterranean coast, its mountains, and its great desert lands are all part of the country's rich history. Algerians live in modern cities, in rural areas, and in the harsh desert. Geography, history, and culture all influence the way people live in Algeria today.

Algeria's History and People

Algeria has had a long and eventful history. Its Mediterranean location provided easy access to the markets of Europe. Algeria has also participated in trade with other parts of Africa for hundreds of years. Because of its location and resources, Algeria has been a treasure both to its people and to foreign invaders.

Early Foreign Occupations Parts of Algeria have long been occupied by outside groups. The earliest known invaders were the Phoenicians (fuh NISH unz), who were sea traders from the region of present-day Lebanon. The Phoenicians were attracted to Algeria's coast as early as two to three thousand years ago. With help from the Berbers, a North African ethnic group, the Phoenicians set up a trading post on the site of Algiers (al JEERZ). Today, Algiers is the capital of Algeria.

In the A.D. 100s, the Romans invaded Algeria. Berber farmers paid Roman taxes in grain and rented their land from Roman nobles. In the A.D. 600s, Arabs began to spread across North Africa. The Arabs conquered North Africa gradually, over hundreds of years. As a result, the Berber way of life began to change. For example, peace came to the region only after most Berbers accepted the religion of Islam.

Recent Occupations At different times, Algeria's valuable port cities have been commanded by the Spanish, by local pirates, and by the Ottoman Turks. In 1830, the French captured Algiers. The capture resulted in a long period of French colonial rule. Algeria gained independence from France in 1962.

Algeria's People Today, about 75 percent of Algeria's population is Arab, about 24 percent is Berber, and most of the rest is of European descent. Arabs and Berbers alike are Muslim, but many Berbers have combined Islam with their own traditional religious beliefs.

Arabic, several Berber languages, and French are the country's main languages. Many Algerians speak more than one of these languages. Arabic and Tamazight (TAHM uh zyt), a Berber language, are the country's two official languages.

✓ **Reading Check** What foreign influences have been felt in Algeria?

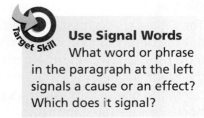

Target Skill

Use Signal Words
What word or phrase in the paragraph at the left signals a cause or an effect? Which does it signal?

City on the Sea
The city of Algiers sits on hills overlooking a bay in the Mediterranean Sea. It has long served as one of Algeria's main ports.
Draw Conclusion *Why do you think the Phoenicians chose the site of Algiers for a trading post?*

Algeria

Both the climate and the physical geography of Algeria vary from place to place. The climate is very different in the south, where the Sahara lies, and along the Mediterranean coast of the north. The Sahara covers most of Algeria's land, but the desert climate is too harsh for most uses. Only northern Algeria, near the Mediterranean Sea, receives enough rainfall to grow crops. Algeria's population is concentrated in the north, in a narrow band of cities and farmland. Study the map and charts to learn more about Algeria's geography.

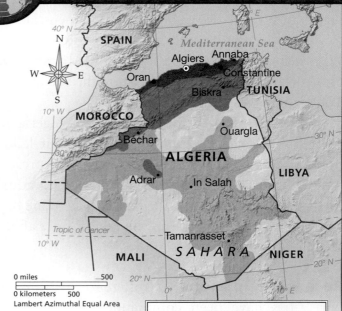

0 miles 500
0 kilometers 500
Lambert Azimuthal Equal Area

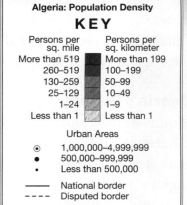

Algeria: Population Density

KEY

Persons per sq. mile	Persons per sq. kilometer
More than 519	More than 199
260–519	100–199
130–259	50–99
25–129	10–49
1–24	1–9
Less than 1	Less than 1

Urban Areas
⊙ 1,000,000–4,999,999
● 500,000–999,999
• Less than 500,000

—— National border
- - - Disputed border

Type of Land

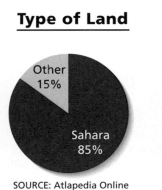

Other 15%
Sahara 85%

SOURCE: Atlapedia Online

Land Use

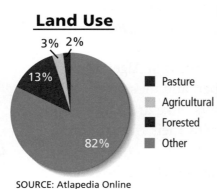

3% 2%
13%
82%

■ Pasture
■ Agricultural
■ Forested
■ Other

SOURCE: Atlapedia Online

Weather Chart for Algiers

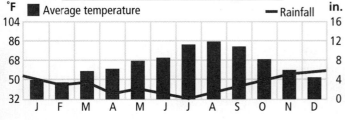

°F
■ Average temperature   —— Rainfall   in.
104   16
86   12
68   8
50   4
32 J F M A M J J A S O N D   0

SOURCE: DK World Desk Reference

Map and Chart Skills

1. **Identify** In which three months does Algiers receive the greatest amount of rainfall?
2. **Draw Conclusions** Why do you think such a small percent of Algeria's land is used for agriculture?
3. **Synthesize Information** Why do most Algerians live near the Mediterranean Sea?

Use Web Code lae-5402 for **DK World Desk Reference Online.**

Algeria's Geography

Most Algerians live in the country's coastal region, called the Tell. Algeria's best farmland is located in this region, as are most of its cities. More than half of Algeria's people live in cities.

Urban Living Many of the Algerians who live in cities are Arab, while some of them are Berber. At the heart of the cities are mosques and open-air marketplaces called **souqs** (sooks). In these souqs, merchants sell food, traditional crafts, and a variety of other goods from their stalls. Older parts of the cities are called **casbahs** (KAHZ bahz). The houses and stores in the casbahs are close together. Children play outside on the narrow, winding streets. Newer parts of the cities are modern, with wide streets and tall buildings made of steel and glass.

Rural Areas Most Berbers and many Arabs live in the countryside. Although the farmland tends to be of poor quality, about one third of Algerians are farmers. Algeria's farmers grow wheat and barley and raise livestock. In the mountains, they build **terraces,** or flat platforms of earth cut into a slope, one above another, for their crops. The terraces increase the amount of farmland and prevent the soil from washing away in the rain.

Traditionally, Algerians live with their extended families. In both urban and rural areas, homes feature several rooms with high walls surrounding an inner courtyard. Family members gather in the courtyard, which might have a garden or fountain.

Desert Dwellers Algeria is more than 80 percent desert. Among the small number of Algerians living in the desert, most settle in oasis towns, where water is available. There, people grow dates or citrus fruits.

Some people who live in the desert work for companies that produce oil and natural gas, Algeria's two main resources. Other desert dwellers are nomads, herding camels and other livestock suited to the climate. Like people in many parts of the world, these nomadic Algerians adapt to their climate by resting during the hottest hours of the day. By being resourceful, Berber and Arab nomads are able to survive the harsh desert conditions.

✔ **Reading Check** How do Algerian desert dwellers make a living?

Finding Land to Farm
Much work goes into building terraces for farming, but the benefits are enormous in areas that are hilly or mountainous. Here, Algerian farmers work the fields below a terraced hillside. **Compare** *How do you think farming on flat land is different from farming on terraced hillsides?*

Algeria Today

Throughout the long periods of outside rule, native Algerians preserved many of their traditions. For example, while French was Algeria's official language, many people kept Arabic and Berber languages alive in their homes. Today, Algerians continue to express their customs and traditions.

Modern Home Life In both urban and rural areas, Algerians continue to value family. Many Algerians live with their extended families. However, young couples in urban areas are having fewer children than people did in previous generations. Urban Algerians also tend to live in smaller family groups.

Educating Algeria's Youth While under French rule, few non-European children received a good formal education. Since gaining independence, the Algerian government has worked hard to improve education for its children and young people. Most instruction is in Arabic. Children from ages 6 to 15 are required by law to attend school. Attendance is high in city schools but is lower in rural areas. New universities have been built to educate Algeria's young people. Some students attend colleges in other countries.

An Algerian family

✓ **Reading Check** Which language is used in most Algerian classrooms today?

Section 2 Assessment

Key Terms

Review the key terms at the beginning of this section. Use each term in a sentence that explains its meaning.

Target Reading Skill

Review the section Algeria's History and People on pages 118 and 119. Find the words that signal causes or effects related to the foreign occupation of Algeria.

Comprehension and Critical Thinking

1. (a) Name What foreign groups have played a role in the history of Algeria?

(b) Explain What roles did Arabs and Berbers play in the history of Algeria?

2. (a) Identify In which geographic area do most Algerians live?

(b) Compare and Contrast Compare life for Algerians living in urban, rural, and desert areas. How are their lives similar? How are they different?

3. (a) Recall Describe education in Algeria today.

(b) Draw Conclusions What do you think is the importance of the language that is spoken in schools?

Writing Activity

Write an interview that you could conduct with someone living in Algeria today. Think of five questions you would like to ask this person. Try to ask questions that cover a number of different topics.

> **Writing Tip** Try to avoid questions that could be answered with a *yes* or a *no*. Questions that begin with words such as *why* or *how* often lead to more interesting answers.

Review and Assessment

♦ Chapter Summary

Section 1 : Egypt

- Islam influences many parts of daily life in Egypt, including daily practices and the country's laws.
- Most of Egypt's population is centered along the Nile River, the country's main source of water in both urban and rural areas.

Cairo, Egypt

Section 2: Algeria

- At times over thousands of years, a variety of foreign groups have occupied Algeria.
- Most Algerians live in modern cities or in rural areas. A small number of Algerians, however, live in the desert.
- Family and education are both valued by Algerians today.

Algerian desert

♦ Key Terms

Each of the statements below contains a key term from the chapter. If the statement is true, write *true*. If it is false, change the highlighted term to make the statement true.

1. A traditional Egyptian open-air market is called a casbah.

2. Egypt's rural farmers are called fellaheen.

3. Souqs are platforms cut into the side of a slope.

4. Islamic law is called Cairo.

5. In Algeria, open-air markets may be called terraces.

6. The old section of Algiers is called the bazaar.

7. Sharia is the capital of Egypt.

◆ Comprehension and Critical Thinking

8. (a) **Recall** What are some common Islamic religious practices in Egypt?
(b) **Analyze Information** What is the importance of Sharia to Muslims in Egypt?

9. (a) **Identify** What is the main source of Egypt's water supply?
(b) **Conclude** How does the Aswan High Dam affect Egypt's water supply?

10. (a) **Describe** What is life like in Cairo?
(b) **Make Generalizations** Why do so many Egyptians move from rural areas to cities such as Cairo?
(c) **Identify Effects** What are some of the effects of overcrowding in Cairo?

11. (a) **Recall** Describe the geography of Algeria.
(b) **Explain** How have people adapted to the geography and climate of Algeria?
(c) **Summarize** What has been the importance of Algeria's coastal location throughout its history?

12. (a) **Identify** What languages are spoken in Algeria today?
(b) **Apply Information** How do these languages reflect the history of Algeria?

13. (a) **Explain** How has the traditional view of family changed for urban Algerians?
(b) **Predict** Do you think rural Algerians will change their view of family in a similar way? Explain why or why not.

◆ Skills Practice

Distinguishing Fact and Opinion In the Skills for Life activity in this chapter, you learned how to distinguish fact from opinion.

Review the steps you followed to learn this skill. Next, read a magazine article. List several facts and several opinions that are given in the article. Write down a way that each fact you listed can be proved. Then explain whether facts or reasons are given to support each opinion.

◆ Writing Activity: Science

Do research to learn about how people have used science to help them live in desert climates. Find out about nomadic living as well as life in an oasis town. Write a report describing your findings.

MAP MASTER™ Skills Activity

Place Location For each place listed below, write the letter from the map that shows its location.
1. Cairo
2. Algeria
3. Mediterranean Sea
4. Egypt
5. Sahara

Go Online
PHSchool.com Use Web Code **lap-5420** for an interactive map.

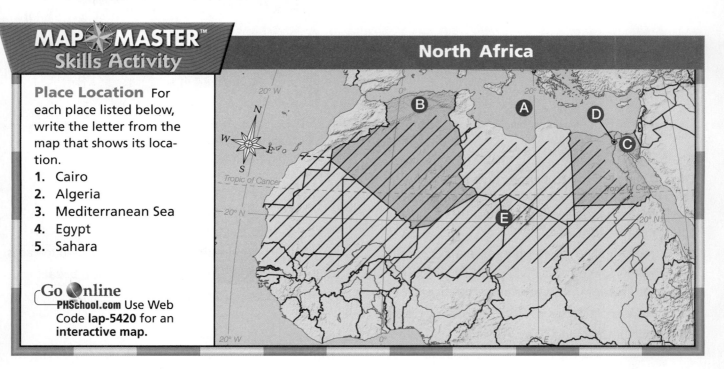

North Africa

Standardized Test Prep

Test-Taking Tips

Some questions on standardized tests ask you to identify main ideas. Read the paragraph below. Then follow the tips to answer the sample question.

> A Berber household can include grandparents, parents, sons, daughters, and cousins. Family members all share one courtyard. Each married couple within the family has a house that opens onto the courtyard. All the windows of the house face the courtyard. The head of each family is a member of the village assembly that makes village laws.

TIP Some paragraphs have a topic sentence that states the main idea. Every sentence in the paragraph supports this idea.

Pick the letter that best answers the question.

Which topic sentence is missing from this passage?

TIP The best way to be sure you have picked the right answer is to read all four answer choices before deciding on one.

A The Berbers and the Arabs are Algeria's two main ethnic groups.

B An extended Berber family includes more than just a mother, a father, and children.

C Most Berbers from Algeria live in villages.

D Family is central to every part of Berber village life.

Think It Through By reading the paragraph, you will find that every sentence tells about Berber life. You can rule out A because the paragraph is not about Arabs. You can rule out C because the paragraph is not mainly about villages. That leaves B and D. B is about Berber families, but it could be a detail sentence in the paragraph; not all the sentences are about family members. The correct answer is D.

Practice Questions

Use the tips above and other tips in this book to help you answer the following questions. Read the paragraph below to answer Question 1. Choose the letter of the best answer.

> Some desert dwellers work for companies that produce oil and natural gas. Others are nomads who herd camels and other livestock that are suited to the hot, dry climate. Like people in many parts of the world, these Algerians adapt to their climate by resting during the hottest hours of the day.

1. Which topic sentence is missing from the paragraph above?

   A Oil and natural gas are Algeria's two most important natural resources.

   B Algerians have found ways to work and survive in the desert.

   C It is difficult to live in the desert.

   D Agriculture and fuel industries thrive in the desert.

2. In Egypt, most people live

   A in Cairo.

   B in Alexandria.

   C in the valley and delta regions of the Nile.

   D in the Nile delta region.

3. Which of the following statements is true?

   A In Algeria, all Arabs and Berbers are Muslims.

   B In Algeria, Arabs and a small percentage of Berbers are Muslims.

   C In Egypt, most people are Coptic Christians.

   D In Egypt, almost half of the people are Coptic Christians.

Go Online PHSchool.com

Use Web Code laa-5400 for **Chapter 4 self-test**.

Chapter Preview

This chapter will introduce you to some of the countries of West Africa.

Country Databank
The Country Databank provides data and descriptions of each of the countries in the region: Benin, Burkina Faso, Cape Verde, Chad, Gambia, Ghana, Guinea, Guinea-Bissau, Ivory Coast, Liberia, Mali, Mauritania, Niger, Nigeria, Senegal, Sierra Leone, and Togo.

Section I
Nigeria
Land of Diverse Peoples

Section 2
Ghana
Leading Africa to Independence

Section 3
Mali
Desert Living

Target Reading Skill

Main Idea In this chapter you will focus on understanding main ideas. Identifying main ideas and their supporting details will help you learn as you read.

► The large, mud-brick Great Mosque in Djenné, Mali, is a source of pride for many West Africans.

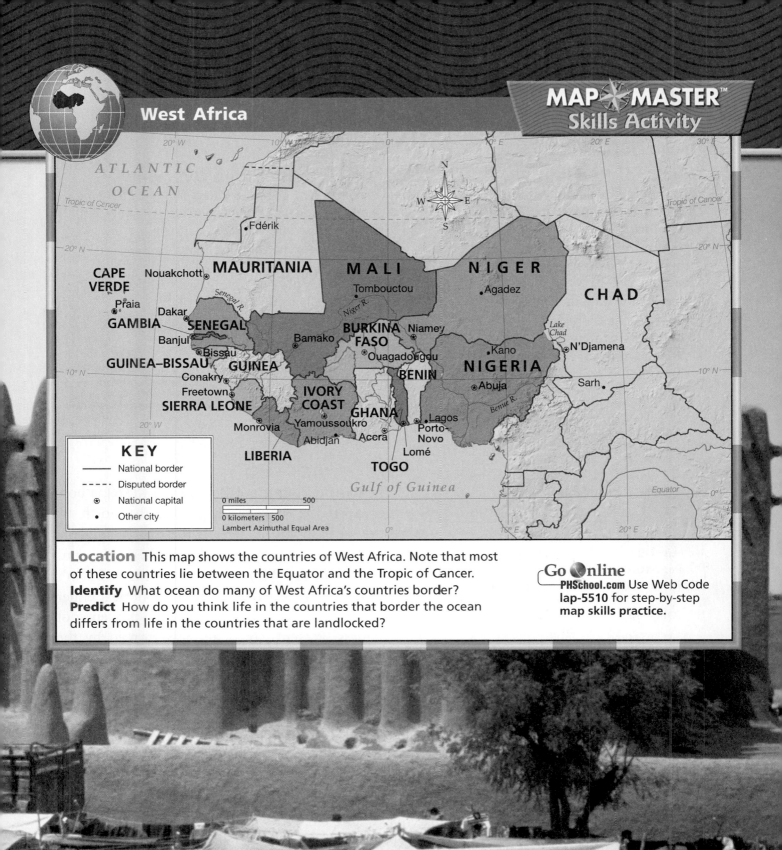

KEY

—— National border
----- Disputed border
⊛ National capital
• Other city

0 miles 500
0 kilometers 500
Lambert Azimuthal Equal Area

Location This map shows the countries of West Africa. Note that most of these countries lie between the Equator and the Tropic of Cancer.
Identify What ocean do many of West Africa's countries border?
Predict How do you think life in the countries that border the ocean differs from life in the countries that are landlocked?

Go Online
PHSchool.com Use Web Code
lap-5510 for step-by-step
map skills practice.

Guide for Reading

This section provides an introduction to the 17 countries that make up the region of West Africa.

- Look at the map on the previous page and then read the paragraphs below to learn about each nation.
- Analyze the data to compare the countries.
- What are the characteristics that most of the countries share?
- What are some key differences among the countries?

Viewing the Video Overview

View the World Studies Video Overview to learn more about each of the countries. As you watch, answer these questions:

- What are some common features of the region?
- How does the climate of West Africa affect the people living there?
- What natural resources are important to the countries of West Africa?

Explore the geography of West Africa.

Benin

Capital	Porto-Novo
Land Area	42,710 sq mi; 110,620 sq km
Population	6.9 million
Ethnic Group(s)	42 ethnic groups, including Fon, Adja, Yoruba, Bariba
Religion(s)	traditional beliefs, Muslim, Christian
Government	republic
Currency	CFA franc
Leading Exports	cotton, crude oil, palm products, cocoa
Language(s)	French (official), Fon, Bariba, Yoruba, Adja, Houeda, Somba

The narrow country of Benin (beh NEEN) is bordered on the west by Togo, on the north by Burkina Faso and Niger, on the east by Nigeria, and on the south by the Atlantic Ocean. Seasons are rainy or dry. More than two thirds of Benin's people live in the south. Most live in or near either Porto-Novo, the capital, or Cotonou, the center of business. Present-day Benin was formed by the French in the late 1800s. Since it gained independence in 1960, it has been on a shaky path to democracy and stability. In 1990, Benin successfully opened politics to multiple parties.

Near Porto-Novo, Benin

Burkina Faso

Capital	Ouagadougou
Land Area	105,714 sq mi; 273,800 sq km
Population	12.6 million
Ethnic Group(s)	Mossi, Gurunsi, Senufo, Lobi, Bobo, Mande, Fulani
Religion(s)	traditional beliefs, Muslim, Christian
Government	parliamentary republic
Currency	CFA franc
Leading Exports	cotton, animal products, gold
Language(s)	French (official), Mossi, Fulani, Tuareg, Dyula, Songhai

Burkina Faso (bur KEE nuh FAH soh) is bordered on the west and north by Mali, on the east by Niger and Benin, and on the south by Togo, Ghana, and Ivory Coast. The hot, dry north receives plentiful sunshine. The south is tropical, with more rainfall and a greater range of temperatures. Ninety percent of the population is rural—a higher percentage than in any other West African country. A French colony beginning in the 1890s, it gained independence as Upper Volta in 1960. Its name changed to Burkina Faso in 1984.

Cape Verde

Capital	Praia
Land Area	1,557 sq mi; 4,033 sq km
Population	408,760
Ethnic Group(s)	Creole, black, white
Religion(s)	Roman Catholic, Protestant
Government	republic
Currency	Cape Verde escudo
Leading Exports	fuel, shoes, garments, fish, hides
Language(s)	Portuguese (official), Portuguese Creole

West Africa's smallest nation, Cape Verde (kayp vurd), lies in the Atlantic Ocean, west of Senegal. It consists of ten islands and five islets. One of them, Fogo Island, is home to an active volcano that last erupted in 1995. Throughout its history, periods with little rainfall have brought hardship on the nation. Cape Verde has been inhabited since 1462, when its first settlers arrived from Portugal. They brought enslaved Africans as well. In 1975, Cape Verde gained independence. Today, about half of Cape Verdeans live on the island of São Tiago.

Chad

Capital	N'Djamena
Land Area	486,177 sq mi; 1,259,200 sq km
Population	9 million
Ethnic Group(s)	200 distinct groups, including Arab, Sara
Religion(s)	Muslim, Christian, traditional beliefs
Government	republic
Currency	CFA franc
Leading Exports	cotton, cattle, gum arabic
Language(s)	Arabic (official), French (official), Sara, Maba

Chad (chad) is Africa's fifth-largest country. It is bordered on the west by Cameroon, Nigeria, and Niger; on the north by Libya; on the east by Sudan; and on the south by the Central African Republic. Its northern lands are covered by the Sahara and are spotted with extinct volcanoes. In the south, the Sahel gets slightly more rain. Lake Chad, in the west, was historically a stop for traders crossing the Sahara. The French controlled the region from 1900 to 1960, when it became independent. Chad has since faced civil wars and military takeovers of the government.

Introducing West Africa

Gambia

Capital	Banjul
Land Area	3,861 sq mi; 10,000 sq km
Population	1.5 million
Ethnic Group(s)	Mandinka, Fulani, Wolof, Jola, Serahuli
Religion(s)	Muslim, Christian, traditional beliefs
Government	republic
Currency	dalasi
Leading Exports	peanuts and peanut products, fish, cotton lint, palm kernels
Language(s)	English (official), Mandinka, Fulani, Wolof, Jola, Sonike

At 295 miles (475 kilometers) in length and 15 to 30 miles (24 to 48 kilometers) in width, Gambia (GAM bee uh) is a narrow country. It is surrounded by Senegal except on the west, where it borders the Atlantic Ocean. The Gambia River flows the entire length of the country. Gambia's economy depends on peanuts as a cash crop. Great Britain ruled Gambia from the early 1600s until 1965. In the early years after independence, Gambia's smooth transition from colonial rule to stable democracy stood as a model for other African nations. Although the government was overthrown in 1994, Gambia has since returned to a stable democracy.

Ghana

Capital	Accra
Land Area	89,166 sq mi; 230,940 sq km
Population	20.2 million
Ethnic Group(s)	Akan, Moshi-Dagomba, Ewe, Ga, Gurma, Yoruba, white
Religion(s)	Christian, traditional beliefs, Muslim
Government	constitutional democracy
Currency	cedi
Leading Exports	gold, cocoa, timber, tuna, bauxite, aluminum, manganese ore, diamonds
Language(s)	English (official), Twi, Fanti, Ewe, Ga, Adangbe, Gurma, Dagomba (Dagbani)

Ghana (GAH nuh) is bordered on the west by Ivory Coast, on the north by Burkina Faso, on the east by Togo, and on the south by the Atlantic Ocean. Ghana is rich in natural resources. It was originally referred to as the Gold Coast because of its abundant supply of gold. In addition, Ghana is viewed as a leader in African politics. The country became independent in 1957, making it the first African nation south of the Sahara to achieve independence as well as the first former European colony to be governed by black leaders.

Gold ornaments from Ghana

Guinea

Capital	Conakry
Land Area	94,925 sq mi; 245,857 sq km
Population	7.8 million
Ethnic Group(s)	Peuhl, Malinke, Soussou
Religion(s)	Muslim, Christian, traditional beliefs
Government	republic
Currency	Guinea franc
Leading Exports	bauxite, alumina, fish, diamonds, coffee, gold, agricultural products
Language(s)	French (official), Fulani, Malinke, Soussou

Guinea (GIH nee) is neighbored by Guinea-Bissau, Senegal, Mali, Ivory Coast, Sierra Leone, and Liberia. The western border of the country runs along the Atlantic Ocean. Three major rivers—the Gambia, the Senegal, and the Niger—all have their sources in Guinea. The country is rich in natural resources. At least one third of the world's supply of bauxite comes from Guinea, which is the world's second-largest producer of the mineral, after Australia. Farming is also a dominant industry in Guinea, where many people produce cash crops as well as crops to support their families.

Guinea-Bissau

Capital	Bissau
Land Area	10,811 sq mi; 28,000 sq km
Population	1.4 million
Ethnic Group(s)	Balanta, Fula, Manjaca, Mandinga, Papel, white, mixed white and black
Religion(s)	traditional beliefs, Muslim, Christian
Government	republic
Currency	CFA franc
Leading Exports	cashew nuts, shrimp, peanuts, palm kernels, sawn lumber
Language(s)	Portuguese (official), Portuguese Creole, Balante, Fulani, Malinke

The mainland of Guinea-Bissau (GIH nee bih SOW) is bordered by the Atlantic Ocean on the west, Senegal on the north, and Guinea on the east and south. The country also includes a group of islands off its Atlantic coast. Guinea-Bissau's economy revolves mostly around farming. Rice is the main food crop, and cashews are the country's main export. Guinea-Bissau is one of the world's poorest countries. It gained independence from Portugal in 1975 after years of warfare. Since then, it has suffered from civil war and a series of military takeovers. Guinea-Bissau's instability has made it more difficult for the country to escape poverty.

Ivory Coast

Capital	Yamoussoukro
Land Area	122,780 sq mi; 318,000 sq km
Population	16.8 million
Ethnic Group(s)	Akan, Voltaiques (Gur), Northern Mandes, Krous, Southern Mandes
Religion(s)	Muslim, Christian, traditional beliefs
Government	republic
Currency	CFA franc
Leading Exports	cocoa, coffee, timber, petroleum, cotton, bananas, pineapples, palm oil, cotton, fish
Language(s)	French (official), Akan, Kru, Voltaic

Ivory Coast (EYE vur ee kohst) is one of the largest countries on West Africa's coast. It is bordered on the west by Liberia and Guinea, on the north by Mali and Burkina Faso, on the east by Ghana, and on the south by the Gulf of Guinea. Mountains cover most of its western edge. Cocoa and coffee are major agricultural products. Since a 1999 coup, Ivory Coast has faced political instability and violence. A civil war between the government and rebel forces lasted from 2002 to 2003. Despite the presence of African, UN, and French peacekeeping troops, the country remains unstable.

Introducing West Africa

**Spot-nosed
monkey
in Liberia**

Liberia

Capital	Monrovia
Land Area	37,189 sq mi; 96,320 sq km
Population	3.3 million
Ethnic Group(s)	Kpelle, Bassa, Gio, Kru, Grebo, Mano, Krahn, Gola, Gbandi, Loma, Kissi, Vai, Dei, Bella, Mandingo, Mende, Americo-Liberians, Congo People
Religion(s)	traditional beliefs, Christian, Muslim
Government	republic
Currency	Liberian dollar
Leading Exports	rubber, timber, iron, diamonds, cocoa, coffee
Language(s)	English (official), Kpelle, Vai, Kru Bassa, Grebo, Kissi, Gola, Loma

Liberia (ly BIHR ee uh) never experienced European rule. It was Africa's first republic, founded in 1847 by freed slaves from the United States. It is bordered on the northwest by Sierra Leone, on the north by Guinea, on the east by Ivory Coast, and on the south and west by the Atlantic Ocean. It has rain forests in which animals such as monkeys and crocodiles live. Beginning in 1990, a chaotic civil war engulfed Liberia. A peace deal was signed in 2003, but about 15,000 UN peacekeeping soldiers remain in the country. Today, 95 percent of Liberians are of African descent. The rest are mostly Americo-Liberians, descendants of the country's American-born founders.

Mali

Capital	Bamako
Land Area	471,042 sq mi; 1,220,000 sq km
Population	11.3 million
Ethnic Group(s)	Mande, Peul, Voltaic, Songhai, Tuareg, Moor
Religion(s)	Muslim, traditional beliefs, Christian
Government	republic
Currency	CFA franc
Leading Exports	cotton, gold, livestock
Language(s)	French (official), Bambara, Fulani, Senufo, Soninke

Mali (MAH lee) is one of West Africa's few landlocked countries. It is bordered on the west by Senegal and Mauritania, on the north by Algeria, on the east by Niger and Burkina Faso, and on the south by Ivory Coast and Guinea. The northern third of Mali is covered by the Sahara. To the south lies the Sahel, where cattle graze widely. The Senegal and Niger rivers flow through Mali. The country is named after an empire that flourished there 700 years ago.

Cattle herders in Mali

Mauritania

Capital	Nouakchott
Land Area	397,837 sq mi; 1,030,400 sq km
Population	2.8 million
Ethnic Group(s)	Maur, black, mixed
Religion(s)	Muslim
Government	republic
Currency	ouguiya
Leading Exports	iron ore, fish, fish products, gold
Language(s)	Arabic (official), Hassaniyah Arabic, Wolof, French

Mauritania (mawr uh TAY nee uh) is bordered on the west by the Atlantic Ocean, on the north by Western Morocco and Algeria, on the east and south by Mali, and on the south by Senegal. About two thirds of the country is covered by the Sahara. Many nomads once lived in the desert, but frequent droughts prevented many of them from staying there. For that reason, the population of the city of Nouakchott (nwahk SHAHT) has grown to around one million people.

Niger

Capital	Niamey
Land Area	489,073 sq mi; 1,226,700 sq km
Population	11.3 million
Ethnic Group(s)	Hausa, Djerma, Songhai, Fula, Tuareg, Beri Beri, Arab, Toubou, Gourmantche
Religion(s)	Muslim, traditional beliefs, Christian
Government	republic
Currency	CFA franc
Leading Exports	uranium ore, livestock products, cowpeas, onions
Language(s)	French (official), Hausa, Djerma, Fulani, Tuareg, Teda

Niger (NY jur) is bordered on the west by Burkina Faso and Mali, on the north by Algeria and Libya, on the east by Chad, and on the south by Nigeria and Benin. Much of the country is arid Sahara or Sahel, although there are savannas in the south. Niger has often faced drought. Also, the country has faced long-term conflict between the northern and southern ethnic groups. Although politically stable after gaining independence in 1960, Niger has struggled to establish democracy. In 1990, seeking fairer treatment, the Tuareg people of the north rebelled against the government. The signing of a peace treaty in 1995 resolved the conflict.

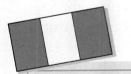

Nigeria

Capital	Abuja
Land Area	351,648 sq mi; 910,768 sq km
Population	129.9 million
Ethnic Group(s)	250 distinct groups, including Hausa, Fulani, Yoruba, Igbo, Ijaw, Kanuri, Ibibio, Tiv
Religion(s)	Muslim, Christian, traditional beliefs
Government	republic
Currency	naira
Leading Exports	petroleum and petroleum products, cocoa, rubber
Language(s)	English (official), Hausa, Yoruba, Igbo

Nigeria (ny JIHR ee uh) has the largest population of any African country. It is bordered on the west by Benin, on the north by Niger, on the east by Chad and Cameroon, and on the south by the Atlantic Ocean. Members of at least 250 ethnic groups live in Nigeria. The country is one of the world's largest oil producers. It is also one of Africa's leaders in education. About 98 percent of Nigerian children attend elementary school, and the country is home to more than 50 colleges and universities. Still, corrupt government, ethnic conflict, and religious conflict have all troubled modern Nigeria.

Introducing West Africa

Senegal

Capital	Dakar
Land Area	74,131 sq mi; 192,000 sq km
Population	10.6 million
Ethnic Group(s)	Wolof, Pular, Serer, Jola, Mandinka, Soninke, white, Southwest Asian
Religion(s)	Muslim, Christian, traditional beliefs
Government	republic
Currency	CFA franc
Leading Exports	fish, peanuts, petroleum products, phosphates, cotton
Language(s)	French (official), Wolof, Fulani, Serer, Diola, Malinke, Soninke, Arabic

Senegal (SEN ih gawl) is bordered on the west by the Atlantic Ocean, on the north by Mauritania, on the east by Mali, and on the south by Guinea and Guinea-Bissau. Its capital, Dakar, is located on the westernmost reach of the African continent and is an important port for West Africa. Senegal was colonized by the French, and it became independent in 1960. The first president of the country, Léopold Senghor, is known as one of the great African poets.

Léopold Senghor

Sierra Leone

Capital	Freetown
Land Area	27,652 sq mi; 71,620 sq km
Population	5.6 million
Ethnic Group(s)	20 distinct groups, including Temne, Mende, Creole
Religion(s)	Muslim, traditional beliefs, Christian
Government	constitutional democracy
Currency	leone
Leading Exports	diamonds, rutile, cocoa, coffee, fish
Language(s)	English (official), Mende, Temne, Krio

Sierra Leone (see EHR uh lee OHN) is bordered on the west by the Atlantic Ocean, on the north and east by Guinea, and on the south by Liberia. Its capital city, Freetown, lies beside a huge natural harbor surrounded by low mountains. In 1787, the British established Sierra Leone as a place for freed African slaves to live. It later became a British colony and then gained independence in 1961. Since the 1990s, the country has suffered through intense civil wars. The people of Sierra Leone are known for the carved wooden masks they wear during performances, as well as for their carved ivory figures.

Carved wooden mask from Sierra Leone

Togo

Capital	Lomé
Land Area	20,998 sq mi; 54,385 sq km
Population	5.2 million
Ethnic Group(s)	37 distinct groups, including Ewe, Mina, Kabre, white, Southwest Asian
Religion(s)	traditional beliefs, Christian, Muslim
Government	republic
Currency	CFA franc
Leading Exports	cotton, phosphates, coffee, cocoa
Language(s)	French (official), Ewe, Kabye, Gurma

Baobab tree

Togo (TOH goh) is bordered on the west by Ghana, on the north by Burkina Faso, on the east by Benin, and on the south by the Atlantic Ocean. The small country includes coastal lands, mountains, rivers, and plateaus. Many trees cover the southern plateaus, including baobab (BAY oh bab) trees, which are famous for their huge trunks. Togo is one of the world's largest producers of the mineral phosphate. Politically, one party has dominated since 1967. In the 1990s, however, the country made the formation of other political parties legal.

SOURCES: DK World Desk Reference Online; CIA World Factbook Online, 2002; *The World Almanac,* 2003

Assessment

Comprehension and Critical Thinking

1. Compare and Contrast Compare and contrast the histories of these countries.

2. Summarize What are some characteristics that most of the countries share?

3. Analyze Information What are some key differences among the countries?

4. Categorize What kinds of products are the major exports of this region?

5. Predict How might the region be affected by the presence of a great number of ethnic groups?

6. Make a Circle Graph Create a circle graph showing the forms of government held by the countries of West Africa and the percentage each form represents.

Prepare to Read

Objectives

In this section you will
1. Learn to identify Nigeria's three main ethnic groups.
2. Understand the major events in Nigeria's history.
3. Find out about the conflicts Nigeria faced on its path to democracy.

Taking Notes

As you read this section, look for details about Nigeria's three main ethnic groups. Copy the chart below, and use it to record your findings.

Nigeria's Ethnic Groups		
Hausa-Fulani	Yoruba	Igbo
• •	• •	• •

Target Reading Skill

Identify Main Ideas It is impossible to remember every detail that you read. Therefore, good readers identify the main idea in every paragraph or section.

The main idea is the most important point in the section. For example, on page 141, the main idea of the paragraph under the heading Oil is stated here: "Another notable source of tension in Nigeria is the country's wealth of oil resources." All the other information in the paragraph supports this main idea.

Key Terms

- **multiethnic** (mul tee ETH nik) *adj.* having many ethnic groups living within a society
- **Hausa-Fulani** (HOW suh foo LAH nee) *n.* Nigeria's largest ethnic group
- **Yoruba** (YOH roo buh) *n.* Nigeria's second-largest ethnic group
- **Igbo** (IG boh) *n.* Nigeria's third-largest ethnic group

Nigerian youth

If you were planning to travel to Spain, you might learn Spanish. If you were planning to travel to Greece, you might try to learn Greek. But if you were traveling to Nigeria, would you study Nigerian? No, you would not even try to, because there is no such language. In fact, out of the more than 1,000 languages spoken in Africa, at least 200 are spoken in Nigeria alone.

If you find it hard to believe that so many languages can be heard in just one country, picture this: Nigeria is a little larger than the states of California, Oregon, and Washington combined. That means Nigeria could fit inside the United States about 11 times. But Nigeria has nearly half the population of the whole United States. At about 130 million people, Nigeria's population is the largest in Africa.

Ethnic Groups of Nigeria

Nigeria is **multiethnic,** which means that many ethnic groups live within its borders. In fact, it is home to more than 250 ethnic groups—most of whom speak different languages. English is the official language of Nigeria. However, the languages of Nigeria's major ethnic groups dominate the country.

These ethnic groups have inhabited Nigeria for many centuries. As you can see on the map in the Country Profile on page 139, the people of each group tend to live in certain parts of the country. Most members of Nigeria's largest ethnic group, the **Hausa-Fulani** (HOW suh foo LAH nee), live in the northwest. Nigeria's second-largest ethnic group, the **Yoruba** (YOH roo buh), make their home in the southwest. And the **Igbo** (IG boh), Nigeria's third-largest ethnic group, live mainly in the southeast. In addition, many smaller ethnic groups live in central Nigeria, and others are scattered throughout the country.

The Hausa-Fulani In the early 1800s, the Fulani entered northern Nigeria and conquered the Hausa there. The Fulani then ruled over the Hausa. But instead of imposing their own culture, many of the Fulani adopted the Hausa's language and practices. Over time, many Hausa and Fulani have intermarried, and the two groups have come to be known as the Hausa-Fulani.

The majority of Hausa-Fulani live in the countryside. Some herd cattle, while others farm crops such as peanuts and a grain called sorghum (SAWR gum). Still others produce crafts that are traded in markets. Trade has been an important part of the Hausa economy for hundreds of years—since long before the Fulani arrived. The Hausa built trading cities in northern Nigeria, each of which was enclosed by walls and housed a central market. Today, some of these cities, such as Kano, still thrive as centers of commerce.

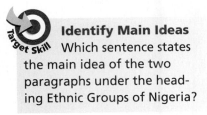

Identify Main Ideas Which sentence states the main idea of the two paragraphs under the heading Ethnic Groups of Nigeria?

Trading City Still Thrives
Kano has been a center of trade for more than 1,000 years. Today, people from around the world visit Kano's Kurmi Market. Vendors sell everything from fabrics (below right) to carved calabash bowls (below left).
Draw Conclusions *Why do you think trading centers such as Kano have been able to last so long?*

A Yoruba farming family

Wole Soyinka Wole Soyinka (WOH lay shaw YING kuh) is a Yoruba man who is known as one of Africa's most talented writers. In 1986, he won the Nobel Prize in Literature—the world's most celebrated prize for writing. Soyinka has written numerous plays, novels, poems, and autobiographical and nonfiction works. In his works, Soyinka often comments on Nigerian society in both serious and humorous ways. He also includes Yoruba folklore and traditions in his writing.

The Yoruba Historically, the Yoruba have been the most urban of Nigeria's major ethnic groups. The Yoruba tradition of building cities began around 1100 and continued for hundreds of years. Each Yoruba city was ruled by a king and was densely populated, including traders and many skilled artisans. Currently, the majority of residents of one of Africa's largest cities, Lagos, are Yoruba. The city was founded in the 1400s and served as the capital of Nigeria from 1960 to 1991.

Today, many Yoruba also live outside cities. Often they are farmers, traders, or craftspeople. The farmers tend to grow cash crops such as cacao. They also grow food for their own families. Yoruba families live in large compounds made up of several houses built around a shared yard. A Yoruba community has many of these compounds.

The Igbo The Igbo have traditionally been rural. They have not built large cities but rather live in small farming villages. The people in a village work closely together. Each village is ruled democratically by a council of elders that the people select. Council members work together to solve problems.

Today, many Igbo also live in cities. Throughout much of the past century, they have served as members of Nigeria's local and federal governments. As you will read, Nigeria became an independent country in 1960, and its first president, Benjamin Nnamdi Azikiwe (NUM dee ah ZEE kway), was Igbo.

✓ **Reading Check** Which of Nigeria's ethnic groups is known as the most urban?

Nigeria

Nigeria is Africa's most heavily populated country and one of its most diverse. The country is rich in culture, but the differences can result in clashes. With more than 250 ethnic groups, tensions between the different groups have been hard to avoid. In addition, Muslim communities in the north and Christian communities in the south often face conflict today. Many northern states have adopted Islamic law. At the same time, Christian churches have drawn millions of new members. Study the map and charts to learn more about Nigeria's diverse population.

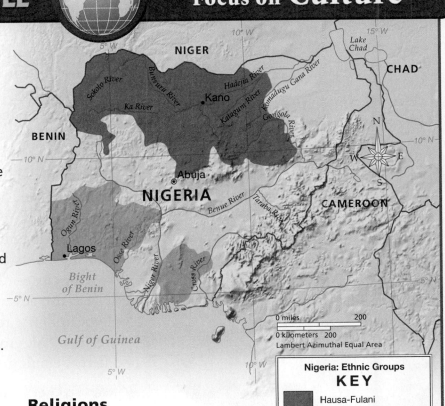

Ethnic Groups

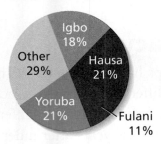

Igbo 18%
Other 29%
Hausa 21%
Yoruba 21%
Fulani 11%

SOURCE: DK World Desk Reference

Religions

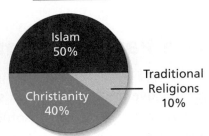

Islam 50%
Christianity 40%
Traditional Religions 10%

SOURCE: *DK World Desk Reference*

Nigeria: Ethnic Groups
KEY

- Hausa-Fulani
- Igbo
- Yoruba
- Other
- National border
- ⊛ National capital
- • Other city

Tall, carved drums like these are made by Igbo people in Nigeria.

Map and Chart Skills

1. **Identify** What are two factors that make Nigeria a diverse country?
2. **Infer** Using the information given in the paragraph and the map above, which of Nigeria's ethnic groups can you infer are Muslim?
3. **Evaluate** Southern Nigeria has large oil reserves. How could this oil wealth play a role in the country's tensions?

Use Web Code **lae-5501** for **DK World Desk Reference Online.**

Nigeria's History

For thousands of years, the region of present-day Nigeria was ruled by many different African peoples who formed their own governments. In the late 1400s, however, Portugal began trading for slaves in West Africa. Soon, Great Britain and the Netherlands began trading in the region as well. By 1914, Great Britain had taken over Nigeria's government.

In 1960, Nigeria became an independent nation, with Lagos as its capital. Ethnic groups that had always lived separately had to learn to live and work together as one nation. In 1991, to help unify the country, Nigeria's government moved its capital from Lagos, in the south, to the city of Abuja (uh BOO juh). The new capital has two advantages. It is located in the middle of the country, relatively close to each of the three major ethnic groups. In addition, members of many different ethnic groups live in Abuja.

✔ **Reading Check** What city became Nigeria's new capital in 1991?

Lagos, Nigeria

The Path to Democracy

Unifying Nigeria's many ethnic groups has not been easy. These groups live in different areas, speak different languages, practice different religions, and sometimes have access to different amounts of economic resources. Only a few years after independence, conflicts began to arise. In 1966, a military group took over the government. The next year, civil war broke out as the Igbo tried to separate from Nigeria and form their own country. In 1970, after thousands had been killed or injured, the Igbo surrendered. The fighting ended, and Nigeria remained united. However, tensions remained high, and military control of the country continued for years.

Religion A key source of the tension in Nigeria is the religious diversity among the various ethnic groups. Most of the Hausa-Fulani practice Islam, while some Yoruba practice Islam and others practice Christianity. The Igbo are primarily Christian. Some members of these groups, as well as members of hundreds of others, also practice traditional African religions. Such religious diversity makes Nigeria rich in culture, but it also challenges national unity.

Oil Another notable source of tension in Nigeria is the country's wealth of oil resources. Nigeria's economy, which is one of the strongest in Africa, revolves around oil. Ninety-five percent of the income Nigeria earns from its exports to other countries comes from oil. However, while the government and the oil companies earn large profits from oil, the people who live on the oil-rich land do not. That is because most of the oil companies are foreign and use foreign workers. Many Nigerians want to gain a share of the work or income generated by the oil industry.

Democracy for Nigeria Since Nigeria gained its independence in 1960, many Nigerians have struggled to create a democratic government free of military rule. Finally, Nigeria's military leaders gave up their power. On May 29, 1999, an election was held for the first time in more than 15 years. Olusegun Obasanjo (oh loo SEG oon oh bah SAHN joh) was elected president of Nigeria. He was re-elected in 2003.

Oil workers in Port Harcourt, Nigeria

✓ **Reading Check** **Which different religions do people in Nigeria practice?**

Section 1 Assessment

Key Terms
Review the key terms at the beginning of this section. Use each term in a sentence that explains its meaning.

Target Reading Skill
State three main ideas from Section 1. Tell whether each is the main idea of a paragraph or of a section under a red heading.

Comprehension and Critical Thinking
1. (a) Recall What are the three largest ethnic groups in Nigeria, and in which region does each group live?

(b) Evaluate Information Identify one feature that is unique to each of Nigeria's three major ethnic groups.

2. (a) Locate In what part of Nigeria is the country's capital, Abuja, located?

(b) Identify Causes Why did Nigeria's government think it was necessary to move the country's capital to Abuja?

3. (a) Name Which ethnic group tried to separate itself from Nigeria in 1967?

(b) Synthesize Information How is being a multiethnic country both good and bad for Nigeria?

(c) Predict What can Nigerians do in the future to resolve the conflicts in their country?

Writing Activity
Suppose that you are a Nigerian newspaper editor. Write an editorial supporting a movement for all Nigerians to use one common language. Be sure to say whether you think the common language should be English or another language, and explain why you think so.

For: An activity on Nigeria
Visit: PHSchool.com
Web Code: lad-5501

Prepare to Read

Objectives

In this section you will
1. Learn about the years of British colonial rule in the area that is now called Ghana.
2. Find out about the beliefs that helped move Ghana toward independence.
3. Discover how Ghana changed after achieving independence.

Taking Notes

As you read this section, look for details about events in the history of Ghana's government. Copy the timeline below, and use it to record your findings.

```
├────────┼────────┼────────┼────────┤
1874                                    2000
```

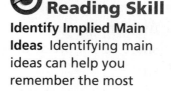

Target Reading Skill

Identify Implied Main Ideas Identifying main ideas can help you remember the most important ideas in your text. Sometimes the main ideas are not stated directly. In those cases, you must add up all the details in a paragraph or section, and then state the main idea yourself.

Key Terms

- **Kwame Nkrumah** (KWAH mee un KROO muh) *n.* founder of Ghana's independence movement and Ghana's first president
- **sovereignty** (SAHV run tee) *n.* political control
- **coup d'état** (koo day TAH) *n.* the sudden overthrow of a government by force

Kwame Nkrumah

In 1935, a 26-year-old student traveled by ship from Ghana to the United States. At that time, Ghana was called the Gold Coast because of its abundant supply of gold. The region had been ruled by Great Britain for more than 60 years. The student's visit to the United States was a turning point in his life. He was well aware that the people of his country did not have true freedom or equality. When he saw the Statue of Liberty for the first time, he felt determined to bring freedom to both his country and his whole continent. As he looked at the statue, he thought to himself, "I shall never rest until I have carried your message to Africa." The student's name was **Kwame Nkrumah**, and in 1957, he would become the leader who steered Ghana to independence.

Asante Legacy The Asante did not submit to colonial rule without a struggle. In 1900, Yaa Asantewa (YAH ah uh sahn TEE wah), the Asante king's mother (at the right), led a war against the British. Even with more powerful weapons, the British took four months to defeat the queen mother's troops. After the war, the British began to treat the Asante more respectfully. Asante children still sing a song about "Yaa Asantewa, the warrior woman who carries a gun and a sword of state into battle."

The Colonial Years

For hundreds of years, many Africans in the Gold Coast had wanted their people to be free to rule themselves. While the Europeans were trading gold and slaves on the Gold Coast, some members of a large local ethnic group called the Akan (AH kahn) formed the Asante (uh SAHN tee) kingdom. This kingdom became very rich from trade. It controlled parts of the northern savanna and the coastal south. The Asante used their wealth and power to try stopping the European takeover of their kingdom. Despite these efforts, in 1874 Great Britain succeeded in colonizing the Gold Coast. Great Britain then ruled the colony through chiefs it appointed or who already held authority.

Effects of British Control When the British colonized the Gold Coast, their main interest was controlling the colony's economy. They encouraged farmers to grow cacao beans, from which they produced cocoa. The British sent the cocoa to factories in Britain where it was made into chocolate. The British also exported timber and gold.

The export of raw materials led to problems that became common throughout colonial Africa. For example, people began growing fewer food crops for themselves and more cash crops such as cacao, which brought in more money. Soon, Gold Coast Africans could no longer supply enough food for their own needs, so they had to import it.

A related problem was that processing cacao brought in more money than growing it did. Therefore, most of the profit was gained in Britain, not in the Gold Coast. Yet another concern was that people began spending more time farming and less time making traditional crafts. As a result, Gold Coast people began to depend on buying factory-made goods from the British.

A Symbol of Pride
Colorful kente (KEN tay) cloth was invented in Ghana in the 1100s as a cloth to be worn by royalty. Over time, it became common for all people in Ghana to wear kente. Many West Africans and African Americans wear kente today with great pride.
Analyze Information *Why would a piece of cloth serve well as a way to show pride in one's heritage?*

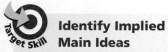
Identify Implied Main Ideas
In one sentence, state what all the details in the paragraph at the right express.

Mixing Old and New The British brought changes to some aspects of Gold Coast culture. For example, they built schools in the Gold Coast. Foreign missionaries ran the schools. Christianity began to replace traditional religions in many areas. Over the years, new ideas and ways of doing things came to traditional communities. Many people blended the new ways with the old African ways. For example, Kwame Nkrumah was born a Christian. But he also believed in parts of the traditional African religion. Nkrumah's respect for the old and the new ways helped him govern when Ghana became independent.

✓ **Reading Check** What goods did the British export from the Gold Coast?

Moving Toward Independence

During the 1900s, Africans whose countries were under colonial rule organized to demand independence. The European countries, however, resisted giving up their colonies. Some Europeans claimed that the colonies were not ready to rule themselves. Nkrumah challenged this argument with a reminder that traditional African governments had ruled Africa's lands for thousands of years. The Akan, for example, had long governed much of the Gold Coast.

A Symbolic Seat
Stools such as this one carry important symbolism for the Akan. When a new ruler takes office, the people say he has been "enstooled." They believe the stool the ruler sits on contains the soul of the nation.
Draw Conclusions *Why do you think people would consider a seat an important symbol?*

Traditional Government The Akan are the largest ethnic group in Ghana today. Historically, Akan elders selected their rulers from members of the royal family. If the leader did not rule fairly, the elders had the right to choose another ruler. Each new ruler received this warning about how to behave:

❝Tell him that
We do not wish greediness
We do not wish that he should curse us
We do not wish that his ears should be hard of hearing
We do not wish that he should call people fools
We do not wish that he should act on his own initiative [act alone] . . .
We do not wish that it should ever be said 'I have no time. I have no time.'
We do not wish personal abuse
We do not wish personal violence.❞

—*Akan statement of political expectation*

Nkrumah Takes Action In 1947, after more than a decade of schooling in the United States and England, Nkrumah returned home. He found a region that was poor, despite an abundance of natural resources. Nkrumah believed that people should benefit from the wealth of their land. He traveled throughout the Gold Coast, convincing people to demand independence.

✓ **Reading Check** How did the Akan system of government aim to assure good government?

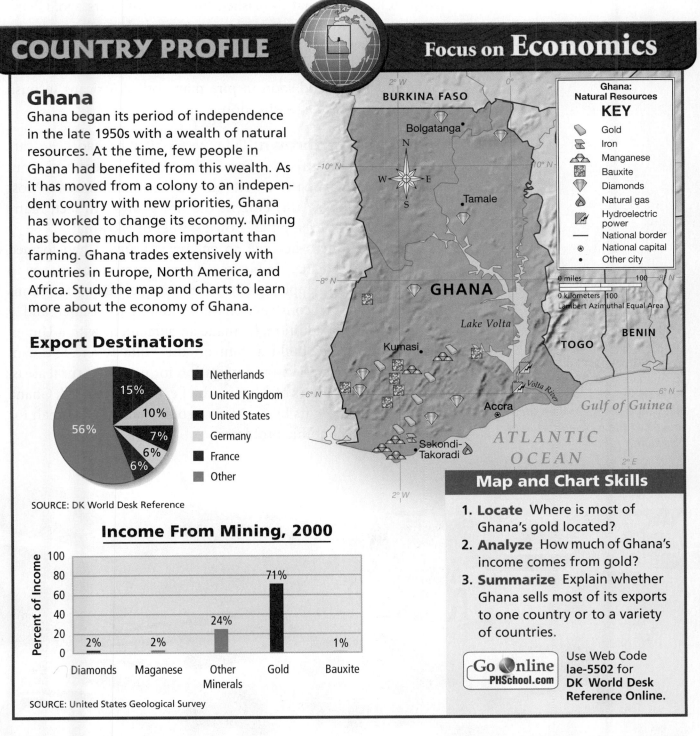

COUNTRY PROFILE

Focus on Economics

Ghana

Ghana began its period of independence in the late 1950s with a wealth of natural resources. At the time, few people in Ghana had benefited from this wealth. As it has moved from a colony to an independent country with new priorities, Ghana has worked to change its economy. Mining has become much more important than farming. Ghana trades extensively with countries in Europe, North America, and Africa. Study the map and charts to learn more about the economy of Ghana.

Ghana: Natural Resources
KEY
- Gold
- Iron
- Manganese
- Bauxite
- Diamonds
- Natural gas
- Hydroelectric power
- National border
- ⊛ National capital
- • Other city

0 miles 100
0 kilometers 100
Lambert Azimuthal Equal Area

BURKINA FASO
Bolgatanga
Tamale
GHANA
Lake Volta
Kumasi
Volta River
Accra
Sekondi-Takoradi
TOGO
BENIN
Gulf of Guinea
ATLANTIC OCEAN

Export Destinations

- Netherlands 15%
- United Kingdom 10%
- United States 7%
- Germany 6%
- France 6%
- Other 56%

SOURCE: DK World Desk Reference

Income From Mining, 2000

Percent of Income

Diamonds	Manganese	Other Minerals	Gold	Bauxite
2%	2%	24%	71%	1%

SOURCE: United States Geological Survey

Map and Chart Skills

1. **Locate** Where is most of Ghana's gold located?
2. **Analyze** How much of Ghana's income comes from gold?
3. **Summarize** Explain whether Ghana sells most of its exports to one country or to a variety of countries.

Go Online PHSchool.com
Use Web Code lae-5502 for DK World Desk Reference Online.

Independence Achieved

In 1957, some 22 years after making his pledge at the Statue of Liberty, Nkrumah gave a moving speech to his people. Great Britain, he said, had finally agreed to grant them **sovereignty** (SAHV run tee), or political control of their own country. Cheering, the people carried Nkrumah through the streets. Crowds sang victory songs to celebrate a dream come true.

Nkrumah became the leader and later the president of the new country. The government named the country Ghana after an African kingdom that flourished hundreds of years ago. Ghana was the first West African colony to gain independence. It was also the second country in all of Africa to become independent of European rule, after South Africa. The achievement of Ghana's independence would soon inspire many other Africans to push hard for—and achieve—freedom.

Nkrumah Overthrown Nine years after he had been carried through the streets a hero, Nkrumah was removed from office by a military **coup d'état** (koo day TAH), or takeover. Most Ghanaian (guh NAY un) citizens did not protest. In fact, many celebrated. Some even pulled down statues of Nkrumah.

How did a hero become an enemy? Nkrumah had formed great plans for Ghana. He borrowed huge amounts of money to make those plans happen quickly. For example, he spent millions of dollars on the construction of a conference center and a superhighway. In addition, he made an agreement with a United States company to build a dam on the Volta River. The dam would provide electricity and irrigation for people in rural areas. But when world prices of Ghana's chief export, cocoa, fell, Ghana could not pay back its loans. Many people blamed Nkrumah for the country's economic problems.

Nkrumah Toppled
Pulled down by angry citizens, the headless statue of Nkrumah lies on the ground in Accra, Ghana. After his overthrow, Nkrumah lived in Guinea and did not return to Ghana before his death. **Draw Inferences** *What do you think Ghanaians thought when they looked at the toppled statue of Nkrumah?*

A Hero Again Nkrumah's downfall did not end Ghana's problems. The country alternated between military and democratically elected governments. Few were successful. Over time, people began to think well again of Nkrumah. Many felt that he had done his best to help the country, especially by leading Ghana to independence. When he died in 1972, he was hailed as a national hero. Leaders around the world mourned his death.

Ghana's Government and Economy Today In 1981, Jerry Rawlings seized power, becoming Ghana's second long-term president. Rawlings, an Air Force pilot, had previously overthrown the government and ruled for a few months. As president from 1981 to 2000, Rawlings tried to reform the politics and economy of Ghana. He stressed the importance of Ghana's traditional values of hard work and sacrifice. Ghanaians supported Rawlings, and Ghana's economy began to grow.

Today, Ghana's economy continues to be dependent on the sale of cocoa. Even so, the economy has grown strong enough that Ghana has been able to build better roads and irrigation systems. The government under John Kufuor, who was democratically elected president in 2000, has continued implementing improvements in Ghana.

✓ **Reading Check** How did Nkrumah lose his position as president?

After Nkrumah's death, this mausoleum was built as a national monument in his honor.

Section 2 Assessment

Key Terms
Review the key terms at the beginning of this section. Use each term in a sentence that explains its meaning.

Target Reading Skill
State an implied main idea from Section 2 other than the one you identified on page 144.

Comprehension and Critical Thinking
1. (a) Explain How did the Gold Coast's economy change after the British began encouraging farmers to grow cacao beans?
(b) Summarize While the British ruled the Gold Coast, did traditional ways stay the same, disappear, or blend with the new?
2. (a) Recall When arguing for independence, how did Kwame Nkrumah respond to the European claim that the African colonies were not ready to rule themselves?
(b) Identify Causes Why did the economic conditions of the Gold Coast under colonial rule lead Africans there to believe they should rule themselves?
3. (a) Note Compared to other African colonies, when did Ghana gain independence?
(b) Identify Cause and Effect What caused people's attitudes toward Nkrumah to change before and after his death?

Writing Activity
Work with a partner to write about one or two changes you would like to see happen in your country or community. Consider obstacles to making these changes. Then write a plan that explains each change, how you would make it, and how you would overcome any obstacles.

For: An activity on Ghana
Visit: PHSchool.com
Web Code: lad-5502

Julia's neighbor, Mrs. Gonzalez, owns a dog that Julia loves to play with. One day Mrs. Gonzalez offered to pay Julia for walking the dog every morning and afternoon. That sounded to Julia like a fun way to earn some money. But she was already considering joining the swim team. Walking the dog twice a day as well as going to swim practice seemed like too many commitments. Julia realized she would have to decide between the two—but how?

Playing with Buster in the backyard

Some decisions are easy to make because one choice clearly has more to offer than the other. On the other hand, many decisions are difficult to make because all the choices have both positive and negative outcomes. Making good decisions means considering all the options before you decide.

Learn the Skill

Use these steps to make a good decision.

1. **Identify the issue.** Write a question explaining what needs to be decided.

2. **List the alternatives.** When you make a decision, you are choosing between at least two alternatives, or choices.

3. **For each alternative, list the likely outcomes, both positive and negative.** Every decision has outcomes, or effects. Use a decision-making grid like the one on page 149 to list the possible outcomes.

4. **Put a check mark (✓) next to the most important outcomes.** Marking the outcomes that matter most to you can help you reach your decision.

5. **Choose the option that seems best.** Write your decision in a sentence.

My Decision-Making Grid

Decision: Should I take the dog-walking job or join the swim team?

Alternatives	Likely Positive Outcomes	Likely Negative Outcomes
Take the dog-walking job.	Earn money. Get to play with a dog. Help my neighbor.	Don't have time for other activities. Don't get to spend time with friends.
Join the swim team.	Get exercise. Have fun. Meet new people.	Don't have time for other activities. Don't get to spend time with animals.

Practice the Skill

Suppose you win a contest at school and receive money as a prize. There is a certain item you have wanted to buy, and now you can afford it. But in three months your class is taking a field trip, and you know you will need to have some money for the trip. Follow the steps below to decide what to do with your prize money.

1 What is the decision you will make? Write down a question explaining what needs to be decided.

2 List the alternatives that you have to choose from. Are there two alternatives, or more?

3 Create a decision-making grid like the one above. Fill in the likely outcomes.

4 Put a check mark next to the outcomes that are most important to you.

5 Decide which alternative seems best to you. Write down an explanation of your reasoning.

Apply the Skill

Think of an important decision that you might have to make in the near future. It might have to do with school, friends, family, or something else. Create a decision-making grid to analyze the alternatives and outcomes. Then state your decision and your reasons for making it.

Section 3

Mali
Desert Living

Prepare to Read

Objectives

In this section you will

1. Discover how Mali's environment affects its economy.
2. Find out how desert can spread across the land.
3. Learn about the importance of preserving Mali's environment.

Taking Notes

As you read this section, look for details about the role of the Sahel in the life of the people of Mali. Copy the diagram below, and use it to record your findings.

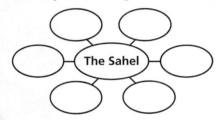

The Sahel

Target Reading Skill

Identify Supporting Details The main idea of a paragraph or section is supported by details that give further information about it. These details may explain the main idea by giving examples or reasons. As you read, note the details that support each main idea in the text.

Key Terms

- **desertification** (dih zurt uh fih KAY shun) *n.* the process by which fertile land becomes too dry or damaged to support life
- **overgrazing** (oh vur GRAYZ ing) *n.* allowing too much grazing by large herds of animals

Tombouctou, Mali

These days in Tombouctou (tohm book TOO), Mali, sand piles up against buildings. It coats the fur of camels. It gives a yellowish tint to everything in sight. Inside a hotel, a fine layer of red sand coats the lobby. Only a few of the rooms are taken. The manager is waiting for the river to rise, hoping it will bring customers.

But each year, as the climate slowly changes, the river rises a little later. "Ten years ago the first boat arrived on July 1," says Tombouctou politician Moulaye Haidara (moo LAH ee HY dah rah). "Five years ago it was July 15. Now, we're lucky if it's here by early August. In another five years, who knows?"

Mali's Environment

Tombouctou is located in the partly dry lands of the Sahel. As you can see on the map in the Country Profile on page 153, the Sahel lies between the Sahara and the savanna. The Sahara stretches over much of West Africa, and it is expanding all the time. In Mali, the Sahara covers about one third of the land. Few Malians inhabit the Sahara. Some live in the Sahel, while others live in the savanna, the one area of the country that receives abundant rainfall.

Resources of the Sahel The Sahel extends across Africa from Mauritania in the west to Ethiopia in the east. People have lived in the Sahel for thousands of years. They have long used its resources to earn their living. Malians in the Sahel herd animals and raise food crops to feed their families. Many earn extra money by raising cash crops as well. The rainy season, which lasts from May to October, is an ideal time for farming. During the rest of the year, farming is still possible in the Sahel thanks to water sources that exist year-round, such as the Niger River.

A Crossroads Location In the past, the Sahel's location as a crossroads between the Sahara and the savanna helped its economy flourish. For example, the city of Tombouctou was once a convenient stopping point for many camel caravans traveling between North Africa and the savanna. From the 1300s through the 1500s, Tombouctou thrived as one of Africa's wealthy centers of trade.

Today, people still live in Tombouctou, but they no longer practice trade on a large scale. Once European ships began trading along Africa's coast, trade through the Sahel decreased. Transporting goods by ship was faster and easier than sending them by camel. However, Tombouctou is still a crossroads for people traveling through the area.

✓ **Reading Check** Which months are the best for farming in the Sahel?

Table Skills

The table shows some of the groups of people who pass through Tombouctou and the ways they typically make a living. Below, a trader's camels carry salt to Tombouctou. **Identify** Which groups are traders? **Analyze Information** Based on the way they earn their living, what reasons do you think these groups have for passing through Tombouctou?

Activity in Tombouctou

Ethnic Group	Activities
Bambara	Farmers, traders
Berbers	Nomads
Fulani	Cattle herders
Mandingo	Farmers, traders
Songhai	Traders, gardeners
Tuareg	Nomads

Identify Supporting Details

The main idea under the red heading The Desert Spreads is that desertification is threatening the ways people in Mali make a living. Which details in the paragraphs at the right tell about this problem?

Diagram Skills

Overgrazing in the Sahara is the result of too much grazing by animals such as sheep, goats, camels, and cattle. **Identify** How does the soil become loosened when animals graze? **Predict** Do you think there are ways in which the people of the Sahara could avoid overgrazing their animals?

The Desert Spreads

Mali has little industry. Most people make their living through trading, farming, or herding. However, these types of work are being threatened by **desertification,** the change of fertile land into land that is too dry or damaged to support life. In Mali and other countries of the Sahel, the desert is spreading south. Even the wetter lands in southwest Mali are at risk of becoming desert. But how does fertile land turn into desert? Scientists have identified two causes of desertification that may be at work in Mali.

Overgrazing One cause of desertification is **overgrazing,** or allowing too much grazing by large herds of animals. When animals graze, they often eat the roots of plants, which hold the soil in place. With the roots gone, the fierce winds of the Sahara erode the soil. The soil then blows into the air, creating yellow dust clouds. This loose soil is one reason that Tombouctou is slowly being covered in sand—the desert is taking over the land.

Drought Another cause of desertification is drought, which you will recall is a long period of little or no rain. Droughts can turn land into desert. Over the last 30 years, the Sahel has received much less rain than it did before. Some scientists argue that a few years of good rainfall could stop desertification.

✓ **Reading Check** What does desertification do to fertile land?

Overgrazing

The roots of a plant hold the soil in place.

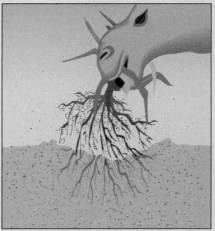
As a camel eats the plant and pulls up the roots, the soil is loosened.

Wind lifts the loosened soil from the ground and into the air.

Mali

From north to south, Mali's climate changes from the dry desert of the Sahara to the moderately wet savanna. In between lies the Sahel, a zone where farmers and herders face challenges from year to year due to unpredictable rainfall. The boundaries of the three regions are shifting as the Sahel grows drier and the desert expands southward. Human activity has also endangered farmland and vegetation in the Sahel. Study the map and charts to learn more about the importance of water in shaping the human geography of Mali.

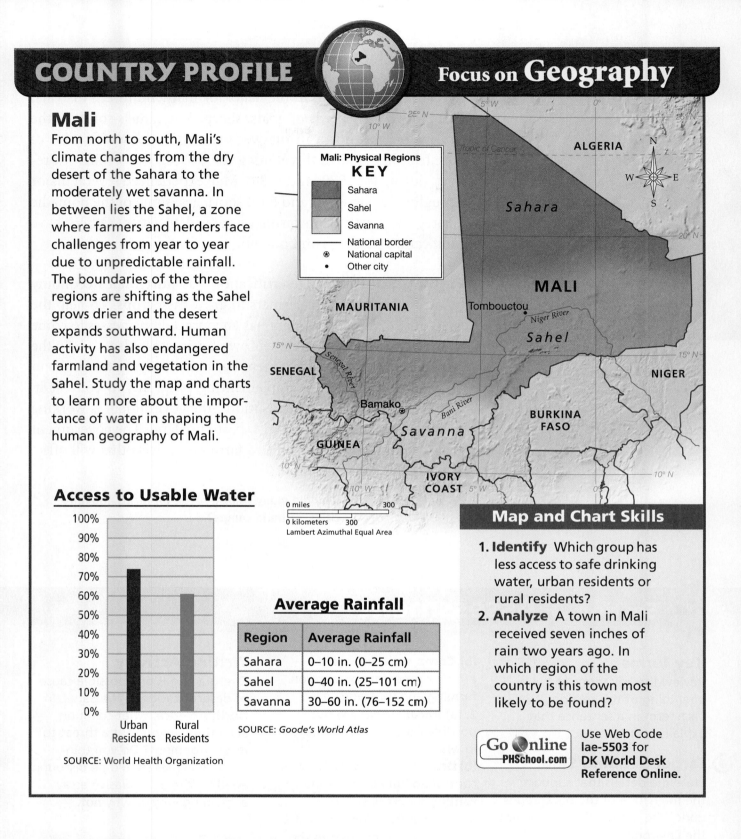

Mali: Physical Regions
KEY
- Sahara
- Sahel
- Savanna
- National border
- ⊗ National capital
- • Other city

0 miles 300
0 kilometers 300
Lambert Azimuthal Equal Area

Access to Usable Water

SOURCE: World Health Organization

Average Rainfall

Region	Average Rainfall
Sahara	0–10 in. (0–25 cm)
Sahel	0–40 in. (25–101 cm)
Savanna	30–60 in. (76–152 cm)

SOURCE: *Goode's World Atlas*

Map and Chart Skills

1. **Identify** Which group has less access to safe drinking water, urban residents or rural residents?
2. **Analyze** A town in Mali received seven inches of rain two years ago. In which region of the country is this town most likely to be found?

Go Online
PHSchool.com

Use Web Code lae-5503 for DK World Desk Reference Online.

Preserving the Environment

Many people around the world are concerned about the future of the Sahel. The United Nations has created a committee to help prevent desertification. Before the problem of desertification can be resolved, however, people living in the Sahel must learn how to avoid practices that make the problem worse.

Like this woman, most Tuaregs wear blue from head to toe.

A Way of Life in Danger Many people who live in the Sahel are nomads. The Tuareg (TWAH reg), for example, have lived in the desert and in the Sahel for many hundreds of years. They move their herds of goats, sheep, and camels south in the dry season and north in the wet season. The desertification of countries like Mali is threatening the Tuareg way of life. Moreover, during the 1970s and 1980s, Mali experienced several major droughts. Facing water and food shortages, some of the nomadic Tuareg have settled on farms or moved to cities. Others have built camps outside Tombouctou.

Finding Solutions Desertification has hurt Mali's economy by making it harder for farmers to grow cash crops. To help the economy, Mali's government has encouraged businesses to come to Mali and people to start their own businesses. Also, to help the environment, Mali's government has been studying the problem of desertification and is implementing programs to combat it. With the help of the United Nations, the government is working to educate people about better ways to use land. The government is also sponsoring irrigation and farming projects that will offset the effects of desertification.

✓ **Reading Check** Why did many Tuareg settle on farms, move to cities, or build camps?

Section 3 Assessment

Key Terms
Review the key terms at the beginning of this section. Use each term in a sentence that explains its meaning.

Target Reading Skill
State the details that support the main idea of the paragraphs under the red heading Preserving the Environment.

Comprehension and Critical Thinking
1. (a) Identify Name two ways in which the environment of the Sahel makes farming in the region possible.

(b) Compare Compare the effects of the environment on farming and on trade.

2. (a) Recall What are two possible causes of desertification in Mali?

(b) Draw Conclusions How much control do humans have in preventing desertification?

3. (a) Describe How has Mali's government responded to the negative effects of desertification on the economy?

(b) Predict If the government's efforts succeed, do you think some of the Tuareg will be able to return to their nomadic way of life?

Writing Activity
Overgrazing is one possible cause of desertification in the Sahel. In North America, what common activities may present a threat to its environment? Do you think those activities should be discouraged? Write a persuasive essay explaining why or why not.

> **Writing Tip** Be sure to use persuasive language in your essay. Include reasons and examples that clearly support your argument.

Review and Assessment

◆ Chapter Summary

Section 1: Nigeria

- Nigeria is home to more than 250 ethnic groups. The largest are the Hausa-Fulani, the Yoruba, and the Igbo.
- After thousands of years of self-rule, Nigeria became a British colony in 1914. It gained independence from Great Britain in 1960.
- During Nigeria's move toward democracy, Nigerians have faced conflicts over religion and over the wealth gained by the oil industry.

Kano, Nigeria

Section 2: Ghana

- In 1874, the British colonized the Gold Coast. They took control of the economy, built schools, and brought Christianity to the region.
- During the 1900s, Africans under colonial rule began organizing for independence. Kwame Nkrumah led the independence movement in the Gold Coast.
- In 1957, Ghana became the first West African country to become independent.

Section 3: Mali

- People in the Sahel have long relied on its resources and its location as a crossroads for trade.
- Desertification is occurring in Mali and other countries of the Sahel. Two possible causes are overgrazing and drought.
- Desertification threatens the ways of life of many people living in the Sahel. Mali's government is working to find solutions to this problem.

Tuareg woman

◆ Key Terms

Match the definitions in Column I with the key terms in Column II.

Column I

1. Nigeria's second-largest ethnic group
2. having many ethnic groups living within a society
3. the process by which fertile land becomes too dry or damaged to support life
4. Ghana's first president
5. a sudden overthrow of a government by force
6. political control

Column II

A Kwame Nkrumah

B Yoruba

C sovereignty

D coup d'état

E desertification

F multiethnic

◆ Comprehension and Critical Thinking

7. **(a) Name** List the three largest ethnic groups that live in Nigeria.
   (b) Explain What are two sources of conflict in Nigeria today?
   (c) Predict How might Nigeria's government help resolve the country's conflicts?

8. **(a) Recall** During the colonial years, why did people in the Gold Coast have to start importing their food?
   (b) Synthesize Information When the British changed the structure of the Gold Coast's economy, how did the lifestyles of the people living there also change?
   (c) Infer According to Kwame Nkrumah's beliefs, did those lifestyle changes matter in the discussion of independence?

9. **(a) Explain** How did Tombouctou's location in the Sahel allow it to develop as a major trading center in the 1300s?
   (b) Summarize Did large-scale trading in Tombouctou end because of environmental change or because of social change? Explain.

◆ Skills Practice

Decision Making In the Skills for Life activity in this chapter, you learned how you can make good decisions.

Review the steps you followed to learn this skill. Then suppose that you have to make a choice between two after-school activities, such as writing for the school newspaper and acting in the school play. Create a decision-making grid. Put check marks next to the most important outcomes. Review the check marks and choose the option that seems best. Write a sentence stating your decision.

◆ Writing Activity: Geography

In the Sahel, overgrazing may be a cause of desertification. It might seem that a simple solution is to stop overgrazing. However, many people of the Sahel make their living from the animals that they graze. To prevent overgrazing, these people would have to change their ways of life. They would have to stop herding animals, herd fewer animals, or move elsewhere to herd their animals. Write a newspaper editorial explaining how you think this problem could be solved.

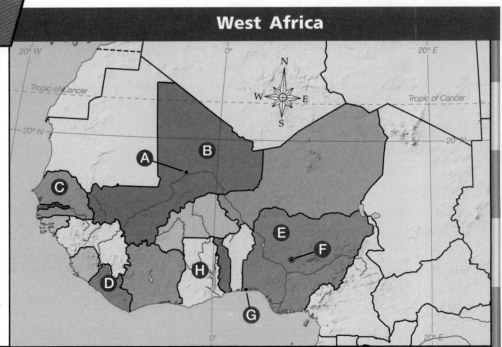

MAP★MASTER™
Skills Activity

Place Location For each place listed below, write the letter from the map that shows its location.

1. Nigeria
2. Ghana
3. Liberia
4. Tombouctou
5. Lagos
6. Abuja
7. Senegal
8. Mali

Go Online
PHSchool.com Use Web Code lap-5520 for an **interactive map.**

West Africa

Standardized Test Prep

Test-Taking Tips

Some questions on standardized tests ask you to analyze an outline. Study the outline below. Then follow the tips to answer the sample question.

> I. The Hausa-Fulani
>   A. Cattle herders, farmers, craftspeople
>   B. Built trading cities
> II. The Yoruba
>   A. Very urban
>   B. Also many farmers, traders, craftspeople
> III. _____
>   A. Rural farmers
>   B. Governed by democratic councils

TIP Pay attention to the organization of the outline. Use that information to help you answer the question.

Pick the letter that best answers the question.

Which of the following major topics belongs next to III?

A The Nigerians
B Ethnic groups of Nigeria
C The Igbo
D Christians

TIP Use what you know about history, geography, or government to find the BEST answer.

Think It Through This outline is organized by major topics and details. The question asks you to find major topic III. Answer B is too general; it could be the subject of an entire outline. Answer D is not an ethnic group. That leaves A and C. You can use your knowledge of geography to help you. Nigerians are a general group—citizens of a country. The Hausa-Fulani and the Yoruba are specific groups—ethnic groups in Nigeria. The Igbo are also a Nigerian ethnic group, so the correct answer is C.

Practice Questions

Use the tips above and other tips in this book to help you answer the following questions. Use the outline below to answer Question 1. Choose the letter of the best answer.

> I. Nkrumah overthrown
>   A. Nkrumah removed from office by a coup d'état
>   B. Nkrumah blamed for economic problems
> II. _____
>   A. Continuing economic problems
>   B. Improvement of public opinion about Nkrumah
> III. Government and economy today

1. According to the outline, which of the following belongs next to II?
   A Independence achieved
   B A hero again
   C Traditional government
   D Mixing old and new

2. Which of the following was Nigeria's first capital after independence?
   A Kano
   B Abuja
   C Lagos
   D Tombouctou

3. How does Mali's savanna differ from the Sahel and the Sahara?
   A It gets less rain.
   B It has a more northern location.
   C It gets more rain.
   D It is inhabited by fewer people.

Go Online
PHSchool.com

Use Web Code laa-5500 for **Chapter 5 self-test.**

Chapter

6

East Africa

Chapter Preview

This chapter will introduce you to some of the countries that make up East Africa.

Country Databank

The Country Databank provides data and descriptions of each of the countries in the region: Burundi, Djibouti, Eritrea, Ethiopia, Kenya, Rwanda, Seychelles, Somalia, Sudan, Tanzania, and Uganda.

Section 1
Ethiopia
Religious Roots

Section 2
Tanzania
Determined to Succeed

Section 3
Kenya
Ties That Bind

⊙ Target Reading Skill

Context In this chapter you will focus on understanding context. Using context clues and recognizing nonliteral meanings will help you learn as you read.

▶ Many of the world's fastest runners are Kenyan. This man is training on the plains of Kenya.

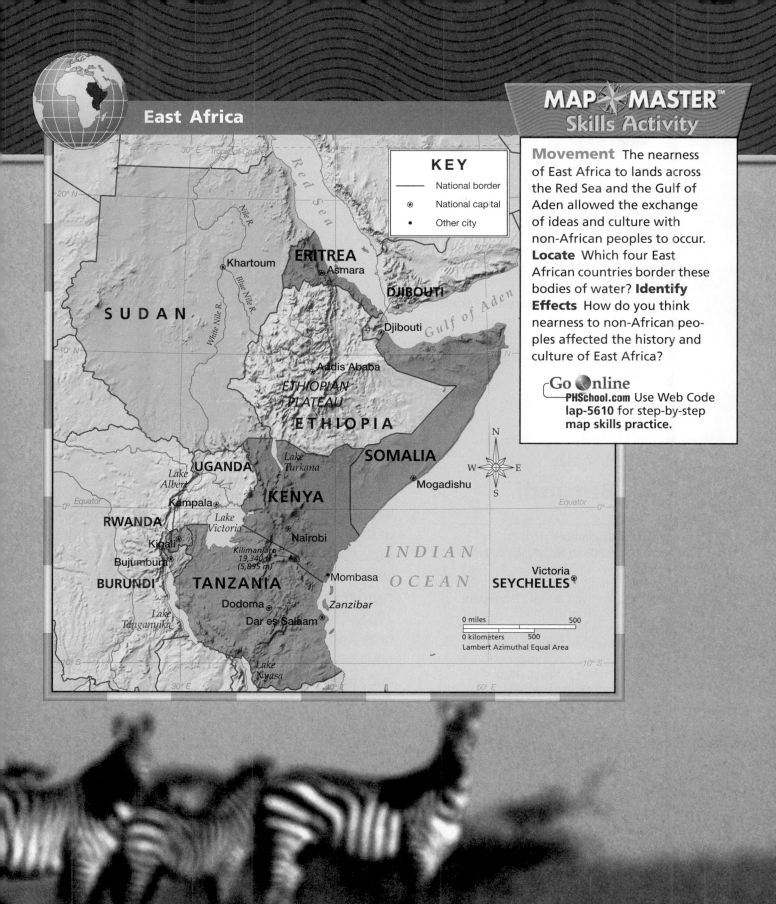

MAP MASTER™
Skills Activity

KEY

— National border

⊛ National capital

• Other city

Movement The nearness of East Africa to lands across the Red Sea and the Gulf of Aden allowed the exchange of ideas and culture with non-African peoples to occur. **Locate** Which four East African countries border these bodies of water? **Identify Effects** How do you think nearness to non-African peoples affected the history and culture of East Africa?

Go Online

PHSchool.com Use Web Code lap-5610 for step-by-step map skills practice.

Map labels: Red Sea, Tropic of Cancer, Nile R., Khartoum, ERITREA, Asmara, DJIBOUTI, Djibouti, Gulf of Aden, SUDAN, White Nile R., Blue Nile R., Addis Ababa, ETHIOPIAN PLATEAU, ETHIOPIA, SOMALIA, Lake Turkana, UGANDA, Lake Albert, KENYA, Mogadishu, Kampala, Equator, RWANDA, Lake Victoria, Kigali, Nairobi, Bujumbura, Kilimanjaro 19,340 ft (5,895 m), INDIAN OCEAN, BURUNDI, TANZANIA, Mombasa, Victoria, SEYCHELLES, Dodoma, Zanzibar, Lake Tanganyika, Dar es Salaam, Lake Nyasa

0 miles 500
0 kilometers 500
Lambert Azimuthal Equal Area

Guide for Reading

This section provides an introduction to the eleven countries that make up the region of East Africa.

- Look at the map on the previous page and then read the paragraphs below to learn about each nation.
- Analyze the data to compare the countries.
- What are the characteristics that most of the countries share?
- What are some key differences among the countries?

Burundi

Capital	Bujumbura
Land Area	9,903 sq mi; 25,650 sq km
Population	6.4 million
Ethnic Group(s)	Hutu, Tutsi, Twa
Religion(s)	Roman Catholic, Protestant, traditional beliefs, Muslim
Government	republic
Currency	Burundi franc
Leading Exports	coffee, tea, sugar, cotton, hides
Language(s)	French (official), Kirundi (official), Kiswahili

The small country of Burundi (boo ROON dee) is bordered on the west by the Democratic Republic of the Congo, on the north by Rwanda, and on the east and south by Tanzania. Beginning in the 1970s, the country faced fierce fighting between two ethnic groups, the Hutu and the Tutsi. In 2002, a new government signed a peace treaty to help end the conflict. However, the country remains unstable, with small conflicts continuing and the economy weakened from the many years of fighting.

Djibouti

Capital	Djibouti
Land Area	8,873 sq mi; 22,980 sq km
Population	472,810
Ethnic Group(s)	Issa, Afar, Somali, white, Arab, Ethiopian
Religion(s)	Muslim, Christian
Government	republic
Currency	Djibouti franc
Leading Exports	reexports, hides and skins, coffee (in transit)
Language(s)	Arabic (official), French (official), Somali, Afar

Djibouti (jih BOO tee) is bordered on the south by Somalia, on the south and west by Ethiopia, on the north by Eritrea and the Red Sea, and on the east by the Gulf of Aden. It was established in 1977, when it gained independence from France. Its capital, Djibouti, is an important port city for the country's economy. Otherwise, the economy is weak because the country has few natural resources. In the early 1990s, fighting broke out between the nation's two main ethnic groups. In 2000, a peace treaty ended the fighting.

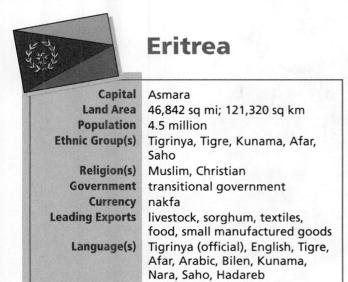

Eritrea

Capital	Asmara
Land Area	46,842 sq mi; 121,320 sq km
Population	4.5 million
Ethnic Group(s)	Tigrinya, Tigre, Kunama, Afar, Saho
Religion(s)	Muslim, Christian
Government	transitional government
Currency	nakfa
Leading Exports	livestock, sorghum, textiles, food, small manufactured goods
Language(s)	Tigrinya (official), English, Tigre, Afar, Arabic, Bilen, Kunama, Nara, Saho, Hadareb

Eritrea (ehr uh TREE uh) is bordered on the west and north by Sudan, on the north and east by the Red Sea, and on the south by Djibouti and Ethiopia. After being ruled by the Italians and then the British during the 1800s and early 1900s, Eritrea was taken over by Ethiopia in 1952. After thirty years of fighting, Eritrea gained its independence in 1993. Then, from 1998 to 2000, Eritrea and Ethiopia fought another destructive war over border disputes. Tensions in the region continue, and Eritrea's economy is weak from many years of war.

An Eritrean girl

Ethiopia

Capital	Addis Ababa
Land Area	432,310 sq mi; 1,119,683 sq km
Population	67.7 million
Ethnic Group(s)	Oromo, Amhara, Tigre, Sidamo, Shankella, Somali, Afar, Gurage
Religion(s)	Muslim, Christian, traditional beliefs
Government	federal republic
Currency	Ethiopian birr
Leading Exports	coffee, qat, gold, leather products, oilseeds
Language(s)	Amharic (official), Tigrinya, Galla, Sidamo, Somali, English, Arabic

Ethiopia (ee thee OH pea uh) is bordered on the west by Sudan, on the north by Eritrea and Djibouti, on the east and south by Somalia, and on the south by Kenya. It is one of the oldest countries in the world. Unlike most African countries, it was never colonized by a European power—at each European attempt, the Ethiopians proved victorious. In the 1990s, Ethiopia became a federal republic with a constitution and free elections. In the past 50 years, the country has experienced war and severe famine, or lack of food. Establishing a stable economy has therefore been difficult.

Introducing East Africa

Cheetahs in a Kenyan national park

Kenya

Capital	Nairobi
Land Area	219,787 sq mi; 569,250 sq km
Population	31.3 million
Ethnic Group(s)	Kikuyu, Luhya, Luo, Kalenjin, Kamba, Kisii, Meru
Religion(s)	Protestant, Roman Catholic, traditional beliefs, Muslim
Government	republic
Currency	Kenya shilling
Leading Exports	tea, horticultural products, coffee, petroleum products, fish, cement
Language(s)	Kiswahili (official), English (official), Kikuyu, Luo, Kamba

Located along the Equator, Kenya (KEN yuh) is bordered on the west by Lake Victoria and Uganda, on the north by Sudan and Ethiopia, on the east by Somalia and the Indian Ocean, and on the south by Tanzania. The Great Rift Valley runs through the western half of the country. Kenya is home to the Kenyan Highlands, one of the most successful farming regions in Africa. The country is also a major center of business and trade in East Africa. In addition, many rare animals and numerous national parks have made tourism a strong industry in Kenya.

Rwanda

Capital	Kigali
Land Area	9,632 sq mi; 24,948 sq km
Population	7.4 million
Ethnic Group(s)	Hutu, Tutsi, Twa
Religion(s)	Christian, Muslim, traditional beliefs
Government	republic
Currency	Rwanda franc
Leading Exports	coffee, tea, hides, tin ore
Language(s)	French (official), English (official), Kinyarwanda (official), Kiswahili

Rwanda (roo AHN duh) is bordered on the west by the Democratic Republic of the Congo, on the north by Uganda, on the east by Tanzania, and on the south by Burundi. It is the most densely populated country in Africa. Fierce civil war erupted in the early 1990s when nearly 1 million Tutsi were massacred by the majority Hutu. As a result of the war, about 2 million Hutus migrated to neighboring countries. After the war's end, many of them returned to Rwanda. The country's economy is slowly improving.

Seychelles

Capital	Victoria
Land Area	176 sq mi; 455 sq km
Population	80,098
Ethnic Group(s)	white, black, South Asian, East Asian, Arab
Religion(s)	Christian
Government	republic
Currency	Seychelles rupee
Leading Exports	canned tuna, cinnamon bark, copra, petroleum products (reexports)
Language(s)	Seselwa (French Creole) (official), English, French

The 115 islands of Seychelles (say SHEL) are located in the Indian Ocean, northwest of Madagascar. The islands are known for their natural beauty and unique plants and animals. They are home to the coco de mer (KOH koh duh mehr), a plant that produces a coconut-like fruit that is one of the largest fruits in the world. In addition, some of the last giant tortoises in the world live there. In 1976, Seychelles gained its independence from the United Kingdom, and in 1993 it became a democracy. Tuna fishing and tourism are the leading economic activities of these islands.

Fishing near Seychelles (left); a giant tortoise (below)

Somalia

Capital	Mogadishu
Land Area	242,215 sq mi; 627,337 sq km
Population	7.8 million
Ethnic Group(s)	Somali, Bantu, Arab
Religion(s)	Muslim
Government	transitional government
Currency	Somali shilling
Leading Exports	livestock, bananas, hides, fish, charcoal, scrap metal
Language(s)	Somali (official), Arabic (official), English, Italian

Somalia (soh MAH lee uh) occupies the Horn of Africa, the easternmost point of the continent. It is bordered on the west by Kenya, Ethiopia, and Djibouti; on the north by the Gulf of Aden; and on the east by the Indian Ocean. Much of Somalia is semiarid desert. There is some fertile land along the coast and in the south near the capital, Mogadishu (moh gah DEE shoo). Most Somalis are farmers or nomadic herders. In recent years, Somalia has faced many severe problems, such as civil war, the collapse of its government, and famine.

Introducing East Africa

Sudan

Capital	Khartoum
Land Area	917,374 sq mi; 2,376,000 sq km
Population	37.1 million
Ethnic Group(s)	black, Arab, Beja
Religion(s)	Muslim, traditional beliefs, Christian
Government	authoritarian regime
Currency	Sudanese pound or dinar
Leading Exports	oil and petroleum products, cotton, sesame, livestock, groundnuts, gum arabic, sugar
Language(s)	Arabic (official), Dinka, Nuer, Nubian, Beja, Zande, Bari, Fur, Shilluk, Lotuko

In land area, Sudan (soo DAN) is the largest country in Africa. It is bordered on the west by the Central African Republic, Chad, and Libya; on the north by Egypt; on the east by the Red Sea, Eritrea, and Ethiopia; and on the south by Kenya, Uganda, and the Democratic Republic of the Congo. Both the Blue Nile and White Nile rivers flow through Sudan. Nearly 50 years of civil war have led to millions of deaths, migrations out of the country, and economic problems.

An ancient pyramid at Meroë, in present-day Sudan

Tanzania

Capital	Dar es Salaam and Dodoma
Land Area	342,099 sq mi; 886,037 sq km
Population	37.2 million
Ethnic Group(s)	Bantu, Asian, white, Arab
Religion(s)	Muslim, traditional beliefs, Christian
Government	republic
Currency	Tanzanian shilling
Leading Exports	gold, coffee, cashew nuts, manufactured goods, cotton
Language(s)	English (official), Kiswahili (official), Sukuma, Chagga, Nyamwezi, Hehe, Makonde, Yao, Sandawe

Tanzania (tan zuh NEE uh) is bordered on the west by Zambia, the Democratic Republic of the Congo, Burundi, and Rwanda; on the north by Uganda and Kenya; on the east by the Indian Ocean; and on the south by Mozambique and Malawi. It is home to Mount Kilimanjaro, Africa's tallest mountain. The Great Rift Valley forms the country's south-western border. In 1964 the newly independent regions of Tanganyika and Zanzibar joined to become Tanzania. It is one of the world's poorest nations, but today Tanzania's manufacturing and mining industries are helping the economy boom.

Uganda

Capital	Kampala
Land Area	77,108 sq mi; 199,710 sq km
Population	24.7 million
Ethnic Group(s)	18 distinct groups, including Baganda, Ankole, Basoga, Iteso, Bakiga, Langi, Rwanda, Bagisu
Religion(s)	Roman Catholic, Protestant, traditional beliefs, Hindu, Muslim
Government	republic
Currency	New Uganda shilling
Leading Exports	coffee, fish and fish products, tea, gold, cotton, flowers, horticultural products
Language(s)	English (official), Luganda, Nkole, Chiga, Lango, Acholi, Teso, Lugbara

SOURCES: DK World Desk Reference Online; CIA World Factbook Online; *The World Almanac*, 2003

Uganda (yoo GAN duh) is bordered on the west by the Democratic Republic of the Congo, on the north by Sudan, on the east by Kenya, and on the south by Tanzania, Lake Victoria, and Rwanda. Uganda gained independence from Britain in 1962. It has since faced difficult political challenges. During the 1970s and 1980s, civil war led to hundreds of thousands of deaths as well as destruction of the country's economy. Since the 1990s, Uganda has been celebrated for its return to economic success. The country has many natural resources, including copper and cobalt, as well as fertile soil and plentiful rain.

Lake Victoria

Assessment

Comprehension and Critical Thinking

1. Draw Conclusions What are some characteristics that most East African countries share?

2. Analyze Information What are some key differences among the countries?

3. Compare Compare the land areas and populations of Burundi and Sudan.

4. Categorize What kinds of products are the major exports of this region?

5. Summarize Which languages are spoken in more than one country in this region?

6. Make a Bar Graph Create a bar graph showing the land area, in square miles, of each of the countries in this region.

Keeping Current

Access the **DK World Desk Reference Online** at PHSchool.com for up-to-date information about all eleven countries in this chapter.

Go Online
PHSchool.com

Web Code: lae-5600

Ethiopia
Religious Roots

Prepare to Read

Objectives

In this section you will
1. Learn about the two major religions practiced in Ethiopia.
2. Understand the contrasts in the daily lives of rural and urban Ethiopians.

Taking Notes

As you read this section, look for details about religion and daily life in Ethiopia. Copy the table below, and use it to record your findings.

Culture of Ethiopia	
Religion	**Daily Life**
• •	• •

Target Reading Skill

Use Context Clues When you come across an unfamiliar word, you can sometimes figure out its meaning from clues in the context. The context refers to the surrounding words and sentences. As you read, look at the context for the word *isolated* in the last paragraph on page 167. Use the sentence that follows it as a clue. What do you think *isolated* means?

Key Terms

• **monastery** (MAHN uh stehr ee) *n.* a place where people, especially men known as monks, live a religious life
• **Geez** (gee EZ) *n.* an ancient Ethiopian language that was once used to write literature and religious texts but is no longer spoken

As a young boy, Iyasus Mo'a (ee YAH soos MOH uh) learned to read and write. Around the year 1241, he traveled from his home in Wag to Tigray (tee GRAY), both in northern Ethiopia. He walked a distance that today would take three days to drive.

Did he plan to enter a university in Tigray? No—at that time there were no universities in Ethiopia. Iyasus entered a Christian monastery. A **monastery** is a place where people, especially men known as monks, live a religious life. As a monk, Iyasus studied hard for many years and eventually also became a famous teacher. His students built monasteries and schools all over the region.

The monastery of Debre Damo, where Iyasus Mo'a became a monk in the 1200s

Major Religions of Ethiopia

Iyasus Mo'a learned Ethiopia's ancient traditions. He studied a language called Geez (gee EZ). **Geez** is one of the world's oldest languages. Much of Ethiopia's history was preserved by monks like Iyasus, who copied books in Geez by hand.

The religion Iyasus studied—Christianity—had spread to Ethiopia along trade routes. Ethiopia was a center of trade. It once included present-day Eritrea as well. These lands border the Red Sea. Look at the physical map of Africa on page 4 of the Regional Overview. Find the Red Sea. As people traded goods along the Red Sea, they also learned about one another's religions. The Red Sea connected Ethiopia with Egypt and Palestine, which were early centers of Christianity.

Establishment of Christianity in Ethiopia Alexandria, a city in Egypt, was one of the first centers of Christianity. By the year A.D. 350, missionaries from Alexandria had brought Christianity to Ethiopia. Over time, Christians in Egypt and Ethiopia came to differ with Christians in Rome and Constantinople about certain beliefs. In A.D. 451, Egyptian Christians separated from the rest of the Christian Church. They formed an Egyptian branch of Christianity called the Coptic Christian Church. Ethiopia's Christians also practiced Coptic Christianity.

Over time, Ethiopian Christians became isolated from Christians in other parts of the world. Ethiopia's mountains made it difficult for people who lived in the interior to travel to other areas. Some people did travel overland or along the Red Sea. However, Ethiopian Christians were cut off from these travel routes in the A.D. 600s, when Muslim Arabs arrived in the region.

Links to
Language Arts

Written Language Ethiopians began writing in Geez by the A.D. 300s. They used Geez to write literature and religious texts such as the one shown below. Ethiopia and Egypt were the only ancient African countries to develop their own writing systems. Many Islamic kingdoms in Africa did produce written documents for religious and government purposes. However, these texts were written in Arabic, which was developed in Arabia.

Underground Churches
Here you see St. George's Church of Lalibela from a side view (above left) and an overhead view (above right). The church was built in the shape of a cross. **Compare** *Compare the effects of looking at the church from the side and from above.*

Target Skill **Use Context Clues**
If you do not know what *reigned* means, consider the word's context. You know that Lalibela reigned for a few decades. You also know that he was the ruler of Roha. You could conclude that *reigned* means "was the ruler of."

Spread of Islam Into Ethiopia The Muslim Arabs who had begun to settle across North Africa did not attempt to take over Ethiopia. But they did move into nearby areas. Over time, Arab traders built cities along the trade routes of the Red Sea coast. Eventually, Muslim Arabs came to control trade in the entire region. And, in time, some Ethiopians adopted the Muslim faith.

A Unique Form of Christianity As Muslim Arabs took control of Ethiopia's coastal regions, Ethiopian Christians began moving farther inland. Finally, Christian Ethiopia became surrounded by Muslim-controlled areas. As a result, Christians in Ethiopia had very little contact with Christians elsewhere. The Ethiopian Christian Church developed into a unique form of Christianity with its own traditions and language, Geez.

Also unique to Ethiopian Christianity are the churches of a town called Lalibela (lah lee BAY lah). Once called Roha, it was the capital of Christian Ethiopia for about 300 years. It was renamed for its most famous ruler, Lalibela, who reigned during the late 1100s and early 1200s. The ruler Lalibela sponsored the construction of eleven churches unlike any others—they were built below the ground and cut out of solid rock. Many Christians today travel to Lalibela to visit the churches and celebrate their faith.

Christian-Muslim Interaction Throughout most of Ethiopia's history, Christians and Muslims have coexisted peacefully. However, they have sometimes fought over religious issues. For example, they went to war with each other in the 1500s. Today, about 35 percent of Ethiopians are Christians and about 45 percent are Muslims. Most other Ethiopians practice traditional African religions, although a small number practice Judaism.

✔ **Reading Check** How did Christianity first come to Ethiopia?

Ethiopia

People have lived in Ethiopia longer than in most other countries on Earth. And for most of its history, the nation has ruled itself. Except for a short period of time before World War II, Ethiopia was never colonized by a European country.

Today, as for thousands of years, Ethiopian cultures have been centered mainly in the country's highlands. Many ethnic groups exist, but a few are much larger than the rest. Members of each ethnic group tend to live near one another. Study the map and charts to learn more about Ethiopia's people today.

Ethiopia: Ethnic Groups
KEY

- Amhara
- Oromo
- Sidamo
- Somali
- Other
- — National border
- ⊛ National capital
- • Other city

0 miles 300
0 kilometers 300
Lambert Azimuthal Equal Area

Population by Age*

- 0-14 years
- 15-64 years
- 65 years and older

44%
54%
3%

*Percentages do not total 100 due to rounding

SOURCE: CIA World Factbook

Ethnic Groups

Oromo 40%
Somali 6%
Sidamo 9%
Amhara 25%
Other 20%

SOURCE: DK World Desk Reference

Map and Chart Skills

1. **Name** What is the largest ethnic group in Ethiopia?
2. **Identify** What percentage of Ethiopia's population is under 14 years of age?
3. **Analyze** What does this percentage tell you about Ethiopian society?

Go Online PHSchool.com Use Web Code lae-5601 for DK World Desk Reference Online.

Contrasts in Daily Life

Today, most Ethiopians, regardless of their religious background, live in rural areas. In fact, only about 16 percent of the population lives in cities. How do rural and urban life in Ethiopia differ? A look at the village of Gerba Sefer reveals many clues about rural life in Ethiopia. The capital city of Addis Ababa (ad is AB uh buh), on the other hand, represents the urban life that some Ethiopians know.

Rural Ethiopia Public services such as electricity and running water are rare in rural Ethiopia. For example, no one in the village of Gerba Sefer has electricity, and more people own donkeys than cars. The people who live in the areas surrounding Gerba Sefer make a living by farming. In some rural areas, people make a living by herding cattle or by fishing. Some families specialize in jobs such as woodworking and beekeeping.

A street in Addis Ababa

Urban Ethiopia Addis Ababa, the capital of Ethiopia, has a population of almost 3 million people. It is located in the center of the country. People in Addis Ababa have access to all the conveniences of city life—for example, running water, electricity, and modern hospitals. The city also has a university and a museum, as well as palaces built by ancient emperors. And Addis Ababa is a center of business and trade that reflects a diverse population, which includes ethnic groups such as the Amhara, Tigrey, Galla, and Gurage. The city also houses the headquarters of several international organizations that work for the economic, political, and social well-being of Africa.

✓ **Reading Check** Do most Ethiopians live in rural or in urban settings?

Section 1 Assessment

Key Terms
Review the key terms at the beginning of this section. Use each term in a sentence that explains its meaning.

Target Reading Skill
Find the word *coexisted* in the last paragraph on page 168. Use context to figure out its meaning. What do you think it means? What clues helped you arrive at its meaning?

Comprehension and Critical Thinking
1. (a) **Recall** When did Christianity first come to Ethiopia?
(b) **Summarize** What led to the unique nature of the Christianity practiced in Ethiopia?
(c) **Predict** What do you think helps Christians and Muslims exist peacefully in Ethiopia today?
2. (a) **Identify** In what ways do rural Ethiopians make a living?
(b) **Contrast** How is life in Ethiopia's rural areas different from life in Addis Ababa?

Writing Activity
Write a paragraph encouraging travelers to visit the historic churches of Lalibela, Ethiopia. In it, explain how the Ethiopian Christian Church has been affected by the country's history.

For: An activity on Ethiopia
Visit: PHSchool.com
Web Code: lad-5601

Section 2

Tanzania
Determined to Succeed

Prepare to Read

Objectives

In this section you will
1. Find out about early reforms that the government of Tanzania made after independence.
2. Learn about continued social, economic, and political progress and reforms that have been made in Tanzania.

Taking Notes

As you read this section, look for details about social, economic, and political reforms in Tanzania. Copy the chart below, and use it to record your findings.

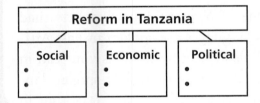

Reform in Tanzania		
Social	**Economic**	**Political**
•	•	•
•	•	•

Target Reading Skill

Use Context Clues You can sometimes clarify the meaning of a word or phrase by using context—the surrounding words, phrases, and sentences. Sometimes the context will give a clear definition or explanation of the word. For example, each word highlighted in blue in this book is followed by a definition. As you read, look for other words that are accompanied by definitions or explanations.

Key Terms

- **lingua franca** (LING gwuh FRANG kuh) *n.* a language used for communication among people who speak different first languages
- **privatization** (pry vuh tih ZAY shun) *n.* the sale of government-owned industries to private companies
- **multiparty system** (MUL tee PAHR tee SIS tum) *n.* a political system in which two or more parties compete in elections

In October 1995, Dar es Salaam (DAHR es suh LAHM), Tanzania, looked ready for a celebration. Flags hung from buildings. People sang in the streets. Was it a holiday? Had a sports team become champions? No—an election was about to start. It would be the first election in more than 30 years to include more than one political party. Finally, voters would have a real choice among candidates with differing views. Tanzanians felt joyful, but they did not know what the future would hold. Other reforms their country had gone through had met with different levels of success.

Early Reforms After Independence

Tanzania lies on the Indian Ocean. This location has made it an important center of trade. Arab traders settled along the coast around 1,200 years ago. In the late 1800s, Germans colonized the entire region. The British took over in the early 1900s. The British named the mainland area Tanganyika (tan guh NYEE kuh). Tanganyika became independent in 1961. In 1964, it joined with the island state of Zanzibar to form Tanzania.

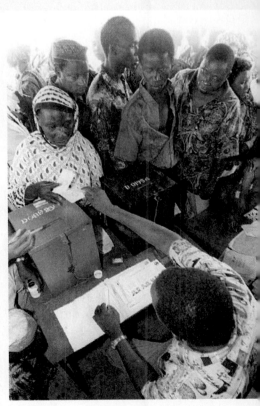

Tanzanians cast their votes.

Chapter 6 Section 2 **171**

Amri Abedi

Amri Abedi was Tanzania's Minister of Justice, the mayor of Dar es Salaam, and the leader of a regional government—all at the same time. He took on so many jobs at once because when Tanzania became independent, it did not have enough educated citizens to run the government. Many of the people who did work in government had to work at more than one job to keep the government running smoothly.

Challenges for the New Nation When Tanzania became independent, most of its people were poor. Few were literate. According to Tanzania's then president, Julius Nyerere, the new republic had serious problems:

> **We had 12 medical doctors in a population of 9 million. About 45 percent of children of schoolgoing age were going to school, and 85 percent of the adult population was illiterate.**
>
> —*Julius Nyerere*

A problem Nyerere wanted to avoid was tension among Tanzania's 120 ethnic groups. In many other African nations, ethnic groups fought against one another after independence. To ensure that ethnic conflicts would not occur in Tanzania, Nyerere adopted unusual social policies. Although some of these policies met with approval both at home and abroad, others were sharply criticized. Even today, debate continues over whether or not Nyerere made good choices for Tanzania.

A National Language One of Nyerere's social policies had to do with language. Various languages are spoken in East African homes, but many people also speak Swahili. As you read in Chapter 2, Swahili is one of Africa's most widely spoken languages. In East Africa, Swahili is a lingua franca (LING gwuh FRANG kuh). A **lingua franca** is a language used for communication among people who speak different first languages. To help unite all of Tanzania's ethnic groups, Nyerere made Swahili the national language.

A One-Party System Nyerere also established a new political system. He feared that political parties in Tanzania would be based on ethnic groups. If so, competition among parties could lead to competition or hatred among ethnic groups. This had happened in other newly independent African nations. Therefore, Nyerere established a one-party system. Elections still involved several candidates, but they were all members of the same party. Critics complained that having just one party encouraged corruption in the government.

Economic Changes Next, Nyerere turned to the economy. He told Tanzanians that independence meant *uhuru na kazi* (oo HOO roo nah KAH zee)—"freedom and work." By this he meant that only hard work could end poverty. Nyerere said that Tanzania should be self-reliant. He did not want the country to depend on other nations for economic support.

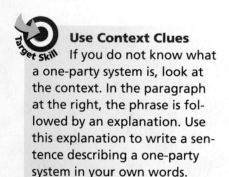

Use Context Clues
If you do not know what a one-party system is, look at the context. In the paragraph at the right, the phrase is followed by an explanation. Use this explanation to write a sentence describing a one-party system in your own words.

Links Across
The World

Kwanzaa In the 1960s, many African Americans began celebrating family, community, and their African heritage with a holiday called Kwanzaa (KWAHN zah). Kwanzaa is based on several traditional African harvest festivals. Its name comes from a Swahili phrase that means "first fruits." The holiday celebrates a set of seven values that also have Swahili names. One of these values is ujamaa. Each night of the week-long holiday, families like the one shown here gather to light a candle and discuss one of the values.

To promote self-reliance, Nyerere established a program of *ujamaa* (oo JAH mah), which is Swahili for "togetherness" or "being a family." Tanzania's economy is based on farming. Nyerere called for all farmers to live in ujamaa villages, where they could work together and share resources. He believed this would help boost farm production. It would also make it easier for the government to provide clean water, education, and other services in an organized way.

✓ **Reading Check** What language is the lingua franca of Tanzania?

Progress and Continued Reform

By the time Nyerere stepped down as president in 1985, Tanzania had changed greatly. The country had a national language and very little ethnic conflict. Education and literacy had improved greatly. Proud of his success, Nyerere commented,

❝When I stepped down, 91 percent of the adult population was literate, 100 percent of the children of school-going age were going to school. . . . We did not have enough engineers, but we had thousands . . . trained by ourselves. We did not have enough doctors, but we had . . . thousands trained by ourselves. That is what we were able to do . . . in a short period of independence.❞

—*Julius Nyerere*

However, Tanzania was still one of the poorest countries in the world. The ujamaa program had failed, and the economy was suffering. Many farm families had refused to move to the new villages. Crop production had decreased throughout the nation.

Tanzania

Like many African nations, Tanzania grows cash crops for export to other countries. The price of these cash crops on the world market greatly influences whether Tanzania's economy improves or declines. When the world price of coffee dropped from about $1.00 per pound in 1996 to less than $.40 per pound in 2003, many Tanzanians suffered. At the same time, the world price of tea rose, helping other Tanzanian farmers. Study the map and charts to learn more about the economy of Tanzania.

Economic Activity

- Services 40%
- Industry 17%
- Agriculture 43%

SOURCE: *CIA World Factbook*

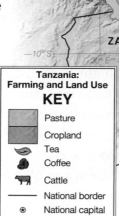

Tanzania: Farming and Land Use
KEY

- Pasture
- Cropland
- Tea
- Coffee
- Cattle
- National border
- ⊛ National capital

Major Cash Crops, 2001

Crop	Exports (billions of Tanzanian shillings*)
Cashews	50.9
Coffee	49.6
Cotton seeds	29.2
Sisal	5.9
Tobacco	32.3

* $1 = approximately 1,000 Tanzanian shillings
SOURCE: Tanzanian Ministry of Agriculture and Food Security

Map and Chart Skills

1. **Identify** (a) Which of Tanzania's cash crops was the most valuable export in 2001? (b) Which was least valuable?

2. **Draw Conclusions** You can see that agriculture makes up the largest part of Tanzania's economy. Name one advantage and one disadvantage of basing an economy on selling cash crops to other countries.

Go Online
PHSchool.com

Use Web Code lae-5602 for DK World Desk Reference Online.

A New Era in Economics After Nyerere retired, Ali Hassan Mwinyi (AH lee hah SAHN um WEEN yee) was elected president. His government replaced some of Nyerere's unsuccessful programs. For example, the government ended Nyerere's failing ujamaa program. The government then encouraged farmers to use new farming methods and types of seeds in order to produce more cash crops. It also asked foreign countries for more help, and a number of them have since loaned money to Tanzania.

The government also decided to try privatization. **Privatization** is the sale of government-owned industries to private companies. Private companies, including some that are foreign-owned, now manage Tanzania's telephone and airline industries. The result of the new economic policies is that Tanzania's economy is improving more quickly and more smoothly than the economies of most other African nations.

Attempts at Political Reform Tanzania's new government also changed the election system. In 1992, the government began to allow new political parties to form. When a country has two or more political parties, it has a **multiparty system.** Tanzania's first elections under the multiparty system were held in October 1995.

But the 1995 and 2000 elections raised some issues that divided people. For example, in both elections, Nyerere's party won the most votes, so power remained with that party. Also, another party suggested that the island of Zanzibar should no longer be part of Tanzania. That would cause exactly the type of social split that Nyerere worried about. Whether Tanzania can achieve the same progress in politics as it has with its economy is still to be seen.

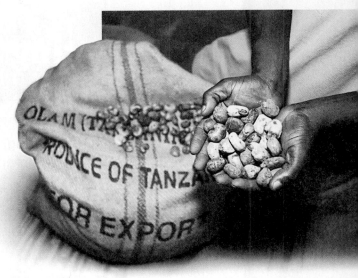

Cashews: A New Cash Crop
Cashew nuts are one of the cash crops that Tanzanian farmers now produce for export to other countries. Coffee and cotton are also major export items.
Summarize *How can producing cash crops for export help improve a country's economy?*

 Reading Check **What political change occurred in 1992?**

Section 2 Assessment

Key Terms
Review the key terms at the beginning of this section. Use each term in a sentence that explains its meaning.

Target Reading Skill
Find the word *self-reliant* on page 172. From its context, what do you think it means?

Comprehension and Critical Thinking
1. (a) Explain Why did Julius Nyerere decide to establish a one-party political system in Tanzania?

(b) Analyze Information In what ways can having a national language help prevent ethnic conflict in a country?
(c) Draw Conclusions If people had not had to move away from their homes, do you think the ujamaa program would have succeeded? Explain.
2. (a) Identify What improvements were made in Tanzania during Nyerere's presidency?
(b) Contrast Contrast the views Nyerere had on foreign involvement in Tanzania with the views that later government leaders had.

Writing Activity
How does Nyerere's slogan uhuru na kazi, or "freedom and work," apply to the kind of independence that you develop as you grow up? Write a paragraph explaining your response to this question.

For: An activity on the Ngorongoro Crater
Visit: PHSchool.com
Web Code: lad-5602

Early each morning, the President of the United States listens to a news briefing prepared just for him. His staff members put the briefing together by reading and listening to news from dozens of newspapers, radio stations, and television networks. They then select the most important stories and write a summary of each one.

Writing a summary of any kind of information involves identifying the main ideas and weaving them together based on what they have in common. Knowing how to write a summary will help you take tests, write essays, and understand what you read.

Learn the Skill

Use these steps to summarize information.

1 **Find and state the main idea of each paragraph or section you want to summarize.** You can often find a main idea in the topic sentence of a paragraph.

2 **Identify what the main ideas have in common.** Look for the ways the ideas are presented—for example, in chronological order, as causes and effects, as comparisons, or as a progression of ideas from simple to complex. Doing this will help you identify the overall focus of the information.

3 **Write a summary paragraph that begins with a topic sentence.** The summary should draw together the main ideas into a broad description of the information. The main ideas will be the supporting details of your topic sentence.

U.S. President George W. Bush discusses the day's events with his staff.

Practice the Skill

Read the section titled Major Religions of Ethiopia on pages 167–168. Then follow the steps below to summarize what you read.

1 Read the heading and subheadings in the section. These titles give you a general idea of the content. You can see that both Christianity and Islam are practiced in Ethiopia. Now read each paragraph and list its main idea.

2 The main ideas in this passage are in chronological order. They cover these dates: 350, 451, the 600s, the 1500s, and today. In what other ways are the main ideas related? What overall idea holds these paragraphs together?

3 You might use this topic sentence for your summary: *Ethiopia's location as a crossroads of trade and ideas has shaped its unique religious history.* Use this topic sentence, or write your own, and then complete the summary paragraph by adding explanations and details. The details will come from the main ideas on your list.

Ethiopian places of worship: the Church of St. Mary of Zion (above) and the Nagash mosque (below)

Apply the Skill

Read the section titled Early Reforms After Independence on pages 171–173. Use the steps in this skill to summarize the information.

Kenya
Ties That Bind

Prepare to Read

Objectives
In this section you will
1. Learn about the peoples of Kenya.
2. Discover what life is like in rural Kenya.
3. Find out what life is like in urban Kenya.

Taking Notes
As you read this section, look for details about daily life in rural and urban Kenya. Copy the chart below, and use it to record your findings.

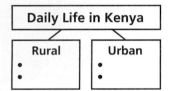

```
Daily Life in Kenya
     |
  ┌──┴──┐
Rural   Urban
  •       •
  •       •
```

Target Reading Skill

Interpret Nonliteral Meanings Literal language is language that means exactly what it says. Nonliteral language uses images or comparisons to communicate an idea.

In this section you will read about "ties that bind" Kenyans together. When you see these words, ask yourself: Are Kenyans really tied together by something physical, or do the words have another meaning?

Key Terms
- **Kikuyu** (kee KOO yoo) *n.* the largest ethnic group in Kenya
- **Maasai** (mah SY) *n.* a seminomadic ethnic group in Kenya
- **seminomadic** (seh mee noh MAD ik) *adj.* combining nomadic wandering and farming in settlements
- **harambee** (hah RAHM bay) *n.* a social policy started by Jomo Kenyatta and meaning "let's pull together" in Swahili

A Maasai family in Kenya standing in front of their land

"**W**here is your shamba?" is a question that two Kenyans usually ask each other when they first meet. A shamba is a small farm owned and run by a Kenyan family. Even Kenyans who move to the city think of the land where they were born as home. They return to it throughout their lives. Land is very important to Kenyans.

Peoples of Kenya

Kenya's highest mountain, Mount Kenya, lies just south of the Equator. Southwest of Mount Kenya is a region of highlands that receives plenty of rain, so the land is good for farming. Most of Kenya's people are farmers. Many of them live in shambas dotting the countryside of the highlands. Others live along Kenya's coast, a warmer area that also has good farmland.

Kenya's Shared Culture Although some Kenyans are of European, Asian, or Arab descent, most come from families that have always lived in Africa. Kenya has plenty of cultural diversity—including more than 40 ethnic groups. Each ethnic group has distinct cultural features. But many groups have features in common, too. For example, some groups speak the same language as one another, and most Kenyans are either Christian or Muslim. Language and religion are some of the ties that bind the peoples of Kenya together.

Many Kenyans also share common values. Most Kenyans value their families as much as they value the land. Some families have six or more children. Members of extended families can be very close, often considering their cousins to be like brothers and sisters.

Kenya's Ethnic Groups The **Kikuyu** (kee KOO yoo) are Kenya's largest ethnic group. Many Kikuyu live in shambas in the highlands near Mount Kenya. They build round homes with mud walls and thatched roofs. The Kikuyu grow food and cash crops such as coffee and sisal, a fiber used to make rope. The **Maasai** (mah SY) are another ethnic group in Kenya, who traditionally make a living by farming and herding. The Maasai are **seminomadic,** which means they sometimes wander as nomads and sometimes live in settlements where they farm.

✔ **Reading Check** How many ethnic groups live in Kenya?

Ethnic Groups of Kenya
These women are Samburu people who, like the Maasai, are seminomadic herders. The women wear traditional Samburu dress—brightly patterned cloths and jewelry made of many colorful beads. **Evaluate** *Why do you think many peoples around the world dress traditionally?*

Life in Rural Kenya

As elsewhere in Africa, the majority of Kenya's farmers are women. They grow fruits and vegetables and herd livestock. Men also farm, but they usually raise cash crops, such as coffee and tea.

The way of life of many Kenyans is changing. As the population increases, many men and some women are moving to the cities to find work. Most women and children, however, stay in rural areas. Women are the primary caretakers of children, and it is expensive for women with children to move to a city. Many find it easier to support their families by farming.

Kenyans Working Together Kenya gained independence from the British in 1963. The first president, Jomo Kenyatta (JOH moh ken YAH tuh), began a social policy he called **harambee** (hah RAHM bay), which in Swahili means "let's pull together." Kenyatta encouraged harambee in many forms, including politics, farming, and education. For example, he had the government pay for a part of each child's education. In response, many villagers worked together to build and support their schools.

COUNTRY PROFILE — Focus on Geography

Kenya

Most Kenyans live in the countryside. The majority of the country's agricultural products are grown in the highlands region, where rainfall is sufficient for farming. An increasing number of Kenyans have moved to major cities. Nairobi, the largest business center in East Africa, is home both to very wealthy families and to people who live in slums. Study the map and charts to learn more about Kenya's land and people.

Major Agricultural Products, 2005

Production (in metric tons)	
Corn	2,800,000
Cassava	910,000
Plantains	452,000
Sugar cane	489,000
Coffee	1,080,000

SOURCE: USDA Foreign Agricultural Service, 2005

Kenya: Yearly Precipitation

KEY

Inches	Millimeters
More than 59	More than 1,499
40–59	1,000–1,499
20–39	500–999
10–19	250–499

— National border
⊛ National capital
• Other city

0 miles 250
0 kilometers 250
Lambert Azimuthal Equal Area

Urban and Rural Population, 1950–2000

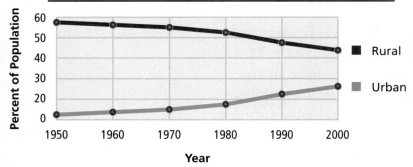

Rural
Urban

SOURCE: United Nations Food and Agriculture Organization

Map and Chart Skills

1. **Identify** What products did Kenya produce more than one million metric tons of in 2005?
2. **Infer** In what region do you think Kenyans farm the least?
3. **Synthesize** Study the population graph. How do you think the trend shown has affected Kenya's agriculture?

Use Web Code lae-5603 for DK World Desk Reference Online.

Women's Self-Help Groups One of the best examples of how harambee is successful in Kenya is the rise of women's self-help groups in rural areas. Women in rural areas all over Kenya have formed these groups to solve problems in their communities. For example, many women felt it was not easy to farm, chop firewood, haul water, and take care of children all in one day. One woman commented, "My children were educated through the sweat of my brow."

These self-help groups do a great variety of work. Some women's groups grow cash crops in addition to the crops they grow for their families to eat. Then they sell the cash crops and save the money as a group. The women meet to decide what to do with the money they have saved. In the mountain village of Mitero, Kikuyu women's groups have built a nursery school and installed water pipes for the community. They also loan money to women who want to start small businesses. Sometimes they give money to women who need to buy such necessities as a cow or a water tank. They also save money individually and use it to educate their children.

✓ **Reading Check** **What is the purpose of women's self-help groups in Kenya?**

Life in Urban Kenya

Kenya's capital, Nairobi (ny ROH bee), is an important business center and one of the largest cities in East Africa. It is also East Africa's most important center of industry and manufacturing. Much of East Africa's banking and trade is centered there as well.

Working in the City Because Nairobi is a thriving city, many Kenyans move there looking for jobs. Every day, people arrive in Nairobi by train, bus, or *matatu* (muh TAH too)—minibus. Nairobi's population grew from one million in 1985 to more than two million in 2000. Many of Nairobi's newcomers walk to their jobs from the outskirts of the city. They may walk as far as ten miles each way because they cannot afford the cost of taking the bus to work.

When men move to Nairobi without their families, they often feel homesick for their loved ones in rural villages. Meanwhile, the women who remain in the villages must do much more work. Many people in Kenya have responded to this situation in the spirit of harambee—by working together.

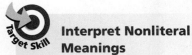

Interpret Nonliteral Meanings
What does the woman mean by saying that her children were educated through the sweat of her brow? Did she use the sweat to teach the children or to pay for their schooling? Restate what she means in your own words.

These Kikuyu women have formed a savings and loan club to support local businesses.

Nairobi, Kenya

City Life Men who move to the city also work together. Many are saving money to buy land in the countryside. Men in Nairobi from the same ethnic group often welcome one another, share rooms, and help one another. Take Moses Mpoke (MOH zuz um POH kay) as an example. Mpoke is a Maasai. He owns land that is too dry for farming or grazing, but he could not move his livestock to find better grazing. After finishing high school, Mpoke moved to Nairobi to work.

Living in the city, Mpoke could have forgotten about his Maasai roots. But every weekend, he returns to his village to see his family and friends. When a visitor in his village asked Mpoke which is the real Moses Mpoke, the one in the city or the one in the village, he answered,

“This is the real Moses Mpoke, but the other is also me. In the week, I can live in the city and be comfortable. At weekends, I can live here [in my village] and be comfortable. The city has not stopped me from being a Maasai. ”

—Moses Mpoke

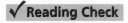 **Reading Check** How do Kenyans living in the city support one another?

Section 3 Assessment

Key Terms
Review the key terms at the beginning of this section. Use each term in a sentence that explains its meaning.

 Target Reading Skill
Find the phrase "in shambas dotting the countryside" on page 179. Explain in your own words what this means.

Comprehension and Critical Thinking
1. (a) Recall In what way do most Kenyans make their living?

(b) Compare What other traits do Kenya's different ethnic groups have in common?

2. (a) Explain Why do most Kenyan women stay in rural villages rather than move to the city?

(b) Summarize How have Kenya's government and Kenya's village women used harambee to help benefit village families?

3. (a) Describe What do many Kenyans who live in the city plan to do with the money they earn?

(b) Analyze Information What different hardships do men and women in Kenya face if the men decide to work in Nairobi?

Writing Activity
Consider the concept of harambee. It means that people work together for a common good. Write an account of how you have seen or would like to see harambee in your community or school.

> **Writing Tip** Start your account with an explanation of what harambee is, so that readers can easily understand how your example fits into the concept.

Review and Assessment

◆ Chapter Summary

Ethiopia

Section 1: Ethiopia

- Ethiopia has two major religions—Christianity and Islam. At times Ethiopian Christians and Muslims have fought each other, but today they live together peacefully.
- Most Ethiopians live in rural areas. Their daily lives are very different from those of Ethiopians in urban areas.

Section 2: Tanzania

- After independence, Tanzania's president Julius Nyerere established Swahili as the country's lingua franca, created a one-party political system, and encouraged farmers to live in ujamaa villages.
- Since Nyerere retired in 1985, Tanzania's government has encouraged privatization and other economic reforms as well as a multiparty political system.

Section 3: Kenya

- Kenyans come from 40 ethnic groups that are distinct but also share some values and characteristics. Many Kenyans are farmers.
- Most Kenyan farmers are women. To help solve community problems, many Kenyan women have formed various self-help groups.
- Many Kenyan men have had to move to the city to find work, but they often return to their villages on weekends or when they retire.

Kenya

◆ Key Terms

Each of the statements below contains a key term from the chapter. If it is true, write *true*. If it is false, change the highlighted term to make the statement true.

1. The Swahili word that means "let's pull together" is harambee.

2. Kikuyu is an ancient Ethiopian language.

3. A place where people live a religious life is a multiparty system.

4. People who speak different languages often communicate by speaking a lingua franca.

5. A country with two or more political parties has a monastery.

◆ Comprehension and Critical Thinking

6. (a) Describe How did Christianity and Islam spread into Ethiopia?
(b) Identify Effects How did the spread of Islam cause Ethiopian Christians to become more isolated?

7. (a) Identify What public services are lacking in Ethiopia's rural areas?
(b) Make Generalizations Do you think the prosperity of Addis Ababa could spread into rural Ethiopia? If it did, how would life change in rural areas?

8. (a) Explain Why did Julius Nyerere establish a lingua franca for Tanzania?
(b) Identify What changes did Julius Nyerere make to Tanzania's economic and political systems?
(c) Contrast What are some advantages of a one-party political system? Of a multiparty system?

9. (a) Recall Has Tanzania had greater success in economics or in politics?
(b) Analyze Information Why has establishing a multiparty political system in Tanzania been a challenge?

10. (a) Recall What are some ties that bind the people of Kenya together?
(b) Summarize How have rural Kenyans worked together to improve their lives?
(c) Identify Effects The movement of men from Kenya's countryside to Nairobi can cause some hardship. How can it also help improve village life?

◆ Skills Practice

Writing a Summary In the Skills for Life activity in this chapter, you learned how to write a summary.

Review the steps you followed to learn this skill. Then reread the part of Section 3 titled Life in Rural Kenya. Find the main idea of each paragraph. Then identify what the main ideas have in common, and write a summary paragraph.

◆ Writing Activity: Language Arts

Think about the community you live in. Is it growing or becoming smaller? Think of reasons why your community may have developed in the way that it has. What are some positive changes that have occurred? What are some negative ones? Use your answers to write a newspaper editorial explaining your opinion on whether your community is developing in a way that benefits its citizens.

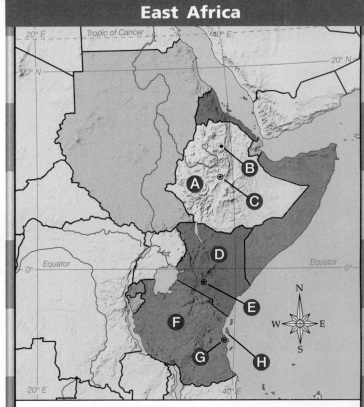

MAP✦MASTER™
Skills Activity

East Africa

Place Location For each place listed, write the letter from the map that shows its location.
1. Ethiopia
2. Nairobi
3. Tanzania
4. Dar es Salaam
5. Zanzibar
6. Kenya
7. Addis Ababa
8. Lalibela

Go Online
PHSchool.com Use Web Code lap-5620
for an **interactive map**.

Standardized Test Prep

Test-Taking Tips

Some questions on standardized tests ask you to analyze a reading selection. Read the passage below. Then follow the tips to answer the sample question.

> Julius Nyerere became the first president of Tanzania in 1964. He made Swahili the national language to help unite his country's many ethnic groups. He encouraged farmers to live together in organized villages and to cooperate. Many more schools were built, and literacy improved dramatically after independence. Many more Tanzanians were trained to be engineers, doctors, and teachers.

TIP Look for topics that are shared by all the sentences in the passage.

Pick the letter that best answers the question.

Which kind of resources in Tanzania does this passage describe?

A natural resources

B human resources

C capital resources

D entrepreneurial resources

TIP Before you read the paragraph, preview the question. Think about it as you read.

Think It Through The question asks what kind of resources the paragraph describes. Skim over each sentence of the paragraph. Each one mentions something about the people of Tanzania. You can eliminate answer A, natural resources, because those are materials found in the environment. You may not know the words *capital* or *entrepreneurial* in C and D, but you probably know that *human* has to do with people. The correct answer is B.

Practice Questions

Use the tips above and other tips in this book to help you answer the following questions. Use the passage below to answer Question 1. Choose the letter of the best answer.

> Lalibela is a town in Ethiopia. People travel there to visit a group of churches for which Lalibela is famous. Many people who live there, however, do not have electricity. Most of them do not own cars. Most of them earn a living by farming.

1. Which is a detail that is described in this passage?

   A The people who live in Lalibela love the churches there.

   B The tourists who visit Lalibela cannot bring cars.

   C Most of the people who live in Lalibela are farmers.

   D Most of Lalibela's visitors are farmers.

2. Which of the following was NOT true of Tanzania's ujamaa program?

   A The program's goal was to boost farm production.

   B People had to work together to make the program successful.

   C The government had to help out with the program.

   D All farm families in Tanzania agreed to take part.

3. Which is the word for a family farm in Kenya?

   A Maasai

   B shamba

   C harambee

   D Kikuyu

Use Web Code laa-5600 for **Chapter 6 self-test.**

A Promise to the Sun
By Tololwa M. Mollel

Prepare to Read

Background Information

Not all stories were written down when they were first told. Myths like the one you are about to read were originally told aloud. They were part of an oral tradition that people passed down from generation to generation.

These myths are meant to entertain the listener. They are also meant to explain something to the listener. Usually, they explain why aspects of the world are as they are. Myths often provide a moral lesson to the listener as well.

This story was written by Tololwa M. Mollel in the style of Maasai myths heard in his youth in Tanzania. Mollel is a well-known storyteller and author.

Objectives

In this section you will
1. Explore the natural world from a point of view that may not be familiar to you.
2. Learn how a storyteller can use animals and natural forces as characters to make a story more meaningful.

savannah alternate spelling of *savanna*
maize (mayz) *n.* corn
shrivel (SHRIH vul) *v.* to wrinkle as moisture is lost
wilt (wilt) *v.* to droop
withered (WITH urd) *adj.* shriveled and shrunken from drying out

Long ago, when the world was new, a severe drought hit the land of the birds. The <u>savannah</u> turned brown, and streams dried up. <u>Maize</u> plants died, and banana trees <u>shriveled</u> in the sun, their broad leaves <u>wilting</u> away. Even the nearby forest grew <u>withered</u> and pale.

The birds held a meeting and decided to send someone in search of rain. They drew lots to choose who would go on the journey. And they told the Bat, their distant cousin who was visiting, that she must draw, too. "You might not be a bird," they said, "but for now you're one of us." Everyone took a lot, and as luck would have it, the task fell to the Bat.

Over the trees and the mountains flew the Bat, to the Moon. There she cried, "Earth has no rain, Earth has no food, Earth asks for rain!"

A full moon rises over the Kenyan landscape.

The Moon smiled. "I can't bring rain. My task is to wash and oil the night's face. But you can try the Stars."

On flew the Bat, until she found the Stars at play. "Away with you!" they snapped, angry at being interrupted. "If you want rain, go to the Clouds!"

The Clouds were asleep but awoke at the sound of the Bat arriving. "We can bring rain," they yawned, "but the Winds must first blow us together, to hang over the Earth in one big lump."

At the approach of the Bat, the Winds howled to a stop.

"We'll blow the Clouds together," they said, "but not before the Sun has brought up steam to the sky."

As the Bat flew toward the Sun, a sudden scream shook the sky:

"Stop where you are, foolish Bat, before I burn off your little wings!"

The Bat shrank back in terror, and the Sun smothered its fire in rolls of clouds. Quickly the Bat said, "Earth has no rain, Earth has no food, Earth asks for rain!"

"I'll help you," replied the Sun, "in return for a favor. After the rain falls, choose for me the greenest patch on the forest top, and build me a nest there. Then no longer will I have to journey to the <u>horizon</u> at the end of each day but will rest for the night in the cool and quiet of the forest."

The Bat quickly replied, "I'm only a Bat and don't know how to build nests, but the birds will happily make you one. Nothing will be easier—there are so many of them. They will do it right after the harvest, I promise—all in a day!"

And down the sky's sunlit paths the Bat flew, excited to bring the good news to the birds.

The birds readily promised to build the nest.

"The very day after the harvest," said the Sparrow.

"All in a day," said the Owl.

"A beautiful nest it'll be," said the Canary.

"With all the colors of the rainbow," said the Peacock.

So the Sun burnt down upon the earth, steam rose, Winds blew, and Clouds gathered. Then rain fell. The savannah bloomed, and streams flowed. Green and thick and tall, the forest grew until it touched the sky. Crops flourished and ripened—maize, bananas, cassava, millet, and peanuts—and the birds harvested. The morning after the harvest, the Bat reminded the birds about the nest. Suddenly the birds were in no mood for work. All they cared about was the harvest celebrations, which were to start that night and last several days.

Clouds fill the East African sky.

horizon (huh RY zun) *n.* the place where Earth and sky appear to meet

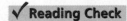

✓ Reading Check

What promise does the Bat make to the Sun?

"I have to adorn myself," said the Peacock.

"I have to practice my flute," said the Canary.

"I have to heat up my drums," said the Owl.

"I have to help prepare the feast," said the Sparrow.

"Wait until after the celebrations," they said. "We'll do it then." But their hearts were not in it, and the Bat knew they would never build the nest.

What was she to do? A promise is a promise, she firmly believed, yet she didn't know anything about making a nest. Even if she did, how could she, all on her own, hope to make one big enough for the sun?

The Sun set, and the Moon rose. The celebrations began. The drums throbbed, the flutes wailed, and the dancers pounded the earth with their feet.

Alone with her thoughts and tired, the Bat fell fast asleep.

She awoke in a panic. The Moon had vanished, the Stars faded. Soon the Sun would rise!

Slowly, the Sun peered out over the horizon in search of the nest.

Certain the Sun was looking for her, the Bat scrambled behind a banana leaf. The Sun moved up in the sky. One of its rays glared over the leaf. With a cry of fear, the Bat fled to the forest.

But even there, she was not long at peace. There was a gust of wind, and the forest opened for a moment overhead. The Bat looked up anxiously. Peeking down at her was the Sun.

She let out a shriek and flew away.

As she flew, a cave came into view below. She dived down and quickly darted in.

There, silent and out of reach, she hid from the glare of the Sun.

She hid from the shame of a broken promise, a shame the birds did not feel.

Outside, the celebrations went on. The Owl's drums roared furiously. The Canary's flute pierced the air. And the Sparrow cheered the Peacock's wild dancing.

The Sun inched down toward the horizon. It lingered over the forest and cast one more glance at the treetops, hoping for a miracle. Then, disappointed, it began to set. The birds carried on unconcerned, the sounds of their festivities reaching into the cave.

throb (thrahb) *v.* to beat

shriek (shreek) *n.* a sharp, shrill sound

Sunrise in Kenya

The Bat did not stir from her hiding place that night. Nor the next day. For many days and nights she huddled in the cave. Then gradually she got up enough courage to <u>venture</u> out—but never in daylight! Only after sunset with Earth in the <u>embrace</u> of night.

Days and months and years went by, but the birds didn't build the nest. The Sun never gave up wishing, though. Every day as it set, it would linger to cast one last, hopeful glance at the forest top. Then, slowly, very slowly, it would sink away below the horizon.

Year after year the Sun continued to drag up steam, so the Winds would blow, the Clouds gather, and rain fall. It continues to do so today, hoping that the birds will one day keep their promise and build a nest among the treetops.

As for the Bat, . . . she made a home in the cave, and there she lives to this day. Whenever it rains, though, she listens eagerly. From the dark silence of her perch, the sound of the downpour, ripening the crops and renewing the forest, is to her a magical song she wishes she could be out dancing to.

And as she listens, the trees outside sway and bow toward the cave. It is their thank-you salute to the hero who helped turn the forests green and thick and tall as the sky.

venture (VEN chur) *v.* to move forward in the face of danger

embrace (em BRAYS) *n.* hug

About the Selection

A Promise to the Sun is a children's book written by Tololwa M. Mollel and published in 1992.

✓ Reading Check

How does the Bat's life change as a result of what happens in the story?

About the Author

Tololwa M. Mollel (b. 1952) is an Arusha-Maasai born in northern Tanzania. He was educated and has taught writing and theater in Tanzania and Canada. Mollel has written more than 15 children's books. He has based his books on African folklore, including traditional Maasai tales and themes from his childhood.

Review and Assessment

Thinking About the Selection

1. (a) Recall What favor did the Sun ask of the Bat?

(b) Explain Why did the Bat not keep her promise?

(c) Analyze What aspects of how a bat lives are explained by this story? What other natural events are explained by this story?

2. (a) Respond Why do you think that the birds did not feel as ashamed as the Bat did?

(b) Analyze What moral lesson does the story teach about making and keeping promises?

Writing Activity

Write a Myth Using this story as a model, write your own myth. You might want to write a myth in which the Bat makes peace with the Sun, or one in which another animal makes a promise to the Moon.

Chapter Preview

This chapter will introduce you to some of the countries of Central and Southern Africa.

Country Databank
The Country Databank provides data and descriptions of each of the countries in the region: Angola, Botswana, Cameroon, Central African Republic, Comoros, Democratic Republic of the Congo, Equatorial Guinea, Gabon, Lesotho, Madagascar, Malawi, Mauritius, Mozambique, Namibia, Republic of the Congo, São Tomé and Príncipe, South Africa, Swaziland, Zambia, and Zimbabwe.

Section 1
Democratic Republic of the Congo
A Wealth of Possibilities

Section 2
South Africa
Struggle for Equality

Target Reading Skill

Sequence In this chapter you will focus on understanding sequence. Identifying sequence and recognizing sequence signal words will help you learn as you read.

▶ Cape Town, South Africa, is an important port and center of industry in Southern Africa.

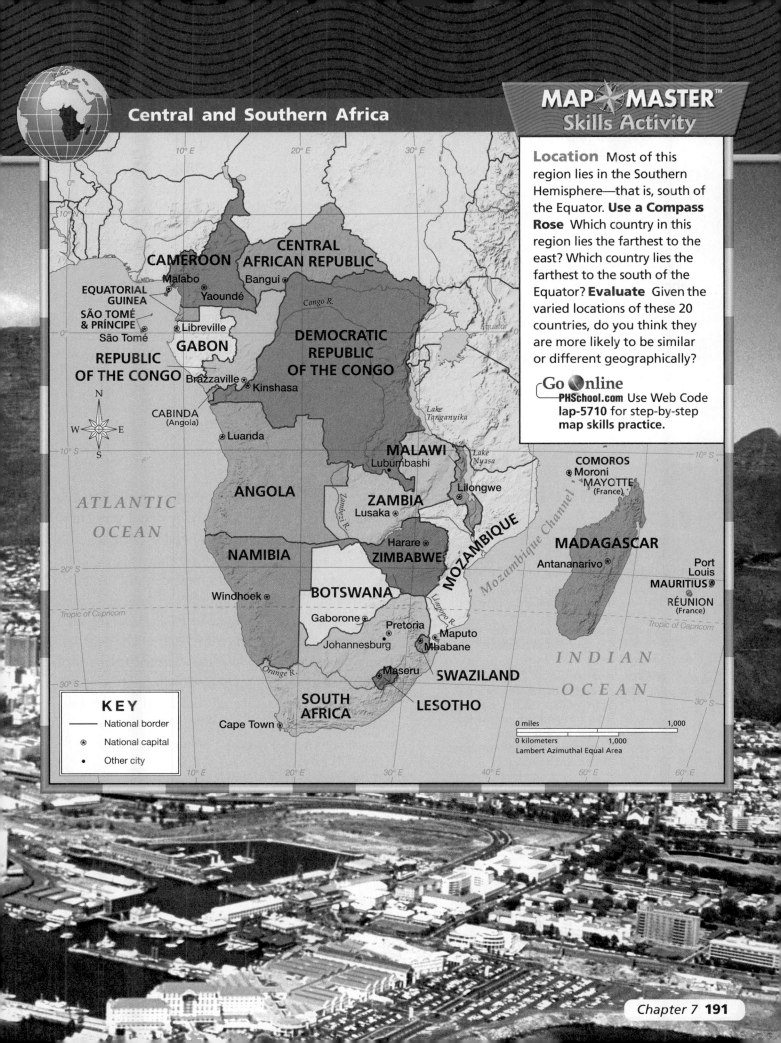

MAP MASTER™
Skills Activity

10° E   20° E   30° E

CAMEROON

CENTRAL
AFRICAN REPUBLIC

Malabo   Bangui ⊛

EQUATORIAL
GUINEA   ⊛ Yaoundé

SÃO TOMÉ
& PRÍNCIPE   ⊛ Libreville   Congo R.

São Tomé   GABON   DEMOCRATIC
                              REPUBLIC
REPUBLIC   OF THE CONGO
OF THE CONGO   Brazzaville ⊛
               ⊛ Kinshasa

N
                CABINDA   Lake
W   E   (Angola)   Tanganyika

S   ⊛ Luanda   Equator

                                              MALAWI   Lake
                                   Lubumbashi •   Nyasa
ATLANTIC   ANGOLA
                                ZAMBIA   ⊛ Lilongwe
OCEAN   Lusaka ⊛
                Zambezi R.

NAMIBIA   Harare ⊛
                                ZIMBABWE   MOZAMBIQUE
                                                      Mozambique Channel
                Windhoek ⊛   BOTSWANA
Tropic of Capricorn
                Gaborone ⊛   Limpopo R.
                         •   ⊛ Maputo
                Johannesburg •   Mbabane ⊛
Orange R.   Maseru ⊛
                                SWAZILAND
30° S
                SOUTH
                AFRICA   LESOTHO
          Cape Town •

COMOROS
⊛ Moroni
MAYOTTE
(France)

MADAGASCAR
Antananarivo ⊛

Port
Louis
MAURITIUS ⊛
RÉUNION
(France)
Tropic of Capricorn

INDIAN
OCEAN

KEY
─── National border
⊛   National capital
•   Other city

0 miles   1,000
0 kilometers   1,000
Lambert Azimuthal Equal Area

Location Most of this region lies in the Southern Hemisphere—that is, south of the Equator. **Use a Compass Rose** Which country in this region lies the farthest to the east? Which country lies the farthest to the south of the Equator? **Evaluate** Given the varied locations of these 20 countries, do you think they are more likely to be similar or different geographically?

Go **Online**
PHSchool.com Use Web Code lap-5710 for step-by-step map skills practice.

Introducing
Central and Southern Africa

Guide for Reading

This section provides an introduction to the 20 countries that make up the region of Central and Southern Africa.

- Look at the map on the previous page and then read the paragraphs below to learn about each nation.
- Analyze the data to compare the countries.
- What are the characteristics that most of the countries share?
- What are some key differences among the countries?

Angola

Capital	Luanda
Land Area	481,551 sq mi; 1,246,700 sq km
Population	10.6 million
Ethnic Group(s)	Ovimbundu, Kimbundu, Bankongo, mixed white and black, white
Religion(s)	traditional beliefs, Roman Catholic, Protestant
Government	republic
Currency	kwanza
Leading Exports	crude oil, diamonds, refined petroleum products, gas, coffee, sisal, fish and fish products, timber, cotton
Language(s)	Portuguese (official), Umbundu, Kimbundu, Kikongo

Angola (ang GOH luh) is bordered on the west by the Atlantic Ocean, on the north by the Democratic Republic of the Congo, on the east by Zambia, and on the south by Namibia. Cabinda is a separate region of Angola that lies between the Atlantic Ocean and the Congo republics. Angola gained independence from Portugal in 1975. However, civil war gripped the country until 2002. The war left many thousands homeless and claimed the lives of an estimated 1.5 million people. Although Angola's economy has been severely damaged by the war, economic recovery is possible. Angola is rich in natural resources, including oil and diamonds.

Thatched-roof houses in Angola

Botswana

Capital	Gaborone
Land Area	226,011 sq mi; 585,370 sq km
Population	1.6 million
Ethnic Group(s)	Tswana, Kalanga, Basarwa, Kgalagadi, white
Religion(s)	traditional beliefs, Christian
Government	parliamentary republic
Currency	pula
Leading Exports	diamonds, copper, nickel, soda ash, meat, textiles
Language(s)	English (official), Tswana, Shona, San, Khoikhoi, Ndebele

Botswana (baht SWAH nuh) is bordered on the west and north by Namibia, on the north and east by Zambia and Zimbabwe, and on the east and south by South Africa. When it was a British colony, Botswana was known as Bechuanaland (bech WAH nah land). After gaining independence in 1966, Botswana's government transformed the economy into one of the fastest-growing in the world. Diamond mining is Botswana's largest industry. AIDS poses a severe health threat to the country. Hundreds of thousands of people have the disease.

Cameroon

Capital	Yaoundé
Land Area	181,251 sq mi; 469,440 sq km
Population	16.1 million
Ethnic Group(s)	Cameroon Highlanders, Bantu, Kirdi, Fulani, Eastern Nigritic
Religion(s)	traditional beliefs, Christian, Muslim
Government	unitary republic
Currency	CFA franc
Leading Exports	crude oil and petroleum products, lumber, cacao beans, aluminum, coffee, cotton
Language(s)	French (official), English (official), Bamileke, Fang, Fulani

Cameroon (kam uh ROON) is bordered on the west by the Atlantic Ocean and Nigeria, on the north by Chad, on the east by the Central African Republic, and on the south by the Republic of the Congo, Gabon, and Equatorial Guinea. It has many forests and rivers and good farmland. Present-day Cameroon was formed in 1961 by merging French Cameroon and a part of British Cameroon. The government has spent the last several decades improving farming conditions and building roads and railways. In terms of oil and agricultural resources, Cameroon is one of Africa's richest countries.

Central African Republic

Capital	Bangui
Land Area	240,534 sq mi; 622,984 sq km
Population	3.6 million
Ethnic Group(s)	Baya, Banda, Mandjia, Sara, Mbouri, M'Baka, Yakoma
Religion(s)	traditional beliefs, Protestant, Roman Catholic, Muslim
Government	republic
Currency	CFA franc
Leading Exports	diamonds, timber, cotton, coffee, tobacco
Language(s)	French (official), Sango, Banda, Gbaya

The Central African Republic (SEN trul AF rih kun rih PUB lik) is bordered on the west by Cameroon, on the north by Chad, on the north and east by Sudan, and on the south by the Democratic Republic of the Congo and the Republic of the Congo. It sits on a low plateau at the southern edge of the Sahel. Once a French colony called Ubangi-Shari (yoo BANG gee SHAH ree), the Central African Republic gained independence in 1960. Since 1993, the government has faced several rebellions. Despite the country's history of instability, the elections of 2005 raised hopes for a more stable future.

Introducing Central and Southern Africa

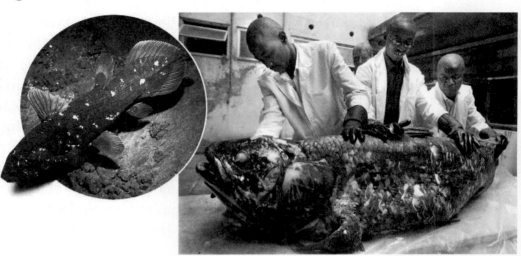

**A live coelacanth (left);
African scientists studying
a dead coelacanth (right)**

Comoros

Capital	Moroni
Land Area	838 sq mi; 2,170 sq km
Population	614,382
Ethnic Group(s)	Antalote, Cafre, Makoa, Oimatsaha, Sakalava
Religion(s)	Muslim, Roman Catholic
Government	independent republic
Currency	Comoros franc
Leading Exports	vanilla, ylang-ylang, cloves, perfume oil, copra
Language(s)	Arabic (official), French (official), Comoran (official)

Comoros (KAH muh rohz) is made up of three islands in the Indian Ocean, off the east coast of Mozambique. Numerous species of birds, animals, and fish live on and around the islands. The most famous of these is the coelacanth (SEE luh kanth), an extremely rare fish. Since gaining its independence from France in 1975, Comoros has experienced several major rebellions and civil wars. It is an extremely poor country. The population is growing rapidly, but the country has few natural resources or economic opportunities. Most of the people of Comoros are subsistence farmers.

Congo, Democratic Republic of the

Capital	Kinshasa
Land Area	875,520 sq mi; 2,267,600 sq km
Population	55.2 million
Ethnic Group(s)	more than 200 distinct ethnic groups, including Bantu, Hamitic
Religion(s)	Roman Catholic, Protestant, Muslim, traditional beliefs
Government	dictatorship
Currency	Congolese franc
Leading Exports	diamonds, copper, coffee, cobalt, crude oil
Language(s)	French (official), Kiswahili, Tshiluba, Kikongo, Lingala

The Democratic Republic of the Congo (dem uh KRAT ik rih PUB lik uv thuh KAHNG goh) lies on the Equator. It is bordered on the west by the Republic of the Congo; on the north by the Central African Republic and Sudan; on the east by Uganda, Rwanda, Burundi, and Tanzania; and on the south by Zambia. The rain forests of the Congo River basin cover much of the country. The country has suffered through years of civil war, which led to the deaths of about 3.5 million people. The nation has the potential for a strong economy, with many mineral resources, farmable land, and good soil.

Congo, Republic of the

Capital	Brazzaville
Land Area	131,853 sq mi; 341,500 sq km
Population	3.3 million
Ethnic Group(s)	Kongo, Sangha, M'Bochi, Take
Religion(s)	Christian, traditional beliefs, Muslim
Government	republic
Currency	CFA franc
Leading Exports	petroleum, lumber, plywood, sugar, cocoa, coffee, diamonds
Language(s)	French (official), Kongo, Teke, Lingala

The Republic of the Congo (rih PUB lik uv thuh KAHNG goh) lies on the Equator. It is bordered on the west by Gabon, on the north by Cameroon and the Central African Republic, on the east and south by the Democratic Republic of the Congo, and on the south by Angola. The Congo River forms the border with the Democratic Republic of the Congo. The Republic of the Congo gained independence from France in 1960. Since then, it has faced years of civil war. The nation has large supplies of oil and timber, and sales of oil have brought the country some wealth.

Equatorial Guinea

Capital	Malabo
Land Area	10,830 sq mi; 28,051 sq km
Population	498,144
Ethnic Group(s)	Bioko, Rio Muni
Religion(s)	Christian, traditional beliefs
Government	republic
Currency	CFA franc
Leading Exports	petroleum, timber, cocoa
Language(s)	Spanish (official), French (official), Fang, Bubi

Equatorial Guinea (ee kwuh TAWR ee ul GIH nee) lies just north of the Equator. It consists of five islands and a mainland area. The mainland is bordered on the west by the Atlantic Ocean, on the north by Cameroon, and on the east and south by Gabon. Many species of animals live on the mainland, including gorillas, leopards, antelopes, crocodiles, and snakes. After almost two hundred years as a Spanish colony, Equatorial Guinea gained independence in 1968. The economy is strong due to recently discovered oil reserves. Forestry, farming, and fishing are also important industries.

Gabon

Capital	Libreville
Land Area	99,489 sq mi; 257,667 sq km
Population	1.2 million
Ethnic Group(s)	Bantu, Fang, Bapounou, Nzebi, Obamba
Religion(s)	Christian, traditional beliefs, Muslim
Government	republic
Currency	CFA franc
Leading Exports	crude oil, timber, manganese, uranium
Language(s)	French (official), Fang, Punu, Sira, Nzebi, Mpongwe

Gabon (gah BOHN) is bordered on the west by the Atlantic Ocean, on the north by Equatorial Guinea and Cameroon, and on the east and south by the Republic of the Congo. The country gained its independence from France in 1960, and it became a democracy in 1990. Oil resources have made Gabon's economy very strong in comparison to the economies of other African countries. People live on only a small portion of Gabon's land. More than three quarters of the country is covered by rain forests that are inhabited by many kinds of animals and plants.

Introducing Central and Southern Africa

Lesotho

Capital	Maseru
Land Area	11,720 sq mi; 30,355 sq km
Population	2.2 million
Ethnic Group(s)	Sotho, white, Asian
Religion(s)	Christian, traditional beliefs
Government	parliamentary constitutional monarchy
Currency	loti
Leading Exports	manufactured goods, wool, mohair, food, live animals
Language(s)	English (off.), Sesotho (off.), Zulu

Lesotho (leh SOO too) is a tiny, mountainous country surrounded on all sides by South Africa. In 1966, the country became independent as a monarchy, or a government led by a king or a queen. Since that time, its government has been unstable. The country has been ruled by a king, by military leaders, and by elected leaders. Lesotho's economy depends heavily on South Africa. Many of Lesotho's men find work in the mines of South Africa. Despite widespread poverty, a large percentage of people in Lesotho are literate.

Madagascar

Capital	Antananarivo
Land Area	224,533 sq mi; 581,540 sq km
Population	16.5 million
Ethnic Group(s)	Malayo-Indonesian, Cotier, white, South Asian, Creole, Comoran
Religion(s)	traditional beliefs, Christian, Muslim
Government	republic
Currency	Malagasy franc
Leading Exports	coffee, vanilla, shellfish, sugar, cotton cloth, chromite
Language(s)	French (off.), Malagasy (off.)

Madagascar (mad uh GAS kur) is the world's fourth-largest island. It lies in the Indian Ocean, east of Mozambique. Before the French colonized Madagascar in 1886, it was an independent kingdom. The nation regained its independence in 1960 and became a democracy in the early 1990s. The nation's economy is based mainly on farming, fishing, and forestry. Madagascar is famous for plants and animals that cannot be found anywhere else on Earth. It is also well known for its spices, including vanilla. A larger percentage of people in Madagascar are literate than in most other African countries.

Malawi

Capital	Lilongwe
Land Area	36,324 sq mi; 94,080 sq km
Population	10.7 million
Ethnic Group(s)	Chewa, Nyanja, Tumbuka, Yao, Lomwe, Sena, Tonga, Ngongi, Ngonde, Asian, white
Religion(s)	Protestant, Roman Catholic, Muslim, traditional beliefs
Government	multiparty democracy
Currency	Malawi kwacha
Leading Exports	tobacco, tea, sugar, cotton, coffee, peanuts, wood products, apparel
Language(s)	English (official), Chichewa (official), Lomwe, Yao, Ngoni

Malawi (MAH lah wee) is bordered on the west, east, and south by Mozambique, on the west by Zambia, and on the north by Tanzania. The dominant geographical feature of this tiny country is Lake Nyasa (NYAH sah), Africa's third-largest body of water. In addition, Malawi lies alongside the Great Rift Valley. Malawi was called Nyasaland while under British rule. It became an independent nation in 1964. Malawi then became a democracy in the mid-1990s. The country's economy is mostly agricultural. Almost 90 percent of Malawians live in rural areas.

Mauritius

Capital	Port Louis
Land Area	784 sq mi; 2,030 sq km
Population	1.2 million
Ethnic Group(s)	Indo-Mauritian, Creole, Sino-Mauritian, Franco-Mauritian
Religion(s)	Hindu, Roman Catholic, Muslim, Protestant
Government	parliamentary democracy
Currency	Mauritian rupee
Leading Exports	iron ore, fish, fish products, gold
Language(s)	English (official), French Creole, Hindi, Urdu, Tamil, Chinese, French

Mauritius (maw RISH ee us) is made up of islands in the Indian Ocean east of Madagascar. The islands were colonized by Portugal in the 1500s. The country was claimed by the Dutch, the French, and the British before it gained independence in 1968. Since that time, it has turned a weak economy based on agriculture into a healthy economy based on manufacturing, banking, and tourism. Mauritius has a stable, democratic government. A majority of the people of Mauritius are descended from Indians who moved to the islands to work on sugar plantations in the 1800s.

Mozambique

Capital	Maputo
Land Area	302,737 sq mi; 784,090 sq km
Population	19.6 million
Ethnic Group(s)	Shangaan, Chokwe, Manyika, Sena, Makha, white, mixed white and black, South Asian
Religion(s)	traditional beliefs, Christian, Muslim
Government	republic
Currency	metical
Leading Exports	prawns, cashews, cotton, sugar, citrus, timber, electricity
Language(s)	Portuguese (official), Makua, Tsonga, Sena, Lomwe

Mozambique (moh zum BEEK) is bordered on the west by South Africa, Zimbabwe, Zambia, and Malawi; on the north by Tanzania; and on the east and south by the Indian Ocean. The Zambezi River divides the country into dry savanna in the south and fertile lands in the north. When it gained independence from Portugal in 1975, Mozambique was one of the world's poorest countries. It suffered through civil war from 1977 to 1992. Heavy flooding in 1999 and 2000 made the poor economy even worse. The people of Mozambique are relying on economic aid from other countries and new policies to improve their situation.

Namibia

Capital	Windhoek
Land Area	318,694 sq mi; 825,418 sq km
Population	1.8 million
Ethnic Group(s)	Ovambo, Kavango, Herero, Damara, Nama, Caprivian, Bushman, Baster, Tswana
Religion(s)	Christian, traditional beliefs
Government	republic
Currency	Namibian dollar
Leading Exports	diamonds, copper, gold, zinc, lead, uranium, cattle, fish
Language(s)	English (official), Ovambo, Kavango, Bergdama, German, Afrikaans

Namibia (nuh MIB ee uh) is bordered on the west by the Atlantic Ocean, on the north by Angola and Zambia, on the east by Botswana, and on the south by South Africa. Its land includes both the Namib and Kalahari deserts. Its economy is dependent on mining. Once a German colony, Namibia fell under South African rule after World War I. It became an independent country in 1990. Namibia still suffers from the effects of the system of racial inequality that South Africa imposed on it for decades. Its government and people are working to overcome these effects.

Introducing **Central and Southern Africa**

São Tomé and Príncipe

Capital	São Tomé
Land Area	386 sq mi; 1,001 sq km
Population	170,372
Ethnic Group(s)	mixed white and black, angolares, forros, servicais, tongas, white
Religion(s)	Christian
Government	republic
Currency	dobra
Leading Exports	cocoa, copra, coffee, palm oil
Language(s)	Portuguese (official), Portuguese Creole

São Tomé and Príncipe (sow toh MEE and PRIN suh pea) is made up of islands in the Gulf of Guinea, west of Gabon. The Portuguese discovered the uninhabited islands in the 1400s. They immediately built plantations and imported slaves to grow the islands' major resource, sugar cane. The islands began exporting coffee and cocoa in the 1800s. The nation gained independence in 1975. The first free elections were held in 1991. Although a poor country, São Tomé and Príncipe has very fertile land and is working to diversify its crops. It is also hoping to make use of oil reserves located in the Gulf of Guinea.

South Africa

Capital	Pretoria, Cape Town, Bloemfontein
Land Area	471,008 sq mi; 1,219,912 sq km
Population	43.6 million
Ethnic Group(s)	black, white, mixed white and black, South Asian
Religion(s)	Christian, traditional beliefs
Government	republic
Currency	rand
Leading Exports	gold, diamonds, platinum, other metals and minerals, machinery and equipment
Language(s)	Afrikaans, English, Ndebele, Pedi, Sotho, Swazi, Tsonga, Tswana, Venda, Xhosa, Zulu (all official)

South Africa (sowth AF rih kuh) occupies the southern tip of the African continent. With a wealth of natural resources, including gold and diamonds, it has the continent's strongest economy. Ruled by the Dutch after 1652 and by the British after 1806, South Africa became independent in 1931. From that time until 1990, the country was known for apartheid, a harsh political system under which the races were separated from each other and discrimination against nonwhites was the law. After years of struggle, nonwhites won equality in 1994, when apartheid ended. The country then focused on healing the wounds of the past.

Swaziland

Capital	Mbabane
Land Area	6,642 sq mi; 17,203 sq km
Population	1.1 million
Ethnic Group(s)	black, white
Religion(s)	Christian, traditional beliefs, Muslim, Jewish
Government	monarchy
Currency	lilangeni
Leading Exports	soft drink concentrates, sugar, wood pulp, cotton yarn, fruit
Language(s)	English (official), siSwati (official), Zulu, Tsonga

Swaziland (SWAH zee land) is a small country that is surrounded by South Africa and Mozambique. More than 95 percent of the population belongs to the Swazi ethnic group. Swaziland gained independence from Great Britain in 1968. The country has a very diversified economy. Because it is landlocked, Swaziland depends mainly on South Africa to move goods in and out of the country. Swaziland is ruled by a king. However, many Swazis have been pressuring the government for democratic reforms, such as having a multiparty political system.

Zambia

Capital	Lusaka
Land Area	285,994 sq mi; 740,724 sq km
Population	10.1 million
Ethnic Group(s)	Bemba, Nyanja, Tonga, Lozi, European, white
Religion(s)	Christian, Muslim, Hindu, traditional beliefs
Government	republic
Currency	Zambian kwacha
Leading Exports	copper, cobalt, electricity, tobacco, flowers, cotton
Language(s)	English (official), Bemba, Nyanja, Tonga, Lunda, Lozi

Zambia (ZAM bee uh) is bordered on the west by Angola, on the north by the Democratic Republic of the Congo and Tanzania, on the east by Malawi and Mozambique, and on the south by Zimbabwe, Botswana, and Namibia. Once a British colony called Northern Rhodesia, Zambia became independent in 1964. For decades, Zambia was under the rule of a single political party. In recent years, it has succeeded in establishing a multiparty democracy. Copper exports have made Zambia prosperous. However, Zambia risks losses if copper prices fall.

Zimbabwe

Capital	Harare
Land Area	149,293 sq mi; 386,670 sq km
Population	11.3 million
Ethnic Group(s)	Shona, Ndebele, Asian, white
Religion(s)	Christian, traditional beliefs, Muslim
Government	parliamentary democracy
Currency	Zimbabwe dollar
Leading Exports	tobacco, gold, ferroalloys, textiles, clothing
Language(s)	English (official), Shona, Ndebele

Zimbabwe (zim BAHB way) is bordered on the west by Botswana and Zambia, on the north by Zambia, on the north and east by Mozambique, and on the south by South Africa. Once the British colony of Southern Rhodesia, Zimbabwe gained independence in 1980. Since then, the country has worked to overcome racial inequality and a troubled economy. Zimbabwe faced additional difficulties under the rule of President Robert Mugabe. These included unfair elections, as well as the destruction of the homes and businesses of about 700,000 people.

SOURCES: DK World Desk Reference Online; CIA World Factbook Online; *The World Almanac*, 2003

Assessment

Comprehension and Critical Thinking

1. Compare and Contrast Compare and contrast the economies of these countries.

2. Summarize What are some characteristics that most of the countries share?

3. Analyze Information What are some key differences among the countries?

4. Infer What can you infer about a country such as South Africa that has eleven official languages?

5. Predict How do you think life in the countries that have no borders on the ocean is different from life in the ones that do?

6. Make a Bar Graph Create a bar graph showing each language that is an official language in this region and how many countries speak that language.

Keeping Current

Access the **DK World Desk Reference Online** at **PHSchool.com** for up-to-date information about all 20 countries in this chapter.

Go Online
PHSchool.com

Web Code: lae-5700

Democratic Republic of the Congo A Wealth of Possibilities

Prepare to Read

Objectives

In this section you will

1. Discover the physical geography and important natural resources of the Democratic Republic of the Congo.
2. Learn about the country's economic and political challenges since independence.
3. Find out how different groups and leaders have reshaped the nation.

Taking Notes

Copy the outline below. As you read this section, look for details about the geography, natural resources, economics, and politics of the Democratic Republic of the Congo. Use the outline to record your findings.

> I. Physical geography and resources
> A. Geographic regions
>   1. _____
>   2. _____
> B. Natural resources

Target Reading Skill

Understand Sequence A sequence is the order in which a series of events occurs. Noting the sequence of important events can help you understand and remember the events. You can track a sequence of events by simply listing the events in the order in which they happened. As you read this section, list the sequence of events in Congo's political history.

Key Terms

- **authoritarian government** (uh thawr uh TEHR ee un GUV urn munt) *n.* a nondemocratic form of government in which a single leader or a small group of leaders has all the power
- **nationalize** (NASH uh nuh lyz) *v.* to transfer ownership of something to a nation's government

An open-pit copper mine in Congo

Copper has been mined in the present-day Democratic Republic of the Congo since ancient times. In the early 1900s, demand for copper brought Europeans to the area. In 1930, a mining company found copper in an area called Kolwezi (kohl WAY zee). The company built a mine and hired miners and a host of other workers. Soon a small city of workers' houses arose. Meanwhile, miners started to dig down into the earth for the copper. They found it, too—right beneath their houses.

The Kolwezi area proved so rich in copper that, at first, miners found they barely had to scratch the surface to find the mineral. As time went on, however, the miners had to dig deeper. Soon they had dug a huge pit in the ground. They built terraces along the sloping walls of the pit. Then they mined each terrace, in a process called open-pit mining. Miners still dig for copper at the Kolwezi mine today.

Physical Geography and Resources

Since the 1930s, the Democratic Republic of the Congo has become one of the world's main sources of copper. Congo, as the country is often referred to, also has many other natural resources. These include gold, diamonds, forests, water, and wildlife. Congo's minerals and other resources have played an important role in the nation's history. (The country's neighbor, the Republic of the Congo, is also referred to as Congo. In this section, all references to Congo are to the Democratic Republic of the Congo.)

Geographic Regions The Democratic Republic of the Congo is Africa's third-largest country. It is equal in size to the area of the United States east of the Mississippi River. The country has four major geographic regions: the Congo basin, the northern uplands, the eastern highlands, and the southern uplands.

The Congo basin is covered by dense rain forest. Most Congolese (kahng guh LEEZ) live in the other three regions. The northern uplands, which run along the country's northern border, are covered in savanna. Grasslands and occasional thick forests spread across the eastern highlands. The southern uplands are high plains of grasslands and wooded areas. In each of these three regions, many people make a living as subsistence farmers.

Natural Resources About two thirds of Congo's people are farmers. However, mining produces most of the country's wealth. The Kolwezi and other huge copper deposits exist in the southern province of Katanga (kuh TAHNG guh). Congo is one of the top producers of diamonds in the world. It also has reserves of other valuable minerals such as gold. In addition, Congo has the potential to develop many hydroelectric plants. These are plants that use swiftly flowing river water to generate electricity.

Links to Science

From Water to Electricity
At a hydroelectric plant, electricity is generated by flowing water. For that reason, these plants are usually built at the bottom of a dam. Water that collects behind the dam flows through turbines, which change the energy of the moving water into electricity. The water is not used up in the process—it continues to flow and can be used again for agriculture and other purposes. A large hydroelectric dam (below) sits on Inga Falls, along the Congo River.

Natural Resources in Congo's History Natural resources have dominated much of the history of the Democratic Republic of the Congo. For example, by the 1400s, the kingdoms of Kongo, Luba, and Lunda ruled much of the area. These kingdoms became powerful largely because they had fertile soil and plentiful rain and their people made iron tools that enabled them to farm more productively. Similarly, when the Portuguese arrived in the area in the 1480s, they came in search of a natural resource—gold.

Some 400 years later, during the scramble for Africa, King Leopold II of Belgium took control of present-day Congo. He ruled brutally, forcing Africans to harvest wild rubber without paying them. Belgium grew wealthy while Africans suffered, starved, and died, probably by the millions. Later, because of an international campaign to end Leopold's abuses, the Belgian government ruled less harshly. But it maintained its interest in Congo's resources, especially its copper and diamonds.

✔ **Reading Check** Which industry produces most of Congo's wealth?

Economic and Political Challenges

In spite of its abundant natural resources, the Democratic Republic of the Congo has faced major economic and political challenges. During the 1900s, both the economy and the government of Congo faced a series of crises.

Congo Gains Independence As you have read, calls for independence echoed throughout the African continent during the mid-1900s. In 1960, the Democratic Republic of the Congo won its independence from Belgium. However, Congo's first years as an independent country proved to be difficult.

Belgium had done little to prepare Congo for self-rule. In addition, various groups fought one another for power. The foreign companies that controlled Congo's mines feared the unrest would hurt business. In 1965, these foreign companies helped a military leader, Joseph Mobutu (muh BOO too), take power. With a strong ruler in control, they thought their businesses would thrive.

Celebrating Independence
At a celebration of the country's independence in 1960, boys carry the flag of the newly formed Democratic Republic of the Congo.
Predict How do you think Congolese people felt when their country gained independence?

Mobutu Makes Changes Mobutu tried to restore order in the country by setting up an **authoritarian government**—a nondemocratic form of government in which a single leader or small group of leaders has all the power. He also tried to cut ties with the colonial past. First, he renamed the country Zaire (zah IHR), a word that has traditional African roots. And he took on a new name for himself, Mobutu Sese Seko (muh BOO too SAY say SAY koh), which he considered more traditionally African. Then he nationalized foreign-owned industries. To **nationalize** is to transfer ownership to the government.

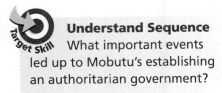

Understand Sequence
What important events led up to Mobutu's establishing an authoritarian government?

COUNTRY PROFILE

Focus on Economics

Democratic Republic of the Congo

Congo's natural resources play a key role in its economy. The country's total earnings from exports in 2002 were around $1.2 billion. Minerals alone made up about 85 percent of those earnings, as they have in most recent years. Most of the economy's diversity comes from the variety of minerals produced. However, Congo does not use all of its natural resources. Thus, the country has potential for greater economic success. Study the map and charts to learn more about Congo's natural resources and economy.

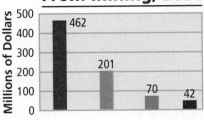

Democratic Republic of The Congo: Natural Resources

KEY
- Gold
- Silver
- Copper
- Tin
- Uranium
- Cobalt
- Coal
- Diamonds
- Petroleum
- Hydroelectric power
- National border
- National capital
- Other city

0 miles 500
0 kilometers 500
Lambert Azimuthal Equal Area

Export Destinations

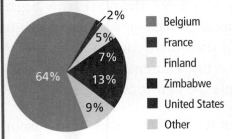

- Belgium
- France
- Finland
- Zimbabwe
- United States
- Other

2%
5%
7%
64%
13%
9%

SOURCE: DK World Desk Reference

Estimated Income From Mining, 2001

Millions of Dollars

- Diamonds: 462
- Petroleum: 201
- Cobalt: 70
- Copper: 42

SOURCE: The Economist Intelligence Unit's *Country Profile 2003*

Map and Chart Skills

1. **Name** Which two countries buy most of Congo's exports?
2. **Identify** Which mineral earns the most income for Congo?
3. **Infer** How does the map support the idea that Congo has greater potential for using its natural resources?

Use Web Code **lae-5701** for **DK World Desk Reference Online.**

Mobutu also borrowed money from foreign countries, such as the United States, for projects to improve Zaire's economy. But most of Mobutu's economic moves failed. Many government officials who ran the nationalized companies proved to be poor managers. Others stole their companies' profits. Mobutu and his supporters, too, kept much of Zaire's wealth for themselves.

Crisis In the mid-1970s, the world price of copper fell sharply. Suddenly Zaire was earning less and less from its major export. It could not pay back the money it had borrowed, and the economy quickly collapsed. Mobutu responded by cutting the amount of money spent by the government. The cutbacks caused hardship, especially for Zaire's poorest people. Fewer jobs were available, so many people could not earn a living. When political groups challenged Mobutu's policies, Mobutu crushed their efforts. He had many of his opponents imprisoned or killed.

✓ **Reading Check** Why did Mobutu change the country's name?

Reshaping the Nation

Throughout the 1980s, Mobutu ruled harshly, and Zaire's economy continually declined. Calls for reform came from inside and outside the country. In the early 1990s, Mobutu's grip on the country finally began to weaken.

Rebellion Against Government In 1996, a minor uprising began in eastern Zaire. A small ethnic group fought with the government's troops. The neighboring countries of Uganda, Rwanda, and Burundi supported the small group. With their help, the uprising turned into a rebellion against Mobutu's government. Zaire's army was unable to put down the rebellion.

Within months, the rebels gained control of much of eastern Zaire. By May 1997, the rebel army began closing in on the capital, Kinshasa. Alarmed, Mobutu fled to Morocco. He died there four months later. A leader of the rebel army, Laurent Kabila (law RAHN kuh BEEL uh), became the new president.

Showing Culture in Currency
The upper bill was printed while the name of the country was Zaire. The lower bill was printed after the name became the Democratic Republic of the Congo. **Analyze Images** *What aspects of the Congo are represented by the images on these bills?*

A New Government Takes Hold The rebel army soon controlled the whole country, which Kabila renamed the Democratic Republic of the Congo. Kabila vowed to establish a new constitution and hold national elections. But months went by without the promised reforms. Criticism quickly erupted. By early 1998, popular support for the new government was fading.

A Second Rebellion In August 1998, another armed rebellion began, this time against Kabila's government. Supported by Uganda and Rwanda, the new rebels threatened to overthrow the government. Angola, Namibia, and Zimbabwe backed Kabila's government. The civil war continued month after month.

Peace and Reform The war in Congo was the first war in post-independence Africa to involve several African nations. In July 1999, the heads of six of these countries met in Zambia to write a peace agreement. However, neither side fulfilled the agreement. Hostilities continued into 2001, when Kabila was killed. His son, Joseph Kabila, became president.

Rwandan President Paul Kagame (left) and Joseph Kabila sign peace agreements in 2002.

The younger Kabila began making significant reforms. He implemented programs to revive the economy. He replaced many corrupt government officials with well-trained officials. He also allowed the United Nations to send peacekeeping troops to Congo. By the end of 2002, many of the disagreements over the terms of peace had been settled. However, small conflicts did continue in the eastern part of the country. Congo has found that the path to peace is neither smooth nor easy.

✓ **Reading Check** How was Congo's civil war unique for Africa?

Section 1 Assessment

Key Terms
Review the key terms at the beginning of this section. Use each term in a sentence that explains its meaning.

Target Reading Skill

Place these events in the correct order: Joseph Kabila becomes president, a rebellion begins, a peace agreement is written.

Comprehension and Critical Thinking
1. (a) List What are some of Congo's natural resources?

(b) Analyze Information What role have these resources played in Congo's history?
2. (a) Describe What changes did Joseph Mobutu make in Congo?
(b) Evaluate What factors prevented Mobutu from bringing stability to Congo?
3. (a) Recall What caused Mobutu to flee the country?
(b) Summarize Once Laurent Kabila became president, how did the civil war in Congo change?
(c) Draw Conclusions In what ways has Joseph Kabila brought positive change to Congo?

Writing Activity
Suppose you are an editor for a newspaper. Write an editorial explaining the challenges Congo has faced and predicting how the country will overcome those challenges once peace returns to the nation.

> **Writing Tip** Be sure to state the opinion you are explaining in your editorial. Then use details to support your opinion.

Analyzing Primary Sources

You have probably played the "telephone game." One person makes up a statement and whispers it to the next person. That person whispers it to the next person, and so on. As the statement is passed along, people do not always hear it correctly and it gets confused. By the end, it might not make any sense. If a sentence can get distorted in a matter of minutes, think what can happen to a sentence uttered by someone hundreds of years ago! That is one reason why primary sources are important.

Examples of primary sources

A primary source is information that comes directly from the person who wrote it, said it, or created it. Diaries, photographs, speeches, and recordings are all examples of primary sources. When information does not come directly from the person who created it, it is a secondary source. Newspapers, history books, and Web sites are examples of secondary sources.

Learn the Skill

Use the steps below to analyze a primary source.

1 **Identify who created the information, when it was created, and why.** Before you use any information, determine the source. Is it a primary source?

2 **Identify the main idea.** Make sure you understand what is being communicated, either in words or in visual form.

3 **Separate facts from opinions.** Facts can be proved or disproved. Opinions indicate personal feelings or judgments. A primary source might contain facts and opinions, and both can be valuable.

4 **Look for evidence of bias, or a one-sided view.** If a person's view is biased, it is influenced by certain factors, such as the person's family, culture, or location.

5 **Evaluate whether the source is reliable and whether it suits your purpose.** For factual evidence, you want a primary source that is believable and accurate. For an opinion, you want one that uses good reasoning.

Practice the Skill

Use the steps below to analyze the source in the box.

1 Read the background information and the quotation. Who is the speaker, and when did he speak these words? Is the quotation a primary source?

2 Write a sentence that summarizes Mandela's main point. What situation is he discussing?

3 Using the background information, identify as many facts and opinions as possible. Overall, is this quotation mostly fact or mostly opinion?

4 Do any parts of Mandela's statement show bias?

5 Would this source be of value if you were writing a history of South Africa? A biography of Nelson Mandela? Explain.

In 1994, democratic elections were held in South Africa for the first time. Never before had all South Africans been allowed to vote. After casting his vote, the man who would be elected president, Nelson Mandela, made this statement:

"This is for all South Africans an unforgettable occasion. It is the realization of hopes and dreams that we have cherished over decades. . . . We are starting a new era of hope, reconciliation [coming together] and nation building. We sincerely hope that by the mere casting of a vote the results will give hope to all South Africans and make all South Africans realize this is our country. We are one nation."

—*Nelson Mandela, April 1994*

Two women in Johannesburg, South Africa, proudly display the identification papers needed for voting in the historic 1994 election.

Apply the Skill

Read the quotation from the South African constitution on page 208.
Follow the steps for analyzing a primary source and answer these questions:

1. What makes the quotation a primary source?
2. What is the main idea?
3. Is the information mostly fact or mostly opinion? Explain.
4. Is the information biased? Explain.
5. For what purpose might you use this source?

Prepare to Read

Objectives

In this section you will
1. Understand how white rule in South Africa began.
2. Learn about the system of apartheid.
3. Find out how South Africans built a new nation after apartheid.

Taking Notes

As you read this section, look for details about South Africa before, during, and after apartheid. Copy the chart below, and use to it to record your findings.

South Africa		
Before Apartheid	**During Apartheid**	**After Apartheid**
• •	• •	• •

Target Reading Skill

Recognize Words That Signal Sequence Signal words point out relationships among ideas or events. To help keep the order of events clear as you read, look for words like *after, then,* and *in 1994* that signal the order in which events took place.

Key Terms

- **apartheid** (uh PAHR tayt) *n.* the legal system of South Africa in which the rights of nonwhites were greatly restricted
- **discriminate** (dih SKRIM ih nayt) *v.* to treat people differently, and often unfairly, based on race, religion, or sex
- **Nelson Mandela** (NEL sun man DEL uh) *n.* black leader of the African National Congress and South Africa's first president after apartheid ended

A choir celebrates the new constitution.

❝ We, the people of South Africa,
   Recognize the injustices of our past;
   Honour those who suffered for justice and
      freedom in our land;
   Respect those who have worked to build and
      develop our country; and
   Believe that South Africa belongs to all who live
      in it, united in our diversity. ❞

—*Preamble to the South African Constitution*

So begins the constitution of South Africa. It was written in 1996, soon after nearly a century of harsh and unequal treatment of nonwhite South Africans had officially ended. The constitution's words were shaped by South Africans who came from many backgrounds and political parties. As a result, the 1996 constitution represents all South Africans in a new, democratic South Africa.

Beginning of White Rule

People have lived in present-day South Africa for thousands of years. In 1652, the first white Europeans arrived in the region and set up a colony. These Dutch settlers called themselves Boers (bohrz), the Dutch word for farmers. As you read in Chapter 3, the descendants of these settlers called themselves Afrikaners. They spoke a language related to Dutch, called Afrikaans.

British and French settlers arrived in South Africa by the late 1700s. For years, black South Africans fought the white settlers, who took their land. But by the late 1800s, the white settlers had forced the Africans off the best land.

Cultures Clash The Afrikaners founded their own states. After diamonds and gold were discovered there, the British wanted control of the land. British prospectors, or people who explore for minerals, pushed Afrikaners off their farms.

The British and Afrikaners fought over the Afrikaner land from 1899 to 1902. The British proved victorious and took control of the Afrikaner states. In 1910, the British created the Union of South Africa by unifying all the land they controlled in the region.

Unequal Treatment The white-led government of the Union of South Africa passed several laws to keep land and wealth in white hands. For example, the government declared that blacks could live and own land in only 8 percent of the country. Blacks could work in white areas, but for very low wages. Other laws passed in the 1920s separated white and black workers. The best jobs and the highest wages were reserved for whites.

✔ **Reading Check** When did the first white Europeans arrive in present-day South Africa?

System of Apartheid

The British granted independence to South Africa in 1931. But in 1948, the Afrikaners took political control of the country from the English-speaking whites when the Afrikaner political party, the National Party, won the election.

New Laws Take Hold The new Afrikaner leaders named the system of treating whites and nonwhites by different rules **apartheid** (uh PAHR tayt). In Afrikaans, the word *apartheid* means "apartness." Apartheid laws made it legal to discriminate on the basis of race. To **discriminate** means to treat people differently, and often unfairly, based on race, religion, or sex.

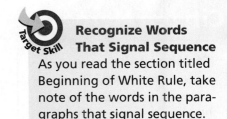

Recognize Words That Signal Sequence
As you read the section titled Beginning of White Rule, take note of the words in the paragraphs that signal sequence.

Keeping People Apart
In this image from the apartheid era, a man sits on a bench designated for Europeans (white South Africans) only. **Analyze Images** *How does this image illustrate discrimination?*

FOR EUROPEANS ONLY

Stephen Biko

Born in 1946 in King William's Town, South Africa, Stephen Biko (BEE koh) studied to become a doctor. Instead, he became a South African hero as a leader of the struggle against apartheid. Biko taught that black South Africans could only become free of white rule if they viewed themselves as equal to whites. His ideas influenced thousands of students and adults throughout South Africa. The white-led government imprisoned Biko for his actions. He died in jail in 1977.

In 1993, Nelson Mandela (left) and F. W. de Klerk (right) together won the Nobel Peace Prize for helping end apartheid.

The laws separated South Africans into four groups—blacks, whites, coloreds, and Asians. Coloreds were people of mixed race. Asians were mainly people from India. Coloreds and Asians, who together made up 12 percent of the popuation, had a few rights. Blacks, who made up 75 percent of the population, had practically no rights at all.

Effects of Apartheid Apartheid affected every aspect of the lives of black South Africans. It forced thousands of them to move to ten poor, rural, all-black areas called homelands. These homelands had the driest and least fertile land in the country. There, blacks lived in poverty. Apartheid also strengthened existing laws that required all blacks to stay in homelands unless they could prove that whites would benefit from hiring them.

In addition, apartheid denied blacks citizenship rights, including the right to vote. The system kept blacks, coloreds, and Asians in low-paying jobs and put them in poor schools. It barred these groups from white restaurants, schools, and hospitals. In short, apartheid kept whites in control of the country.

Struggle to End Apartheid Many South Africans fought apartheid. Starting in the 1950s, blacks and some whites led peaceful protests against it. Over the following decades, South Africa's police met the protesters with deadly force many times. Thousands of men, women, and children were wounded, killed, or imprisoned. Protests, even peaceful ones, were banned. But the demonstrations continued. Many people were willing to risk everything for freedom.

In the 1970s, countries around the world joined the movement against apartheid. Many nations stopped trading with South Africa or lending it money. South Africa's athletes were banned from the Olympic Games. In 1990, these international pressures began to have an effect. F. W. de Klerk, an Afrikaner who was South Africa's president, led the government in abolishing the apartheid laws.

Legally ending apartheid was a major accomplishment. But much work lay ahead to make a reality of legal equality. In 1994, **Nelson Mandela** became South Africa's first black president and the leader who would fight to create a new, more equal system.

✓ **Reading Check** What happened to South Africans who protested against apartheid?

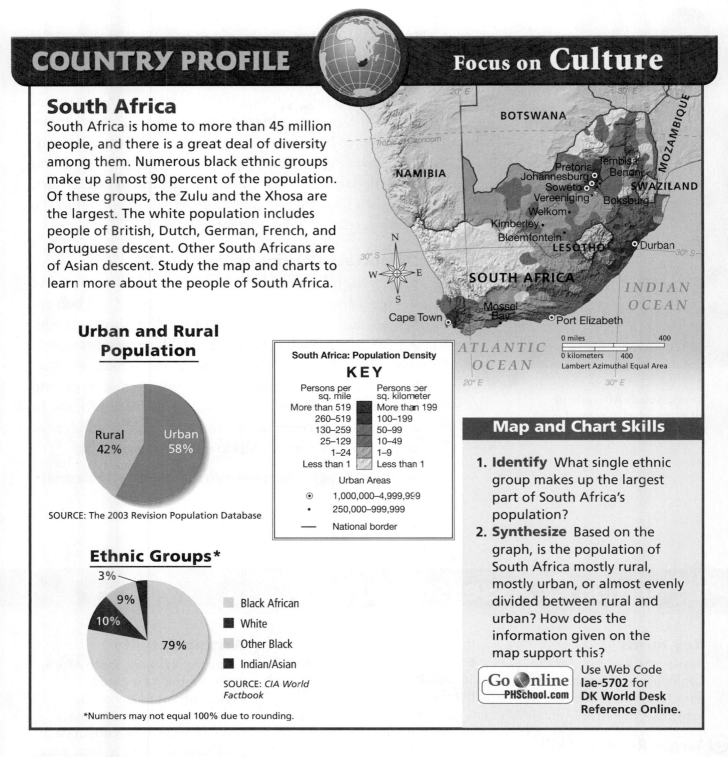

South Africa

South Africa is home to more than 45 million people, and there is a great deal of diversity among them. Numerous black ethnic groups make up almost 90 percent of the population. Of these groups, the Zulu and the Xhosa are the largest. The white population includes people of British, Dutch, German, French, and Portuguese descent. Other South Africans are of Asian descent. Study the map and charts to learn more about the people of South Africa.

Urban and Rural Population

Rural 42%
Urban 58%

SOURCE: The 2003 Revision Population Database

Ethnic Groups*

3%
9%
10%
79%

- Black African
- White
- Other Black
- Indian/Asian

SOURCE: *CIA World Factbook*

*Numbers may not equal 100% due to rounding.

South Africa: Population Density

KEY

Persons per sq. mile	Persons per sq. kilometer
More than 519	More than 199
260–519	100–199
130–259	50–99
25–129	10–49
1–24	1–9
Less than 1	Less than 1

Urban Areas

⊙   1,000,000–4,999,999

·   250,000–999,999

—   National border

Map and Chart Skills

1. **Identify** What single ethnic group makes up the largest part of South Africa's population?
2. **Synthesize** Based on the graph, is the population of South Africa mostly rural, mostly urban, or almost evenly divided between rural and urban? How does the information given on the map support this?

Go Online
PHSchool.com

Use Web Code lae-5702 for DK World Desk Reference Online.

Building a New Nation

Since the 1950s, Mandela had been a leader of the African National Congress (ANC), South Africa's first black-led political party. The ANC had long fought for full voting rights for all South Africans. In 1962, Mandela was sent to prison for life for fighting apartheid. After 28 years of public pressure, de Klerk freed Mandela in 1990. Mandela then became president of the ANC. In April 1994, for the first time, all South Africans were allowed to vote. Mandela and the ANC easily won the presidency.

Today, South Africans of all races attend school together.

New Challenges Blacks and some whites welcomed the end of apartheid. In some ways, however, South Africa has remained a divided society. For example, blacks and whites usually live in different neighborhoods, and whites control most of the country's biggest businesses. Still, new opportunities have been created for millions of blacks, and tensions have eased. Mandela's government proved it was committed to helping all citizens, regardless of race. In fact, the constitution that Mandela's government wrote in 1996 is considered a world model for human rights.

Democracy Continues In June 1999, South Africa held its second election in which all South Africans were free to vote. Mandela retired, and Thabo Mbeki (TAH boh em BEK ee), also a long-term leader of the ANC, became South Africa's next president. With the equality movement set into motion by Mandela, Mbeki has been able to focus on other important issues as well. He has put great energy into improving the economic situations of all South Africans. In addition, he has continued to strengthen South Africa's new, democratic government. Mbeki was reelected in 2004.

✓ **Reading Check** What was unique about the 1994 election?

Section 2 Assessment

Key Terms
Review the key terms at the beginning of this section. Use each term in a sentence that explains its meaning.

Target Reading Skill
Review the section titled Struggle to End Apartheid on page 210. Find the words that signal the sequence of events that helped end apartheid.

Comprehension and Critical Thinking
1. (a) Name Which groups of white Europeans settled in present-day South Africa?

(b) Compare How was the clash between white settlers and black South Africans similar to the clash between the white groups?

2. (a) Describe Describe the system of apartheid.

(b) Draw Conclusions What do you think it was about the system of apartheid that made the struggle to end it take so long?

3. (a) Explain How did apartheid finally end?

(b) Analyze Information Why do you think South Africans chose someone who was black as their first president after apartheid?

Writing Activity
Suppose you live in South Africa. Write a letter to a friend explaining your view of the changes that have taken place there. Include details about what has changed as well as how you think people have responded to the changes.

For: An activity on South Africa
Visit: PHSchool.com
Web Code: lad-5702

◆ Chapter Summary

Section 1: Democratic Republic of the Congo

- The Democratic Republic of the Congo is rich in natural resources. These resources have helped shape the country's history.
- From the 1960s to the 1990s, Congo suffered under the authoritarian rule of Joseph Mobutu. It also suffered in the 1970s, when world prices of copper fell.
- During the 1990s, Congo faced civil wars that involved rebels in Congo. A number of neighboring countries also took part in the fighting.

Section 2: South Africa

- The Dutch, the British, and the French settled in South Africa. The British won control of the region and unified its lands as the Union of South Africa in 1910. It became independent in 1931.
- In 1948, the Afrikaners won political control of South Africa and legally established the system of apartheid. Many people who fought against this system were imprisoned, injured, or killed.
- Afrikaner president F. W. de Klerk legally ended apartheid in 1990. Nelson Mandela then became South Africa's first black president. He was followed in office by Thabo Mbeki.

Congolese currency

Nelson Mandela and F. W. de Klerk

◆ Key Terms

Match the definitions in Column I with the key terms in Column II.

Column I

1. the legal system of South Africa in which the rights of nonwhites were greatly restricted
2. black leader of the African National Congress and South Africa's first president after apartheid ended
3. a nondemocratic form of government in which a single leader or a small group of leaders has all the power
4. to treat people differently, and often unfairly, based on race, religion, or sex
5. to transfer ownership of something to a nation's government

Column II

A authoritarian government

B nationalize

C apartheid

D discriminate

E Nelson Mandela

◆ Comprehension and Critical Thinking

6. **(a) Recall** What important natural resources exist in the Democratic Republic of the Congo?
(b) Draw Conclusions If mining produces most of Congo's wealth, why do you think so many Congolese are farmers, not miners?

7. **(a) Identify** What kind of government did Joseph Mobutu establish in Congo?
(b) Draw Inferences How might this form of government have helped cause rebellion?
(c) Analyze Information What caused the second rebellion in Congo?

8. **(a) Name** What name did Mobutu give his country? What name did Laurent Kabila give it?
(b) Make Generalizations Why do you think a leader might want to change a country's name?

9. **(a) Recall** When did the system of apartheid in South Africa begin?
(b) Summarize How did apartheid affect different groups of South Africans?

10. **(a) Define** What was an important form of protest that black South Africans used against apartheid?
(b) Analyze Information How did the South African government respond to these protests?

11. **(a) Explain** How did the legal end to apartheid come about?
(b) Draw Conclusions Why was it significant that South Africa's first president after apartheid was not white?
(c) Predict Now that apartheid is over, do you think that South Africans will stop focusing on racial issues in politics? Explain.

◆ Skills Practice

Analyzing Primary Sources In the Skills for Life activity in this chapter, you learned how to analyze primary sources.

Review the steps you followed to learn this skill. Then reread the quotation from Tanzania's former president, Julius Nyerere, on page 173 of Chapter 6. Explain why the statement was made, what its main idea is, and which details are facts and which are opinions. Then explain whether you can identify any bias based on the background of the speaker.

◆ Writing Activity: History

Choose either South Africa or the Democratic Republic of the Congo. Write a list of five interview questions you would ask someone who has been elected president of the country. Be sure to consider what challenges the new president faces. Then exchange questions with a partner. Pretend that you are the president, and write answers to your partner's questions.

MAP✹MASTER™
Skills Activity

Central and Southern Africa

Place Location For each place listed, write the letter from the map that shows its location.

1. Cape Town
2. Johannesburg
3. Kinshasa
4. Democratic Republic of the Congo
5. South Africa

Go Online
PHSchool.com Use Web Code **lap-5720** for an **interactive map.**

Standardized Test Prep

Test-Taking Tips

Some questions on standardized tests ask you to identify a frame of reference. Read the passage below. Then follow the tips to answer the sample question.

> Apartheid separated South Africa into four groups: blacks, whites, coloreds, and Asians. In 1990, apartheid came to an end. In 1994, South Africa elected Nelson Mandela the nation's first black president. Someone hearing the news shouted, "What a happy day. At last my people will have some opportunities. I never believed this would happen in South Africa."

TIP Think about the author's purpose as you read. Is the author trying to give you information, convince you of something, or teach you how to do something?

Pick the letter that best answers the question.

Which onlooker probably made those comments?

A a white businessman who owned a large diamond mine

B a politician in a pro-Afrikaner party

C a black woman living in a rural homeland

D a white woman who left South Africa to protest apartheid

TIP Watch out for careless errors. Be sure you understand the question and consider each answer choice.

Think It Through Start with the author's purpose: to give you information about the end of apartheid. Then ask yourself: Who would be happy about the end of apartheid? You can rule out A and B because neither was denied opportunities under apartheid. That leaves C and D. A white woman who had left South Africa in protest would probably be happy about the end of apartheid but would not say it meant opportunities for *her* people. The correct answer is C.

Practice Questions

Use the passage below to answer Question 1. Choose the letter of the best answer. Use the tips above and other tips in this book to help you answer the following questions.

> "We need a new government. The one we have now does not rule fairly. It is no better than Mobutu's government. Our neighbors in Rwanda and Uganda agree with us. We must make a change."

1. Who would have been most likely to make this statement?

A Laurent Kabila

B Joseph Kabila

C a member of the first rebellion that occurred in eastern Congo

D a member of the second rebellion that occurred in eastern Congo

2. Which natural resource did NOT play a role in Congo's history?

A diamonds

B silver

C gold

D rubber

3. When did South Africa become independent?

A 1910

B 1931

C 1948

D 1990

Use Web Code laa-5700 for **Chapter 7 self-test.**

Projects

Create your own projects to learn more about Africa. At the beginning of this book, you were introduced to the **Guiding Questions** for studying the chapters and special features. But you can also find answers to these questions by doing projects on your own or with a group. Use the questions to find topics you want to explore further. Then try the projects described on this page or create your own.

1 **Geography** What are the main physical features of Africa?

2 **History** How have historical events affected the cultures and nations of Africa?

3 **Culture** What features help define different African cultures?

4 **Government** What factors led to the development of different governments across Africa?

5 **Economics** What factors influence the ways in which Africans make a living?

Project

HOLD AN AFRICA CONFERENCE

Africa in the 2000s
As you read about Africa, organize a conference for the rest of your school about present-day life in Africa. Decide on several major topics for the conference, such as literature, arts, religion, and agriculture. Then form committees to plan the conference. One committee can plan an agenda, or list of events. Another can research the selected topics and give speeches at the conference. A publicity team can make posters to let students in other classes know about the conference. A press committee can write news reports about the speeches given at the conference.

Project

RESEARCH AFRICAN ART

African Masks
As you study Africa, find out about the tradition of mask-making in African countries. Look through books and magazines for information about different African mask-making traditions. Research the kinds of masks people make, the ways of making them, and the meanings that they have. Prepare a mini-museum display with pictures or sketches and detailed explanations of the masks and traditions you research. You may want to try making a mask of your own as well.

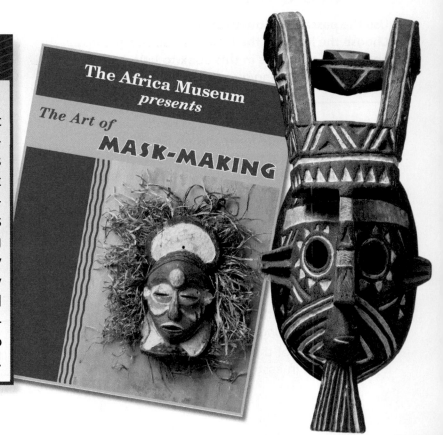

The Africa Museum presents
The Art of MASK-MAKING

Reference

Table of Contents

The World: Political

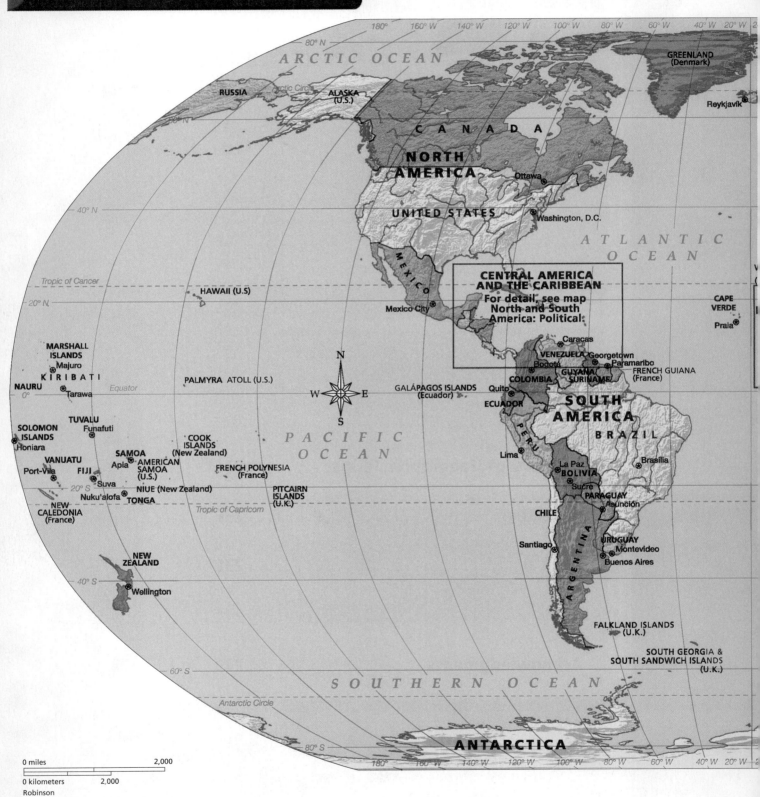

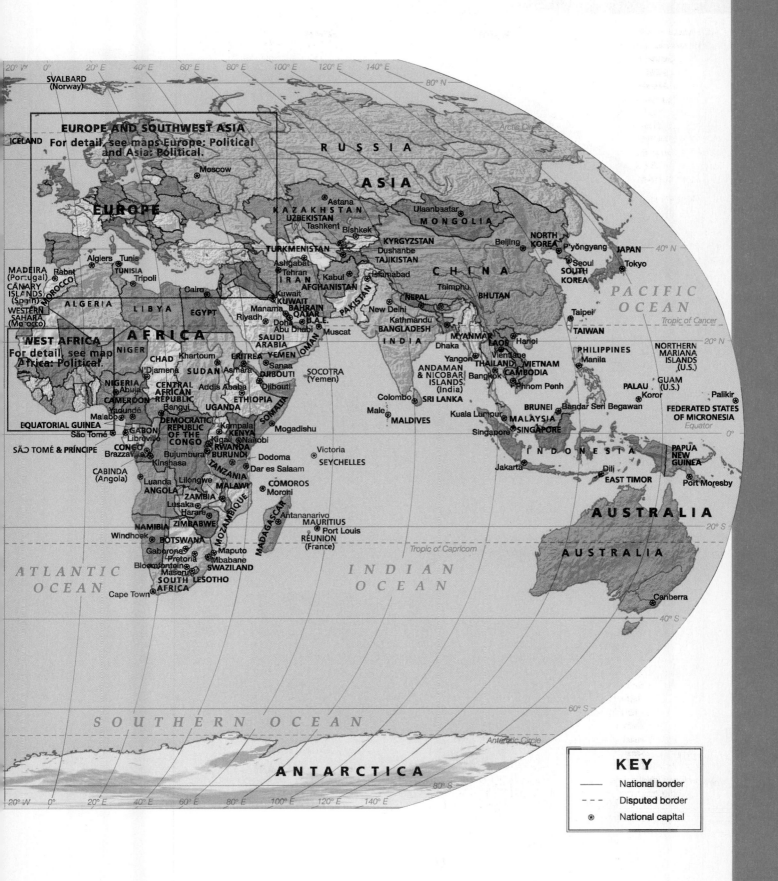

The World: Physical

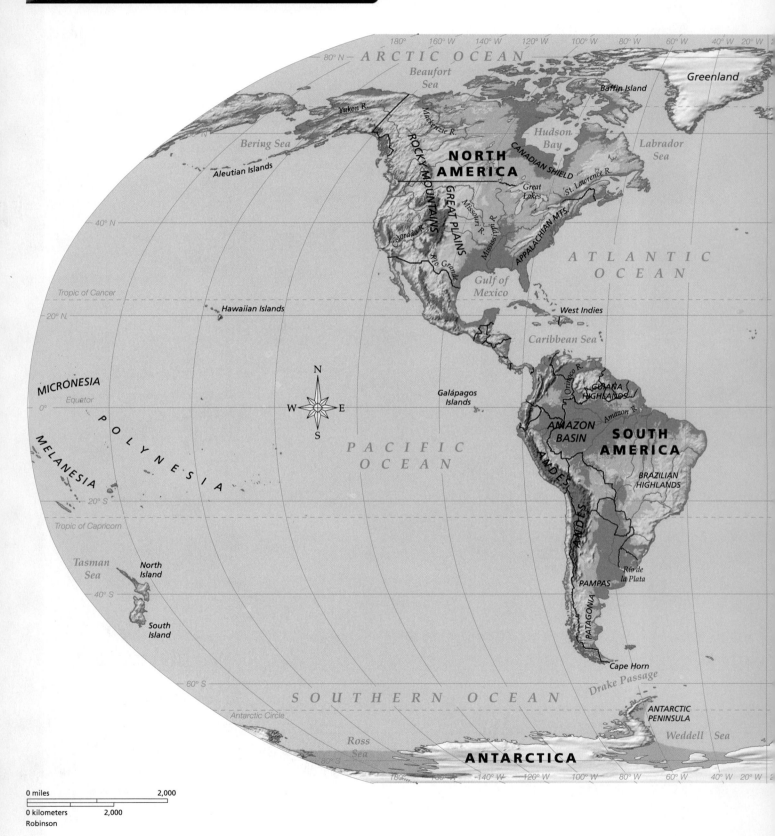

180° 160° W 140° W 120° W 100° W 80° W 60° W 40° W 20° W

80° N ARCTIC OCEAN

Beaufort Sea

Greenland

Baffin Island

Yukon R.

Mackenzie R.

Hudson Bay

Labrador Sea

Bering Sea

ROCKY MOUNTAINS

NORTH AMERICA

CANADIAN SHIELD

Aleutian Islands

GREAT PLAINS

Great Lakes

St. Lawrence R.

40° N

Colorado R.

Missouri R.

Miss. R.

Mississippi R.

APPALACHIAN MTS.

ATLANTIC OCEAN

Rio Grande

Gulf of Mexico

Tropic of Cancer

20° N

Hawaiian Islands

West Indies

Caribbean Sea

MICRONESIA

Equator

0°

N

W   E

S

Galápagos Islands

Orinoco R.

GUIANA HIGHLANDS

Amazon R.

AMAZON BASIN

SOUTH AMERICA

POLYNESIA

PACIFIC OCEAN

ANDES

BRAZILIAN HIGHLANDS

MELANESIA

20° S

Tropic of Capricorn

Tasman Sea

North Island

40° S

South Island

PAMPAS

Rio de la Plata

PATAGONIA

Cape Horn

60° S

SOUTHERN OCEAN

Drake Passage

ANTARCTIC PENINSULA

Weddell Sea

Antarctic Circle

Ross Sea

80° S

ANTARCTICA

180° 160° 140° W 120° W 100° W 80° W 60° W 40° W 20° W

0 miles   2,000

0 kilometers   2,000

Robinson

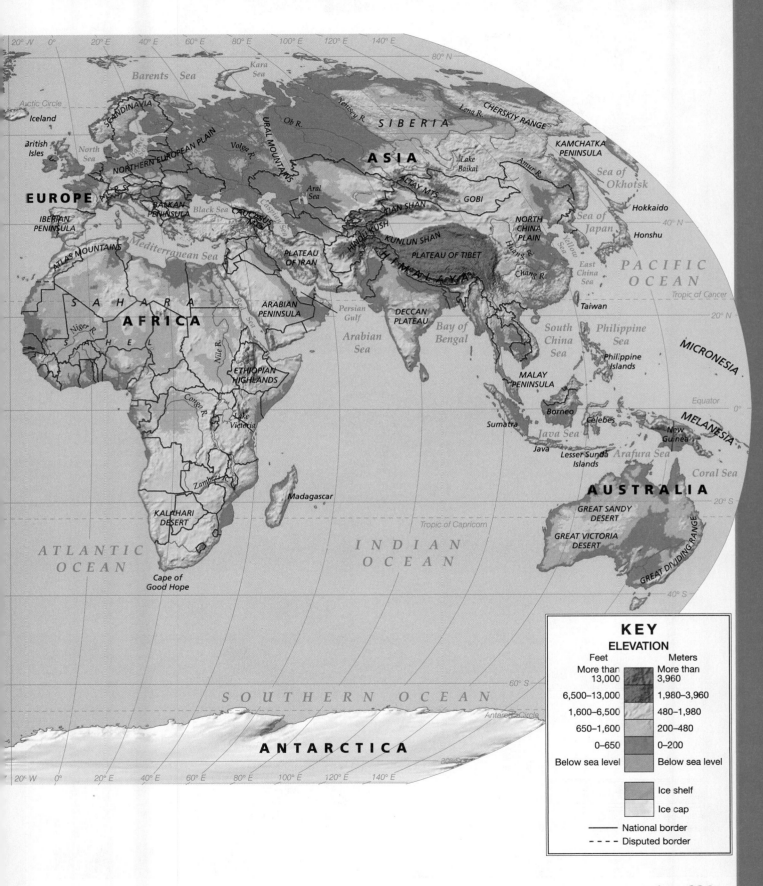

KEY
ELEVATION

Feet		Meters
More than 13,000		More than 3,960
6,500–13,000		1,980–3,960
1,600–6,500		480–1,980
650–1,600		200–480
0–650		0–200
Below sea level		Below sea level

Ice shelf
Ice cap
——— National border
- - - - Disputed border

North and South America: Political

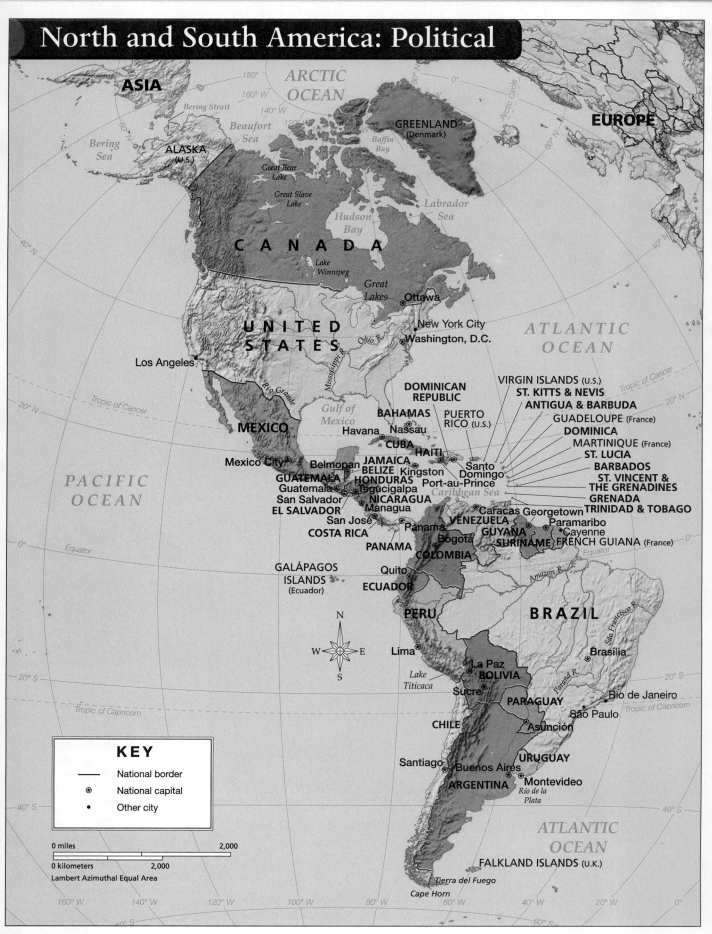

ASIA

ARCTIC OCEAN

180°
160° W
140° W
120° W
0°

Bering Strait

Beaufort Sea

Bering Sea

ALASKA (U.S.)

GREENLAND (Denmark)

Baffin Bay

EUROPE

Great Bear Lake

Great Slave Lake

Hudson Bay

Labrador Sea

60°

40° N

CANADA

Lake Winnipeg

Great Lakes

Ottawa

New York City
Washington, D.C.

ATLANTIC OCEAN

40° N

UNITED STATES

Ohio R.
Mississippi R.

Los Angeles

Rio Grande

Gulf of Mexico

MEXICO

Havana

Nassau

Mexico City

Belmopan

GUATEMALA
Guatemala
San Salvador
EL SALVADOR

BAHAMAS

CUBA

JAMAICA
BELIZE
HONDURAS
Tegucigalpa
NICARAGUA
Managua

Kingston

HAITI

Port-au-Prince

DOMINICAN REPUBLIC

PUERTO RICO (U.S.)

Santo Domingo

VIRGIN ISLANDS (U.S.)
ST. KITTS & NEVIS
ANTIGUA & BARBUDA
GUADELOUPE (France)
DOMINICA
MARTINIQUE (France)
ST. LUCIA
BARBADOS
ST. VINCENT & THE GRENADINES
GRENADA
TRINIDAD & TOBAGO

Tropic of Cancer

20° N

Caribbean Sea

Tropic of Cancer

20° N

PACIFIC OCEAN

San José

COSTA RICA

PANAMA

Panama

Caracas

VENEZUELA

Bogotá

COLOMBIA

Georgetown

GUYANA

SURINAME

Paramaribo
Cayenne
FRENCH GUIANA (France)

Equator

0°

Equator

0°

GALÁPAGOS ISLANDS (Ecuador)

Quito

ECUADOR

PERU

Amazon R.

BRAZIL

São Francisco R.

N
W   E
S

Lima

Lake Titicaca

La Paz
BOLIVIA

Sucre

PARAGUAY

Brasília

Paraná R.

Rio de Janeiro

São Paulo

Tropic of Capricorn

20° S

Tropic of Capricorn

20° S

CHILE

Asunción

URUGUAY

KEY

—— National border

⊛ National capital

• Other city

Santiago

Buenos Aires

ARGENTINA

Montevideo
Río de la Plata

40° S

0 miles   2,000

0 kilometers   2,000

Lambert Azimuthal Equal Area

ATLANTIC OCEAN

FALKLAND ISLANDS (U.K.)

Tierra del Fuego

Cape Horn

40° S

160° W   140° W   120° W   100° W   80° W   60° W   40° W   20° W   0°

North and South America: Physical

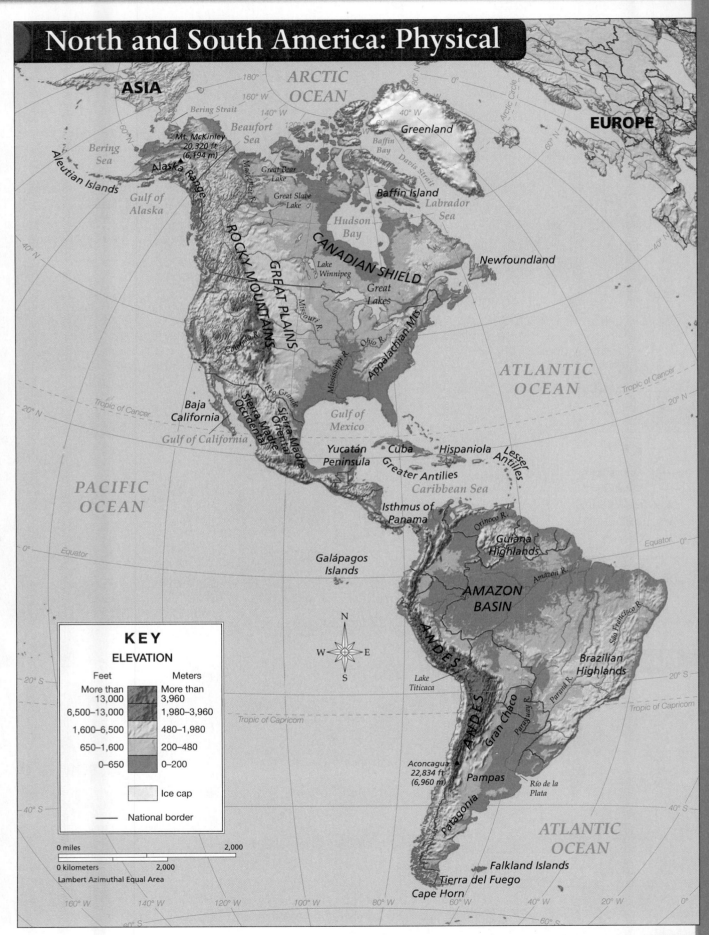

ASIA

ARCTIC OCEAN

180°
160° W
140° W

Bering Strait

Beaufort Sea

Greenland

40° W

EUROPE

Arctic Circle

Bering Sea

Mt. McKinley
20,320 ft
(6,194 m)

Alaska Range

Baffin Bay

Davis Strait

Baffin Island

Labrador Sea

60° N

Aleutian Islands

Gulf of Alaska

Mackenzie R.

Great Bear Lake

Great Slave Lake

Hudson Bay

CANADIAN SHIELD

Newfoundland

40° N

ROCKY MOUNTAINS

GREAT PLAINS

Lake Winnipeg

Great Lakes

Missouri R.

Mississippi R.

Ohio R.

Appalachian Mts.

ATLANTIC OCEAN

Tropic of Cancer

20° N

Colorado R.

Rio Grande

Tropic of Cancer

Baja California

Sierra Madre Occidental

Sierra Madre Oriental

Gulf of California

Gulf of Mexico

Yucatán Peninsula

Cuba

Greater Antilles

Hispaniola

Lesser Antilles

PACIFIC OCEAN

Caribbean Sea

Isthmus of Panama

Galápagos Islands

Orinoco R.

Guiana Highlands

Equator

Equator

0°

AMAZON BASIN

Amazon R.

São Francisco R.

ANDES

Brazilian Highlands

KEY

ELEVATION

Feet		Meters
More than 13,000		More than 3,960
6,500–13,000		1,980–3,960
1,600–6,500		480–1,980
650–1,600		200–480
0–650		0–200

Ice cap

National border

20° S

Lake Titicaca

Tropic of Capricorn

Gran Chaco

Paraguay R.

Paraná R.

Tropic of Capricorn

N
W   E
S

Aconcagua
22,834 ft
(6,960 m)

Pampas

Río de la Plata

40° S

Patagonia

ATLANTIC OCEAN

0 miles   2,000

0 kilometers   2,000

Lambert Azimuthal Equal Area

Falkland Islands

Tierra del Fuego

Cape Horn

160° W   140° W   120° W   100° W   80° W   60° W   40° W   20° W   0°

United States: Political

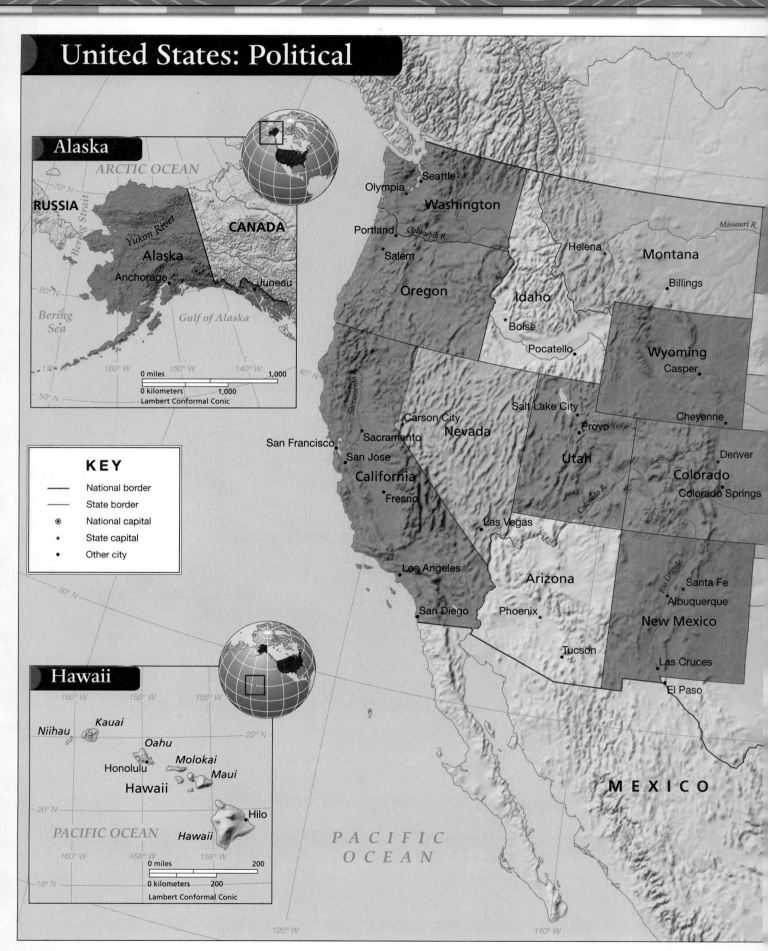

Alaska

ARCTIC OCEAN

RUSSIA

70° N

Bering Strait

Yukon River

CANADA

Arctic Circle

Alaska

Anchorage

Juneau

Bering
Sea

60° N

Gulf of Alaska

Lambert Conformal Conic

170°   160° W   150° W   140° W   1,000

0 miles   1,000
0 kilometers
50° N

KEY

——	National border
——	State border
⊛	National capital
★	State capital
•	Other city

Hawaii

160° W   158° W   156° W

Niihau   Kauai

Oahu

Honolulu   Molokai

Maui

Hawaii

22° N

20° N

PACIFIC OCEAN   Hawaii   Hilo

160° W   158° W   156° W   200

0 miles   200
0 kilometers
18° N

Lambert Conformal Conic

30° N

Seattle

Olympia   Washington

Portland   Columbia R.

Salem   Helena   Montana

Oregon   Idaho   Billings

Boise

Pocatello   Wyoming

Missouri R.

110° W

Carson City   Salt Lake City   Casper

Nevada   Provo   Cheyenne

San Francisco   Sacramento   Utah   Denver

San Jose   Colorado

California   Colorado Springs

Fresno   Colorado R.

Las Vegas

Los Angeles   Rio Grande   Santa Fe

Arizona   Albuquerque

San Diego   Phoenix   New Mexico

Tucson   Las Cruces

El Paso

MEXICO

PACIFIC
OCEAN

120° W   110° W

40° N

Sacramento R.

CANADA

North Dakota
  ★ Bismarck
  • Fargo

Minnesota

South Dakota
  ★ Pierre
  • Sioux Falls

Lake Superior

St. Paul
• Minneapolis
Mississippi R.

Wisconsin

Michigan

Lake Huron

Lake Michigan

Lake Ontario

Maine
  ★ Augusta
  • Portland

Vermont
Montpelier ★

New Hampshire
  • Concord

Albany ★
Boston ★

New York

Buffalo •

Massachusetts
Providence ★
Hartford ★ Rhode Island
Connecticut

• Milwaukee
Madison ★

Grand Rapids •
Lansing ★

Detroit •

Lake Erie

New York City

Iowa
Des Moines ★

Chicago •

Cedar Rapids •

Fort Wayne •

Ohio

Cleveland •
Pittsburgh •

Pennsylvania
Harrisburg ★

New Jersey
★ Trenton
Philadelphia •

Nebraska
  Omaha •
Missouri R.

Lincoln ★

Illinois

Indiana

Columbus ★

Delaware
★ Dover

Baltimore •

Indianapolis •

Washington, D.C. •

Annapolis ★
Maryland

Topeka ★

Kansas City •
Jefferson City ★

Springfield ★

St. Louis •

Cincinnati •
Ohio R.

West
Virginia

Richmond ★

District of Columbia

Kansas

Louisville •

Frankfort ★

Charleston ★

Norfolk •

Arkansas R.

Wichita •

Missouri

Kentucky

Virginia

Raleigh ★

Oklahoma
  Tulsa •

Nashville • Knoxville •

Tennessee

North Carolina
  • Charlotte

Oklahoma City ★

Arkansas
Fort Smith •

Memphis •

Tennessee R.

South Carolina
  • Columbia

Little Rock ★

Atlanta ★

Charleston •

Red R.

Mississippi

Birmingham •

Alabama

Georgia
Columbus •

Dallas •
Fort Worth •

Shreveport •
Louisiana

Jackson ★

Montgomery ★

Savannah •

Texas

Mississippi R.

Baton Rouge ★

Mobile •

Jacksonville •

Austin ★

Gulfport •
New Orleans •

Tallahassee ★

Florida

Houston •

San Antonio •

Orlando •

Gulf of Mexico

Tampa •

ATLANTIC
OCEAN

0 miles   250
0 kilometers   250
Lambert Azimuthal Equal Area

N
W   E
S

Miami •

Europe: Political

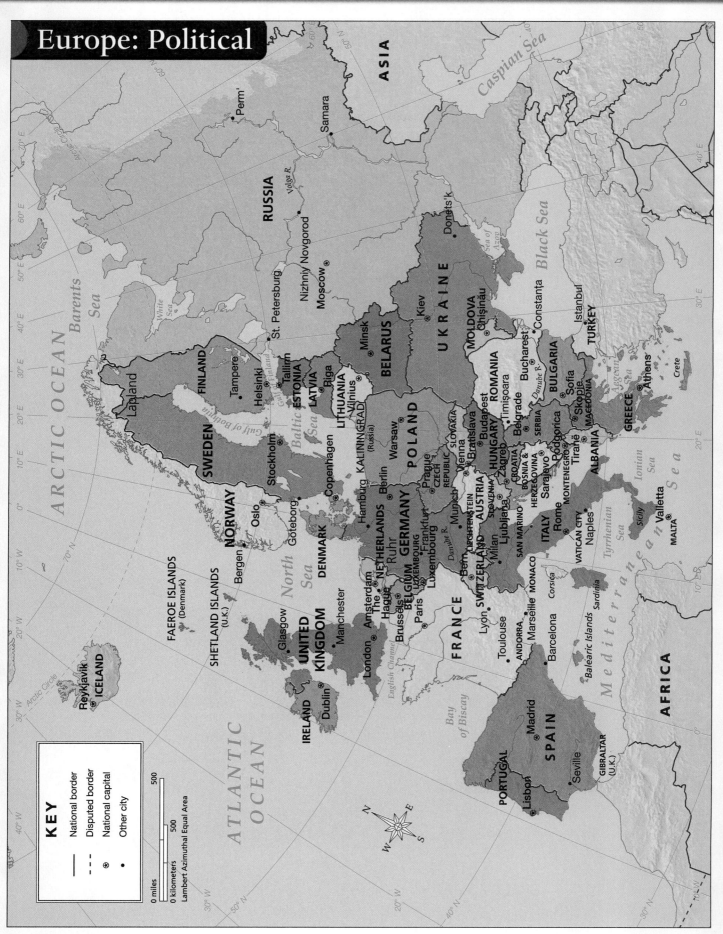

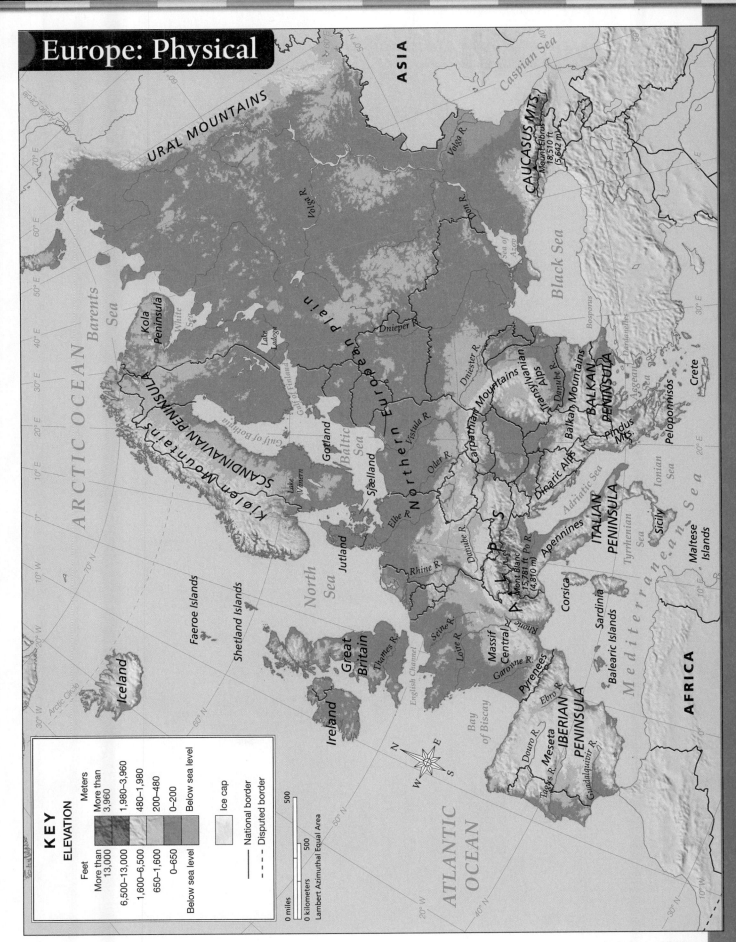

Europe: Physical

KEY

ELEVATION

Feet	Meters
More than 13,000	More than 3,960
6,500–13,000	1,980–3,960
1,600–6,500	480–1,980
650–1,600	200–480
0–650	0–200
Below sea level	Below sea level

Ice cap

—— National border

- - - Disputed border

0 miles 500
0 kilometers 500

Lambert Azimuthal Equal Area

ASIA

URAL MOUNTAINS

Caspian Sea

CAUCASUS MTS.
Mount Elbrus
18,510 ft
(5,642 m)

Volga R.

Don R.

Sea of Azov

Black Sea

ARCTIC OCEAN

Barents Sea

Kola Peninsula

White Sea

Volga R.

Lake Ladoga

Dnieper R.

Northern European Plain

Bosporus

Dardanelles

SCANDINAVIAN PENINSULA

Kjølen Mountains

Gulf of Bothnia

Gulf of Finland

Dniester R.

Carpathian Mountains

Transylvanian Alps

Danube R.

Balkan Mountains

BALKAN PENINSULA

Aegean Sea

Crete

Gotland

Baltic Sea

Sjælland

Vistula R.

Oder R.

Dinaric Alps

Pindus Mts.

Peloponnisos

Lake Vänern

Elbe R.

Danube R.

Adriatic Sea

Ionian Sea

ARCTIC OCEAN

Faeroe Islands

Shetland Islands

North Sea

Jutland

A L P S

Mont Blanc
15,781 ft
(4,810 m)

Apennines

ITALIAN PENINSULA

Tyrrhenian Sea

Sicily

Maltese Islands

Mediterranean Sea

Iceland

Arctic Circle

Ireland

Great Britain

Thames R.

English Channel

Seine R.

Loire R.

Massif Central

Rhône R.

Garonne R.

Bay of Biscay

Pyrenees

Corsica

Sardinia

Balearic Islands

N

Rhine R.

Po R.

ATLANTIC OCEAN

Ebro R.

IBERIAN PENINSULA

Douro R.

Meseta

Tagus R.

Guadalquivir R.

AFRICA

Africa: Political

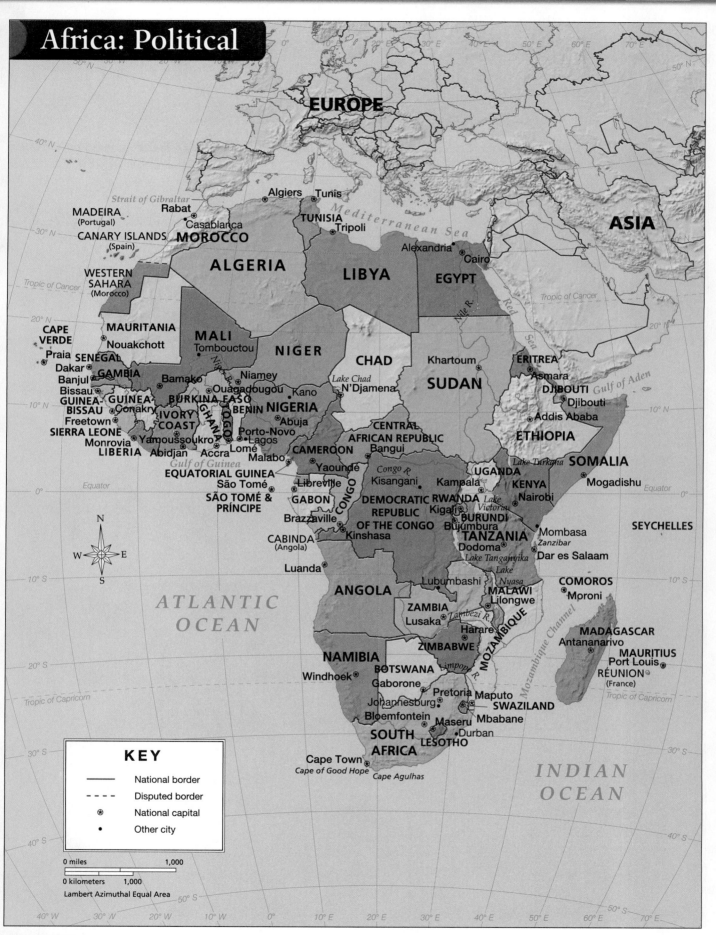

EUROPE

ASIA

Strait of Gibraltar
Algiers • Tunis
Rabat •
MADEIRA
(Portugal)
Casablanca
TUNISIA
Tripoli
Mediterranean Sea
CANARY ISLANDS
(Spain)
MOROCCO
Alexandria • Cairo

WESTERN
SAHARA
(Morocco)
ALGERIA
LIBYA
EGYPT
Nile R.
Red Sea
Tropic of Cancer

CAPE
VERDE
MAURITANIA
MALI
Nouakchott
Tombouctou
NIGER
CHAD
Khartoum •
ERITREA
Asmara •
DJIBOUTI
Gulf of Aden
Praia •
SENEGAL
Dakar •
GAMBIA
Bamako •
Niamey •
Ouagadougou •
Kano •
N'Djamena
Lake Chad
SUDAN
Djibouti •

Banjul
Bissau
GUINEA-
BISSAU
GUINEA
Conakry
BURKINA FASO
BENIN
NIGERIA
Addis Ababa •

Freetown
IVORY
COAST
GHANA
TOGO
Abuja •
CENTRAL
AFRICAN REPUBLIC
Bangui •
ETHIOPIA
SOMALIA

SIERRA LEONE
Monrovia
Yamoussoukro
Porto-Novo
Lagos
Malabo •
CAMEROON
Lake Turkana
Mogadishu •

LIBERIA
Abidjan
Accra
Lomé
Gulf of Guinea
EQUATORIAL GUINEA
São Tomé •
Yaoundé •
Libreville •
Congo R.
Kisangani •
UGANDA
Kampala •
KENYA
Nairobi •

Equator
SÃO TOMÉ &
PRÍNCIPE
GABON
CONGO
DEMOCRATIC
REPUBLIC
OF THE CONGO
RWANDA
Lake Victoria
Kigali •
BURUNDI
Bujumbura •
TANZANIA
Dodoma •
Mombasa •
Zanzibar
SEYCHELLES

Brazzaville •
CABINDA
(Angola)
Kinshasa
Lake Tanganyika
Dar es Salaam •

ATLANTIC
OCEAN
Luanda •
ANGOLA
Lubumbashi •
Lake Nyasa
MALAWI
Lilongwe
COMOROS
Moroni •

ZAMBIA
Lusaka •
Zambezi R.
MOZAMBIQUE
Mozambique Channel
MADAGASCAR
Antananarivo •
MAURITIUS
Port Louis •

NAMIBIA
Windhoek •
BOTSWANA
Gaborone •
Harare •
ZIMBABWE
Limpopo R.
RÉUNION
(France)
Tropic of Capricorn

Tropic of Capricorn
Pretoria
Maputo
Johannesburg
SWAZILAND
Mbabane
INDIAN
OCEAN

Bloemfontein
Maseru
LESOTHO
Durban •

SOUTH
AFRICA
Cape Town •
Cape of Good Hope
Cape Agulhas

KEY

— National border
- - - Disputed border
⊛ National capital
• Other city

0 miles   1,000

0 kilometers   1,000

Lambert Azimuthal Equal Area

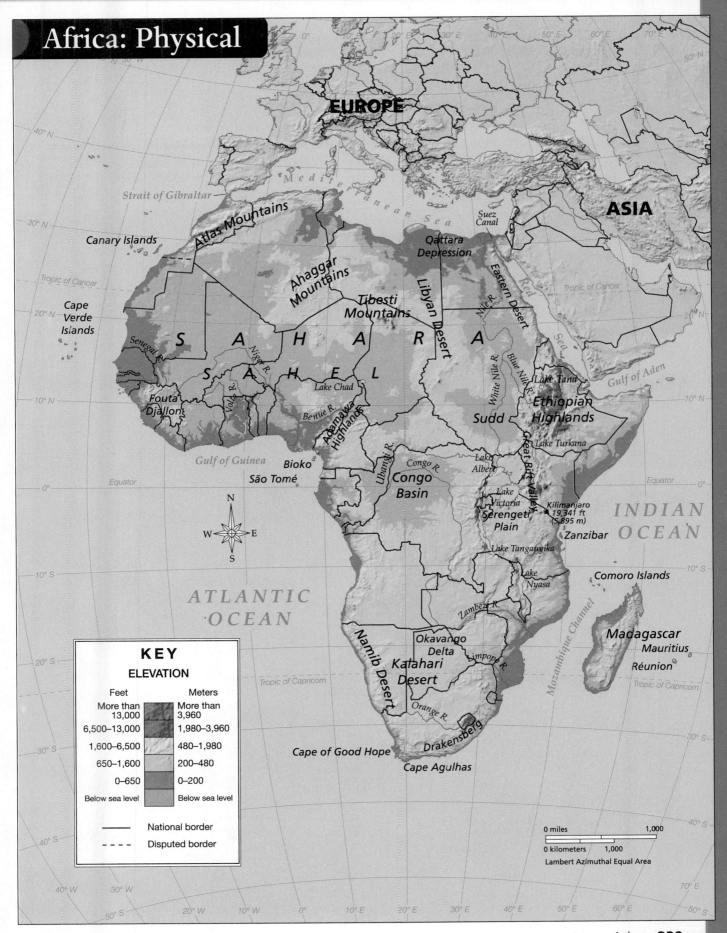

Africa: Physical

EUROPE

ASIA

Strait of Gibraltar

Mediterranean Sea

Atlas Mountains

Canary Islands

Suez Canal

Qattara Depression

Tropic of Cancer

Ahaggar Mountains

Tibesti Mountains

Libyan Desert

Eastern Desert

Red Sea

Tropic of Cancer

Cape Verde Islands

S A H A R A

Senegal R.

Niger R.

S A H E L

Lake Chad

Benue R.

Adamawa Highlands

Nile R.

White Nile R.

Blue Nile R.

Lake Tana

Gulf of Aden

Fouta Djallon

Volta R.

Ethiopian Highlands

Sudd

Gulf of Guinea

Bioko

São Tomé

Ubangi R.

Congo R.

Congo Basin

Lake Albert

Lake Turkana

Great Rift Valley

Equator

Lake Victoria

Serengeti Plain

Kilimanjaro 19,341 ft (5,895 m)

INDIAN OCEAN

Equator

Zanzibar

Lake Tanganyika

ATLANTIC OCEAN

Lake Nyasa

Comoro Islands

Zambezi R.

Mozambique Channel

Madagascar

Mauritius

Réunion

Okavango Delta

Namib Desert

Kalahari Desert

Limpopo R.

Tropic of Capricorn

Tropic of Capricorn

Orange R.

Cape of Good Hope

Drakensberg

Cape Agulhas

KEY

ELEVATION

Feet		Meters
More than 13,000		More than 3,960
6,500–13,000		1,980–3,960
1,600–6,500		480–1,980
650–1,600		200–480
0–650		0–200
Below sea level		Below sea level

— National border

--- Disputed border

0 miles   1,000

0 kilometers 1,000

Lambert Azimuthal Equal Area

N
W E
S

Asia: Political

KEY

— National border
⊛ National capital
• Other city

Note: The southern Kuril Islands, though under Russian administration, are claimed by Japan.

0 miles 1,000
0 kilometers 1,000
Lambert Azimuthal Equal Area

PACIFIC OCEAN

ARCTIC OCEAN

EUROPE

RUSSIA

AFRICA

AUSTRALIA

Oceans & Seas

East Siberian Sea
Sea of Okhotsk
Barents Sea
Kara Sea
Black Sea
Caspian Sea
Aral Sea
Red Sea
Gulf of Aden
Arabian Sea
Bay of Bengal
Andaman Sea
South China Sea
East China Sea
Yellow Sea
Philippine Sea
INDIAN OCEAN

Countries & Cities

Moscow
Yekaterinburg
Omsk
Novosibirsk
Irkutsk
Yakutsk
Siberia
Vladivostok
Sakhalin Island
Kuril Islands

JAPAN
Tokyo
Osaka
Ryukyu Islands

NORTH KOREA
P'yŏngyang
SOUTH KOREA
Seoul
Harbin
Beijing
Tianjin
Shanghai

CHINA
Xi'an
Chongqing
Guangzhou
Hong Kong

MONGOLIA
Ulaanbaatar

TAIWAN
Taipei

PHILIPPINES
Manila

KAZAKHSTAN
Astana
Almaty
Lake Balkhash

UZBEKISTAN
Tashkent
KYRGYZSTAN
Bishkek
TAJIKISTAN
Dushanbe
TURKMENISTAN
Ashgabat

AFGHANISTAN
Kabul
PAKISTAN
Islamabad
Karachi

NEPAL
Kathmandu
BHUTAN
Thimphu
BANGLADESH
Dhaka

INDIA
New Delhi
Kolkata (Calcutta)
Mumbai (Bombay)
Chennai (Madras)

SRI LANKA
Colombo
MALDIVES
Male

MYANMAR (BURMA)
Yangon
THAILAND
Bangkok
LAOS
Vientiane
VIETNAM
Hanoi
Ho Chi Minh City
CAMBODIA
Phnom Penh

MALAYSIA
Kuala Lumpur
SINGAPORE
Singapore
BRUNEI
Bandar Seri Begawan
INDONESIA
Jakarta
Surabaya
Borneo
Celebes
Sumatra
Java

EAST TIMOR
Dili
Timor

PAPUA NEW GUINEA
Port Moresby
New Guinea
New Britain
New Ireland

TURKEY
Ankara
Istanbul
GEORGIA
Tbilisi
ARMENIA
Yerevan
AZERBAIJAN
Baku
CYPRUS
Nicosia
LEBANON
Beirut
ISRAEL
SYRIA
Damascus
Jerusalem
JORDAN
Amman
IRAQ
Baghdad

IRAN
Tehran
Shiraz
KUWAIT
Kuwait
BAHRAIN
Manama
QATAR
Doha
UNITED ARAB EMIRATES
Abu Dhabi
OMAN
Muscat

SAUDI ARABIA
Riyadh
Mecca
YEMEN
Sanaa
SOCOTRA (Yemen)

Rivers & Lakes

Lena R.
Tura R.
Ob R.
Irtysh R.
Yenisey R.
Amur R.
Lake Baikal
Huang R.
Chang R.
Ganges R.

N E
W S

Asia: Physical

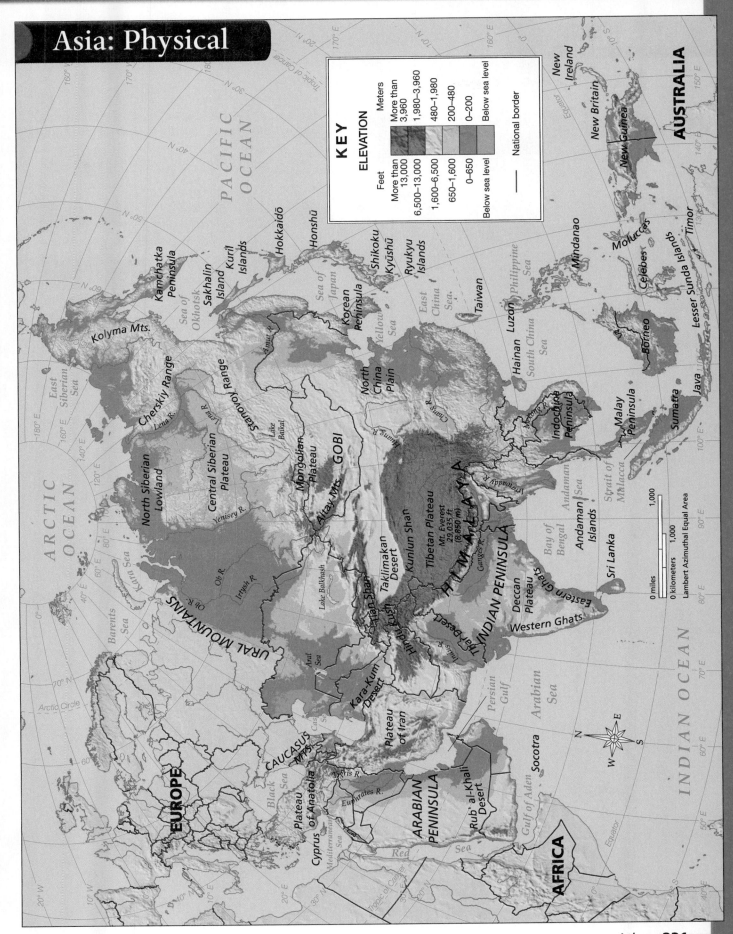

KEY

ELEVATION

Feet	Meters
More than 13,000	More than 3,960
6,500–13,000	1,980–3,960
1,600–6,500	480–1,980
650–1,600	200–480
0–650	0–200
Below sea level	Below sea level

— National border

Lambert Azimuthal Equal Area

Oceania

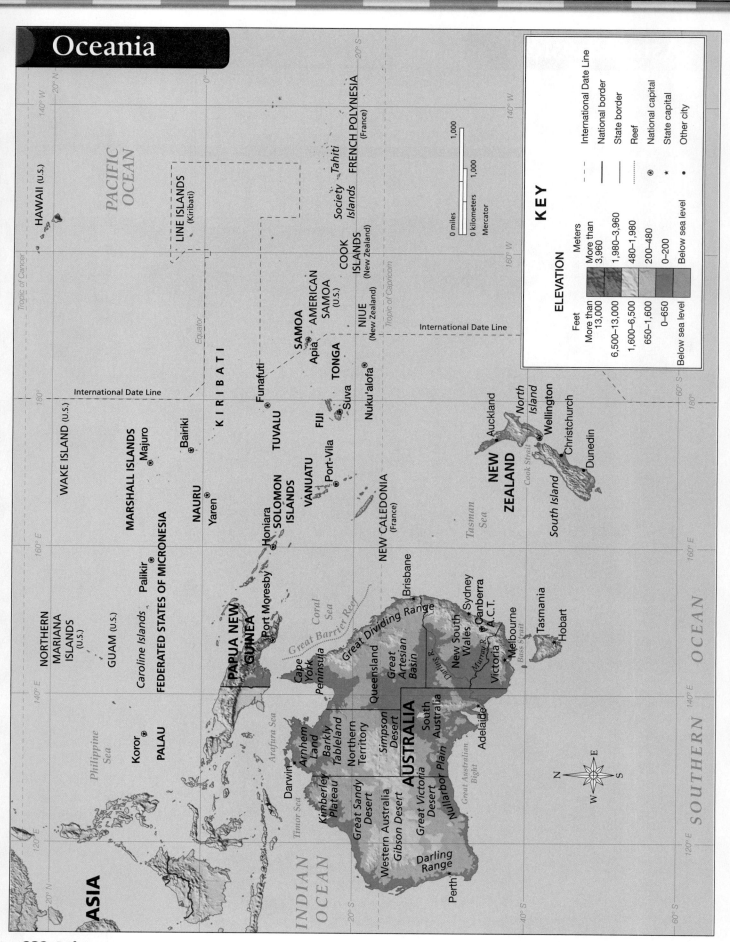

KEY

– – –	International Date Line	
——	National border	
—	State border	
········	Reef	
⊛	National capital	
★	State capital	
•	Other city	

ELEVATION

Feet	Meters	
More than 13,000	More than 3,960	
6,500–13,000	1,980–3,960	
1,600–6,500	480–1,980	
650–1,600	200–480	
0–650	0–200	
Below sea level	Below sea level	

International Date Line

PACIFIC OCEAN

HAWAII (U.S.)

LINE ISLANDS (Kiribati)

FRENCH POLYNESIA (France)

Tahiti
Society Islands

COOK ISLANDS (New Zealand)

SAMOA
Apia
AMERICAN SAMOA (U.S.)

NIUE (New Zealand)

TONGA
Nuku'alofa

Funafuti

TUVALU

FIJI
Suva

KIRIBATI

WAKE ISLAND (U.S.)

MARSHALL ISLANDS
Majuro

Bairiki

NAURU
Yaren

SOLOMON ISLANDS
Honiara

VANUATU
Port-Vila

NEW CALEDONIA (France)

NORTHERN MARIANA ISLANDS (U.S.)

GUAM (U.S.)

Caroline Islands   Palikir

FEDERATED STATES OF MICRONESIA

PAPUA NEW GUINEA
Port Moresby

Koror
PALAU

Philippine Sea

Timor Sea

Arafura Sea

Darwin

Arnhem Land

Kimberley Plateau

Barkly Tableland

Northern Territory

Simpson Desert

Great Sandy Desert

Great Victoria Desert

Gibson Desert

Western Australia

Nullarbor Plain

Great Australian Bight

South Australia

Darling Range

Perth

AUSTRALIA

Queensland

Great Artesian Basin

Cape York Peninsula

Great Dividing Range

Great Barrier Reef

Coral Sea

Brisbane

New South Wales
Sydney
Canberra
A.C.T.

Murray R.
Darling R.
Victoria
Melbourne

Adelaide

Bass Strait

Tasmania
Hobart

Tasman Sea

NEW ZEALAND
North Island
Auckland
Wellington
Cook Strait
South Island
Christchurch
Dunedin

ASIA

INDIAN OCEAN

SOUTHERN OCEAN

Tropic of Cancer

Equator

Tropic of Capricorn

0 miles   1,000
0 kilometers   1,000
Mercator

N E S W

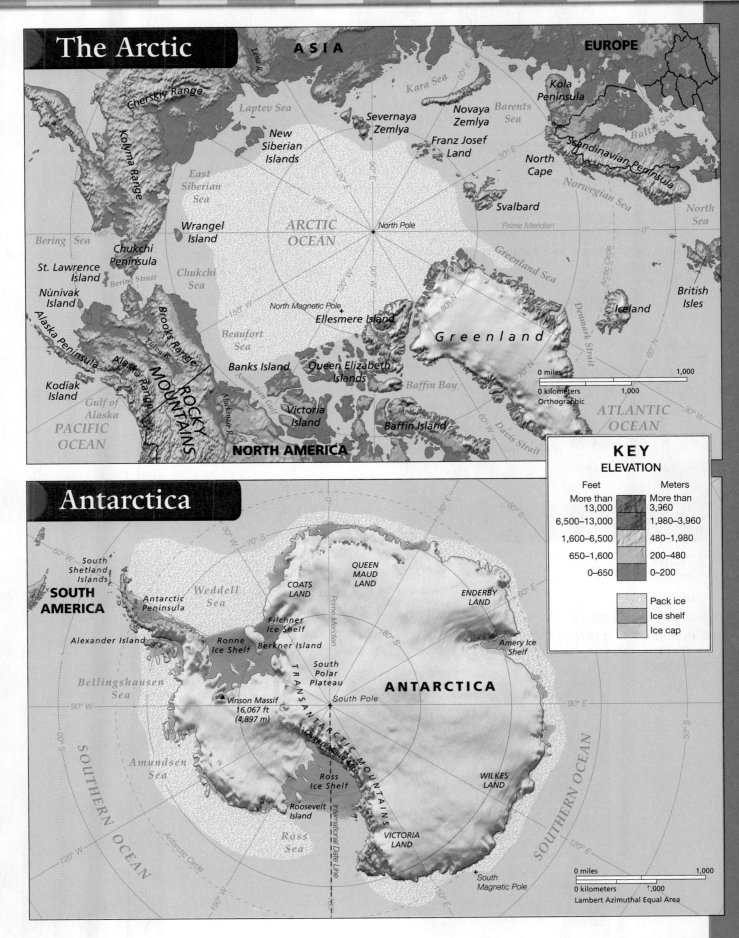

The Arctic

ASIA   EUROPE

Cherskiy Range
Lena R.
Kolyma Range
Laptev Sea
Kara Sea
Severnaya Zemlya
Novaya Zemlya
Barents Sea
Kola Peninsula
New Siberian Islands
Franz Josef Land
Baltic Sea
Scandinavian Peninsula
North Cape
East Siberian Sea
ARCTIC OCEAN
North Pole
Svalbard
Norwegian Sea
Prime Meridian
North Sea
Wrangel Island
Chukchi Peninsula
Bering Sea
Chukchi Sea
Greenland Sea
Iceland
British Isles
St. Lawrence Island
Bering Strait
North Magnetic Pole
Arctic Circle
Nunivak Island
Beaufort Sea
Ellesmere Island
Greenland
Denmark Strait
Alaska Peninsula
Brooks Range
Yukon R.
Banks Island
Queen Elizabeth Islands
Baffin Bay
Kodiak Island
Alaska Range
ROCKY MOUNTAINS
Amundsen Gulf
Mackenzie R.
Victoria Island
Baffin Island
Davis Strait
ATLANTIC OCEAN
Gulf of Alaska
PACIFIC OCEAN
NORTH AMERICA

0 miles 1,000
0 kilometers 1,000
Orthographic

Antarctica

South Shetland Islands
SOUTH AMERICA
Antarctic Peninsula
Weddell Sea
COATS LAND
QUEEN MAUD LAND
ENDERBY LAND
Alexander Island
Filchner Ice Shelf
Ronne Ice Shelf
Berkner Island
Prime Meridian
Amery Ice Shelf
Bellingshausen Sea
Vinson Massif 16,067 ft (4,897 m)
South Polar Plateau
ANTARCTICA
TRANSANTARCTIC MOUNTAINS
QUEEN MAUD MTS.
South Pole
WILKES LAND
Amundsen Sea
Ross Ice Shelf
Roosevelt Island
International Date Line
VICTORIA LAND
SOUTHERN OCEAN
Ross Sea
South Magnetic Pole
Antarctic Circle
SOUTHERN OCEAN

0 miles 1,000
0 kilometers 1,000
Lambert Azimuthal Equal Area

KEY
ELEVATION

Feet		Meters
More than 13,000		More than 3,960
6,500–13,000		1,980–3,960
1,600–6,500		480–1,980
650–1,600		200–480
0–650		0–200

Pack ice
Ice shelf
Ice cap

Glossary of Geographic Terms

basin
an area that is lower than surrounding land areas; some basins are filled with water

bay
a body of water that is partly surrounded by land and that is connected to a larger body of water

butte
a small, high, flat-topped landform with cliff-like sides

▲ **butte**

canyon
a deep, narrow valley with steep sides; often with a stream flowing through it

cataract
a large waterfall or steep rapids

delta
a plain at the mouth of a river, often triangular in shape, formed where sediment is deposited by flowing water

flood plain
a broad plain on either side of a river, formed where sediment settles during floods

glacier
a huge, slow-moving mass of snow and ice

hill
an area that rises above surrounding land and has a rounded top; lower and usually less steep than a mountain

island
an area of land completely surrounded by water

isthmus
a narrow strip of land that connects two larger areas of land

mesa
a high, flat-topped landform with cliff-like sides; larger than a butte

mountain
a landform that rises steeply at least 2,000 feet (610 meters) above surrounding land; usually wide at the bottom and rising to a narrow peak or ridge

▶ **glacier**

◀ **cataract**

◄ **delta**

mountain pass
a gap between mountains

peninsula
an area of land almost completely surrounded by water but connected to the mainland

plain
a large area of flat or gently rolling land

plateau
a large, flat area that rises above the surrounding land; at least one side has a steep slope

river mouth
the point where a river enters a lake or sea

strait
a narrow stretch of water that connects two larger bodies of water

tributary
a river or stream that flows into a larger river

valley
a low stretch of land between mountains or hills; land that is drained by a river

volcano
an opening in Earth's surface through which molten rock, ashes, and gases escape from the interior

▶ **volcano**

Gazetteer

A

Abuja (9°12′ N, 7°11′ E) the capital of Nigeria, p. 140

Addis Ababa (9°2′ N, 38°42′ E) the capital of Ethiopia, p. 170

Aksum an ancient city in northern Ethiopia that was a powerful kingdom and trade center from about A.D. 200 to A.D. 600, p. 43

Algeria (28° N, 3° E) a country in North Africa, officially the Democratic and Popular Republic of Algeria, p. 118

Algiers (36°47′ N, 3°3′ E) the capital of Algeria, p. 119

B

Benin an ancient African kingdom in the forest region of West Africa, p. 49

C

Cairo (30°3′ N, 31°15′ E) the capital and most populous city of Egypt, p. 110

Cape of Good Hope (34°18′ S, 18°26′ E) the cape at the southern end of the Cape Peninsula in South Africa, p. 52

Cape Town (33°48′ S, 18°28′ E) one of the capitals and largest cities in South Africa, p. 98

Carthage an ancient city-state in present-day Tunisia that the Phoenicians established and that controlled Mediterranean trade from the late 500s B.C. through the 200s B.C., p. 46

Central Africa countries in the central region of Africa, p. 11

Congo, Democratic Republic of the (4° S, 25° E) a country in Central Africa; formerly called Zaire, p. 200

Congo River a river in Central Africa that flows into the Atlantic Ocean, p. 13

D

Dar es Salaam (6°48′ S, 39°17′ E) one of two capitals of Tanzania, p. 96

E

East Africa countries in the eastern region of Africa, p. 11

Egypt (27° N, 30° E) a country in North Africa, officially the Arab Republic of Egypt, p. 110

Ethiopia (9° N, 39° E) a country in East Africa, p. 166

G

Ghana an early African empire located in parts of present-day Mauritania and Mali, p. 47

Ghana (8° N, 1° W) a country in West Africa, officially the Republic of Ghana, p. 142

Great Rift Valley the major branch of the East African Rift System, p. 12

Great Zimbabwe an ancient city-state in south-eastern Zimbabwe that was a powerful trade center from about A.D. 1100 to 1500, p. 45

K

Kalahari Desert a desert in Southern Africa, p. 11

Kenya (1° N, 38° E) a country in East Africa, officially the Republic of Kenya, p. 178

Kilwa an Islamic city-state, located on an island off the coast of present-day Tanzania, that was powerful during the A.D. 1300s, p. 45

L

Lagos (6°27′ N, 3°24′ E) a city and main port of Nigeria, p. 140

Lalibela (12°2′ N, 39°02′ E) a town in Ethiopia that is famous for its stone churches carved in the 1100s, p. 168

M

Mali an ancient African empire located in present-day Mali, p. 48

Mali (17° N, 4° E) a country in West Africa, officially the Republic of Mali, p. 150

Mount Kenya (0°9′ S, 37°19′ E) a volcanic mountain in central Kenya, p. 179

Mount Kilimanjaro (3°04′ S, 37°22′ E) the tallest mountain in Africa, located in Tanzania, p. 11

N

Nairobi (1°17′ S, 36°49′ E) the capital of Kenya, p. 181

Namib Desert a desert extending along the Atlantic Coast of Southern Africa, p. 11

Niger River a river in West Africa that flows from Guinea into the Gulf of Guinea, p. 13

Nigeria (10° N, 8° E) a country in West Africa, officially the Federal Republic of Nigeria, p. 136

Nile River the longest river in the world, flowing through northeastern Africa into the Mediterranean Sea, p. 13

North Africa countries in the northern region of Africa, p. 11

Nubia an ancient region in North Africa, p. 39

S

Sahara the largest tropical desert in the world, covering almost all of North Africa, p. 11

Sahel the region in West and Central Africa that forms an intermediate climate zone between the dry Sahara to the north and the humid savannas to the south, p. 21

Songhai an ancient African empire located in present-day Mali, Niger, and Nigeria, p. 48

South Africa (30° S, 26° E) a country in Southern Africa, officially the Republic of South Africa, p. 208

Southern Africa countries in the southern region of Africa, p. 11

T

Tanzania (6° S, 35° E) a country in East Africa, officially the United Republic of Tanzania, p. 171

Tombouctou (16°46′ N, 3°1′ E) a city in Mali near the Niger River; in the past an important center of Islamic education and a stop along trans-Saharan trade routes (also spelled *Timbuktu*), p. 150

W

West Africa countries in the western region of Africa, p. 11

Z

Zambezi River a river in Central and Southern Africa that flows into the Indian Ocean, p. 13

The Zambezi River

Glossary

A

apartheid (uh PAHR tayt) *n.* the legal system of South Africa in which the rights of nonwhites were greatly restricted, p. 209

authoritarian government (uh thawr uh TEHR ee un GUV urn munt) *n.* a nondemocratic form of government in which a single leader or a small group of leaders has all the power, p. 203

B

bazaar (buh ZAHR) *n.* a traditional open-air market with shops or rows of stalls, p. 113

boycott (BOY kaht) *n.* a refusal to buy or use certain products or services, p. 62

C

Cairo (KY roh) *n.* the capital and most populous city of Egypt, p. 110

Cape of Good Hope (kayp uv good hohp) *n.* a former province of the Republic of South Africa; the point of land at the southern end of the Cape Peninsula, South Africa, p. 52

casbah (KAHZ bah) *n.* an old, crowded section of a North African city, p. 121

cash crop (kash krahp) *n.* a crop that is raised for sale, p. 28

city-state (SIH tee stayt) *n.* a city that is also an independent state, with its own traditions, government, and laws, p. 44

civilization (sih vuh luh ZAY shun) *n.* a society that has cities, a central government, and social classes and that usually has writing, art, and architecture, p. 39

clan (klan) *n.* a group of lineages, p. 86

colonize (KAHL uh nyz) *v.* to settle in an area and take control of its government, p. 56

commercial farming (kuh MUR shul FAHR ming) *n.* the large-scale production of crops for sale, p. 67

compound (KAHM pownd) *n.* a fenced-in group of homes, p. 99

coup d'état (koo day TAH) *n.* the sudden overthrow of a government by force, p. 146

cultural diffusion (KUL chur ul dih FYOO zhun) *n.* the spread of customs and ideas from one culture to another, p. 82

cultural diversity (KUL chur ul duh VUR suh tee) *n.* a wide variety of cultures, p. 84

culture (KUL chur) *n.* the way of life of people who share similar customs and beliefs, p. 79

D

democracy (dih MAHK ruh see) *n.* a government over which citizens exercise power, p. 63

desertification (dih zurt uh fih KAY shun) *n.* the process by which fertile land becomes too dry or damaged to support life, p. 152

discriminate (dih SKRIM ih nayt) *v.* to treat people differently, and often unfairly, based on race, religion, or sex, p. 209

diversify (duh VUR suh fy) *v.* to add variety; to expand a country's economy by increasing the variety of goods produced, p. 30

domesticate (duh MES tih kayt) *v.* to adapt wild plants or animals and breed them for human use, p. 38

drought (drowt) *n.* a long period of little or no rain, p. 19

E

economy (ih KAHN uh mee) *n.* a system for producing, distributing, consuming, and owning goods and services, p. 29

elevation (el uh VAY shun) *n.* the height of land above or below sea level, p. 11

Equiano, Olaudah (ek wee AHN oh, oh LOW duh) *n.* an antislavery activist who wrote an account of his enslavement, p. 54

ethnic group (ETH nik groop) *n.* a group of people who share the same ancestors, culture, language, or religion, p. 41

extended family (ek STEN did FAM uh lee) *n.* the part of a family that includes parents, children, and other relatives, p. 86

F

fellaheen (fel uh HEEN) *n.* peasants or agricultural workers in Egypt and other Arab countries, p. 115

fertile (FUR tul) *adj.* rich in the substances plants need to grow well, p. 14

G

Geez (gee EZ) *n.* an ancient Ethiopian language that was once used to write literature and religious texts but is no longer spoken, p. 167

H

harambee (hah RAHM bay) *n.* a social policy started by Jomo Kenyatta and meaning "let's pull together" in Swahili, p. 180

Hausa-Fulani (HOW suh foo LAH nee) *n.* Nigeria's largest ethnic group, p. 137

heritage (HEHR uh tij) *n.* the values, traditions, and customs handed down from one's ancestors, p. 93

hybrid (HY brid) *n.* a plant that is created by breeding different types of the same plant, p. 69

I

Igbo (IG boh) *n.* Nigeria's third-largest ethnic group, p. 137

irrigate (IHR uh gayt) *v.* to supply with water through a ditch, pipe, channel, or sprinkler, p. 19

K

Kikuyu (kee KOO yoo) *n.* the largest ethnic group in Kenya, p. 179

kinship (KIN ship) *n.* a family relationship, p. 86

L

life expectancy (lyf ek SPEK tun see) *n.* the average length of time a person can expect to live, p. 71

lineage (LIN ee ij) *n.* a group of families descended from a common ancestor, p. 86

lingua franca (LING gwuh FRANG kuh) *n.* a language used for communication among people who speak different first languages, p. 172

literate (LIT ur it) *adj.* able to read and write, p. 70

M

Maasai (mah SY) *n.* a seminomadic ethnic group in Kenya, p. 179

Mandela, Nelson (man DEL uh, NEL sun) *n.* black leader of the African National Congress and South Africa's first president after apartheid ended, p. 210

migrant worker (MY grunt WUR kur) *n.* a laborer who travels away from where he or she lives to find work, p. 99

migrate (MY grayt) *v.* to move from one place to settle in another, p. 40

monastery (MAHN uh stehr ee) *n.* a place where people, especially men known as monks, live a religious life, p. 166

multiethnic (mul tee ETH nik) *adj.* having many ethnic groups living within a society, p. 137

multiparty system (MUL tee pahr tee SIS tum) *n.* a political system in which two or more parties compete in elections, p. 175

N

nationalism (NASH uh nul iz um) *n.* a feeling of pride in one's homeland; a group's identity as members of a nation, p. 58

nationalize (NASH uh nuh lyz) *v.* to transfer ownership of something to a nation's government, p. 203

Nkrumah, Kwame (un KROO muh, KWAH mee) *n.* founder of Ghana's independence movement and Ghana's first president, p. 142

nomad (NOH mad) *n.* a person who has no permanent, settled home and instead moves from place to place, p. 22

nuclear family (NOO klee ur FAM uh lee) *n.* the part of a family that includes parents and children, p. 86

O

oasis (oh AY sis) *n.* a fertile place in a desert where there is water and vegetation, p. 19

overgrazing (oh vur GRAYZ ing) *n.* allowing too much grazing by large herds of animals, p. 152

P

Pan-Africanism (pan AF rih kun iz um) *n.* the belief that all Africans should work together for their rights and freedoms, p. 59

pilgrimage (PIL gruh mij) *n.* a religious journey, p. 48

plantation (plan TAY shun) *n.* a large farm where cash crops are grown, p. 53

plateau (pla TOH) *n.* a large, level area that rises above the surrounding land; has at least one side with a steep slope, p. 11

privatization (pry vuh tih ZAY shun) *n.* the sale of government-owned industries to private companies, p. 175

Q

Quran (koo RAHN) *n.* the sacred book of Islam; also spelled *Koran*, p. 80

R

rift (rift) *n.* a deep crack in Earth's surface, p. 12

S

savanna (suh VAN uh) *n.* a region of tall grasses with scattered trees, p. 20

seminomadic (seh mee noh MAD ik) *adj.* combining nomadic wandering and farming in settlements, p. 179

Sharia (shah REE ah) *n.* Islamic law, based on the words and deeds of Muhammad and on comments written by Muslim scholars and lawmakers, p. 111

souq (sook) *n.* an open-air marketplace in an Arab city, p. 121

sovereignty (SAHV run tee) *n.* political control, p. 146

subsistence farming (sub SIS tuns FAHR ming) *n.* raising just enough crops to support one's family, p. 27

Swahili (swah HEE lee) *n.* a Bantu language spoken in much of East Africa, p. 44; an ethnic group in East Africa that resulted from the mixing of African and Arab ways more than 1,000 years ago, p. 93

T

terrace (TEHR us) *n.* a flat platform of earth cut into the side of a slope, used for growing crops in steep places, p. 121

Tombouctou (tohm book TOO) *n.* a city in Mali near the Niger River; also spelled *Timbuktu*, p. 48

tributary (TRIB yoo tehr ee) *n.* a river or stream that flows into a larger river, p. 13

Y

Yoruba (YOH roo buh) *n.* Nigeria's second-largest ethnic group, p. 137

Index

The *m*, *g*, or *p* following some page numbers refers to maps *(m)*, charts, diagrams, tables, timelines, or graphs *(g)*, or pictures *(p)*.

Cover Design

Pronk&Associates

Staff Credits

The people who made up the *World Studies team*—representing design services, editorial, editorial services, educational technology, marketing, market research, photo research and art development, production services, project office, publishing processes, and rights & permissions—are listed below. Bold type denotes core team members.

Greg Abrom, Ernie Albanese, Rob Aleman, Susan Andariese, **Rachel Avenia-Prol,** Leann Davis Alspaugh, Penny Baker, Barbara Bertell, **Peter Brooks,** Rui Camarinha, John Carle, **Lisa Del Gatto,** Paul Delsignore, Kathy Dempsey, Anne Drowns, Deborah Dukeshire, Marlies Dwyer, **Frederick Fellows,** Paula C. Foye, Lara Fox, Julia Gecha, **Mary Hanisco,** Salena Hastings, Lance Hatch, Kerri Hoar, **Beth Hyslip,** Katharine Ingram, Nancy Jones, John Kingston, Deborah Levheim, Constance J. McCarty, **Kathleen Mercandetti,** Art Mkrtchyan, Ken Myett, **Mark O'Malley,** Jen Paley, Ray Parenteau, **Gabriela Pérez Fiato,** Linda Punskovsky, Kirsten Richert, **Lynn Robbins,** Nancy Rogier, Bruce Rolff, Robin Samper, Mildred Schulte, Siri Schwartzman, **Malti Sharma,** Lisa Smith-Ruvalcaba, Roberta Warshaw, Sarah Yezzi

Additional Credits

Jonathan Ambar, Tom Benfatti, Lisa D. Ferrari, Paul Foster, Florrie Gadson, Phil Gagler, Ella Hanna, Jeffrey LaFountain, Karen Mancinelli, Michael McLaughlin, Lesley Pierson, Pronk&Associates, Debi Taffet

DK The DK Designs team who contributed to *World Studies* were as follows: Hilary Bird, Samantha Borland, Marian Broderick, Richard Czapnik, Nigel Duffield, Heather Dunleavy, Cynthia Frazer, James A. Hall, Lucy Heaver, Rose Horridge, Paul Jackson, Heather Jones, Ian Midson, Marie Ortu, Marie Osborn, Leyla Ostovar, Ralph Pitchford, Ilana Sallick, Pamela Shiels, Andrew Szudek, Amber Tokeley.

DK Maps and globes were created by **DK Cartography.** The team consisted of Tony Chambers, Damien Demaj, Julia Lunn, Ed Merritt, David Roberts, Ann Stephenson, Gail Townsley, and Iorwerth Watkins.

Illustrations

Kenneth Batelman: 24, 90; Richard Bonson/DK Images: 68; Richard Draper/DK Images: 114; Jen Paley: 10, 16, 19, 26, 36, 42, 50, 52–53, 57, 65, 66, 78, 80, 84, 87, 91, 92, 97, 103, 110, 112, 117, 118, 120; Jun Park: 152; Pronk&Associates: 136, 139, 142, 145, 149, 150, 151, 153, 169, 171, 174, 178, 180, 200, 203, 208, 211

Photos

Cover Photos

tl, Welsh/firstlight.ca; **tm,** Bridgeman Art Library/SuperStock, Inc.; **tr,** Photodisc/Artbase Inc.; **b,** Juan Biosca/firstlight.ca

Title Page

Juan Biosca/firstlight.ca

Table of Contents

iv–v, Panoramic Images; **vi,** Damien Simonis/Lonely Planet Images; **vii,** F. Lemmens/Masterfile Corporation; **xi,** F. J. Jackson/Alamy Images

Learning With Technology

xiii, Discovery Channel School

Reading and Writing Handbook

RW, Michael Newman/PhotoEdit; **RW1,** Walter Hodges/Getty Images, Inc.; **RW2,** Digital Vision/Getty Images, Inc.; **RW3,** Will Hart/PhotoEdit; **RW5,** Jose Luis Pelaez, Inc./Corbis

MapMaster Skills Handbook

M, James Hall/Dorling Kindersley; **M1,** Mertin Harvey/Gallo Images/Corbis; **M2–3 m,** NASA; **M2–3,** (globes) Planetary Visions; **M6 tr,** Mike Dunning/Dorling Kindersley; **M5 br,** Barnabas Kindersley/Dorling Kindersley; **M10 b,** Bernard and Catherine Desjeux/Corbis; **M11,** Hutchison Library; **M12 b,** Pa Photos; **M13 r,** Panos Pictures; **M14 l,** Macduff Everton/Corbis; **M14 t,** MSCF/NASA; **M15 b,** Ariadne Van Zandbergen/Lonely Planet Images; **M16 l,** Bill Stormont/Corbis; **M16 b,** Pablo Corral/Corbis; **M17 t,** Les Stone/Sygma/Corbis; **M17 b,** W. Perry Conway/Corbis

Guiding Questions

1 t, Christies Images/SuperStock, Inc.; **1 b,** Heini Schneebeli/Bridgeman Art Library

Regional Overview

2 l, G. Hind/Still Pictures; **3 t,** Liba Taylor/Corbis; **4 t,** Chris Lisle/Corbis; **4 b,** Patrick Ward/Corbis; **5 t,** Sharna Balfour/Gallo Images; **5 b,** David Ball/Corbis; **6 ml,** Liba Taylor/Corbis; **6 b,** Leanne Logan/Lonely Planet Images; **7 t,** Geert Cole/Lonely Planet Images; **7 mr,** Harlmut Schwarzbach/Still Pictures; **7 br,** Gallo Images/Corbis

Chapter One

8–9, Tim Davis/Corbis; **10,** Richard Cummins/Corbis; **11 t,** Discovery Channel School; **11 b,** Martin Rogers/Getty Images, Inc.; **12–13,** Jason Lauré/Lauré Communications; **14,** Roger Wood/Corbis; **15,** SuperStock, Inc.; **16,** Jason Edwards/Lonely Planet Images; **18 t,** Hal Beral/Corbis; **18–19 b,** Panoramic Images; **20–21 b,** SuperStock, Inc.; **21 t,** F. Lemmens/Masterfile Corporation; **22,** Lorne Resnick/Getty Images, Inc.; **23,** Robert Patrick/Corbis Sygma; **25,** Ariadne Van Zandbergen/Lonely Planet Images; **26,** Victor Englebert/Victor Englebert Photography; **26 inset,** Dave King/Dorling Kindersley; **28,** Jason Lauré/Lauré Communications; **29 t,** AFP/Corbis; **29 b,** Tim Boyle/Getty Images, Inc.; **30,** Eric Miller/iAfrika Photos; **31,** Martin Rogers/Getty Images, Inc.

Chapter Two

34–35, J. D. Dallet/AGE Fotostock; **36,** Juan Carlos Munoz/AGE Fotostock; **37 t,** Lauros/Giraudon/The Bridgeman Art Library; **37 m,** John Reader/Photo Researchers, Inc.; **37 b,** Robert Sisson/National Geographic Image Collection; **38,** Martin Harvey/Gallo Images/Corbis; **39 t,** Erich Lessing/Art Resource, NY; **39 b,** The Art Archive/Egyptian Museum Turin/Dagli Orti; **41,** David Turnley/Corbis; **42 all,** The Bristish Museum; **44 t,** Anthony Bannister/Gallo Images/Corbis; **44 b,** Corbis; **45,** David Reed/Corbis; **46 both,** Pictor International/Agency ImageState/Alamy; **48 t,** The Granger Collection, New York; **48 b,** Saudi Arabia-Ramadan/AFP/Corbis; **49,** Christie's Images/SuperStock, Inc.; **50,** Yann Arthus-Bertrand/Corbis; **51,** Dorling Kindersley/The Science Museum London; **52 l,** Ingrid Roddis/Lonely Planet Images; **52 r, 53 t,** The Granger Collection, New York; **53 b,** Discovery Channel School; **54 t,** The Granger Collection, New York; **54 b,** Wilberforce Museum, Hull/Dorling Kindersley; **56 l,** The Art Archive/Private Collection; **56 r,** The British Library, London, UK/Topham-HIP/The Image Works; **57,** Chris Steele-Perkins/Magnum Photos; **58 both,** Peter Turnley/Corbis; **59,** UPI/Corbis-Bettman; **61 l,** Hulton-Deutsch Collection/Corbis; **61 r,** M. & E. Bernheim/Woodfin Camp & Associates; **62 t,** Joao Silva/New York Times Pictures; **62–63 b,** Peter Turnley/Corbis; **65,** One Mile Up, Inc./Fotosearch Stock Photography; **66,** Michael S. Lewis/Corbis; **67 t,** A. Ramey/Woodfin Camp & Associates; **67 b,** Charles O. Cecil/Words & Pictures/PictureQuest; **68 t,** Michael S. Lewis/Corbis; **69 t,** Yann Arthus-Bertrand/Corbis; **69 b,** Sandro Vannini/Corbis; **70,** Willem de Lange/PictureNET Africa; **71,** Liba Taylor/Corbis; **72,** Wolfgang Kaehler Photography; **73 l,** Christie's Images/SuperStock, Inc.; **73 r,** Peter Turnley/Corbis

Chapter Three

76–77, Kennan Ward/Corbis; **78,** Getty Images, Inc.; **79,** Glen Allison/Getty Images, Inc.; **80,** Francois Perri/Cosmos/Woodfin Camp & Associates;

81, Jim Erickson/Corbis; 82, Jon Arnold Images/Alamy; 83, Francois Perri/Cosmos/Woodfin Camp & Associates; 84, Jason Lauré/Lauré Communications; 85, M. & E. Bernheim/Woodfin Camp & Associates; 86 t, Craig Pershouse/Lonely Planet Images; 86 b, Robert Frerck/Odyssey Productions, Inc.; 87, Yann Arthus-Bertrand/Corbis; 88 t, M. & E. Bernheim/Woodfin Camp & Associates; 88 b, Discovery Channel School; 89 l, Courtesy of Balla Tounkara; 89 r, Bob Burch/ Index Stock Imagery/PictureQuest; 91 l, Gunter Ziesler/Peter Arnold, Inc.; 91 r, Rich Kirchner/NHPA; 92, Ariadne Van Zandbergen/Lonely Planet Images; 93, Yadid Levy/AGE Fotostock; 94–95 b, Wolfgang Kaehler Photography; 95 t, Peter Marlow/Magnum Photos; 96, Sipa Press; 97, Popperfoto/Alamy Images; 98, Chris Harvey/Stone Allstock/Getty Images Inc.; 99, Ian Murphy/Getty Images, Inc.; 100, Christie's Images, Inc.; 101 l, Jim Erickson/Corbis; 101 r, Ian Murphy/Getty Images

Chapter Four

104–105, Photolibrary.com; 106 t, Discovery Channel School; 106 b, Claudia Wiens/Peter Arnold, Inc.; 107 t, F. J. Jackson/Alamy Images; 107 b, Paul Hardy/Corbis; 108, Damien Simonis/Lonely Planet Images; 109, Patrick Ward/Corbis; 110, Harry Gruyaert/Magnum Photos; 111, Stock Image/SuperStock, Inc.; 112, Nik Wheeler/Corbis; 113, Nik Wheeler; 114 t, Lloyd Cluff/Corbis; 114 b, Dorling Kindersley; 115 t, Discovery Channel School; 115 b, Mark Henley/Panos Pictures; 116, David Young-Wolff/PhotoEdit; 117, Carmen Redondo/Corbis; 118, Robert Everts/Getty Images Inc.; 119, Francoise Perri/Woodfin Camp & Associates; 121 t, Abbas/Magnum Photos; 121 b, Discovery Channel School; 122, Tiziana and Gianni Baldizzone/Corbis; 123 l, Harry Gruyaert/Magnum Photos; 123 r, Robert Everts/Getty Images Inc.

Chapter Five

126–127, Yann Arthus-Bertrand/Corbis; 128 t, Discovery Channel School; 128 b, Art Directors/Jane Sweeney; 130 bl, Ancient Art&Architecture/ DanitaDelimont.com; 130 br, Robert Burch/Bruce Coleman Inc.; 132 tr, Robert Burch; 132 b, AP/WideWorld Photos; 134 mr, AFP/Corbis; 134 b, Beryl Goldberg; 135 tr, Luis Marden/National Geographic/Getty Images, Inc.; 136 bl, Sally Mayman/Getty Images, Inc.; 137 br, Paul Almasy/Corbis; 137 bl, Werner Forman/Art Resource NY; 138 bl, McPherson Colin/Corbis/Sygma; 138 tr, Betty Press/Panos Pictures; 139 b, Hamill Gallery of African Art, Boston MA; 140 tl, Bruno Barbey/Magnum Photos; 141 tr, Campbell William/Corbis/Sygma; 142–143, Dave Starrett/Artbase Inc.; 142 bl, Bettman/Corbis; 143 tr, Hulton-Deutsch Collection/Corbis; 144 bl, Hamill Gallery of African Art, Boston MA; 146 t, Discovery Channel School; 146 b, AP/Wide World Photos; 147 tr, Robert Burch; 148 ml, Imagestate/firstlight.ca; 149 mr, Jonathan Nourok/PhotoEdit Inc.; 149 br, Dave Starrett/Artbase Inc.; 150–151, Ali Atay/Atlas; 150 bl, Wolfgang Kaehler/Corbis; 154 tl, Art Directors/Mary Jelliffe; 155 ml, Paul Almasy/Corbis; 155 mr, Art Directors/Mary Jelliffe

Chapter Six

158–159, Robert Bourgoing; 160, Discovery Channel School; 161 tr, Sheila McKinnon/Mira.com; 162 t, Edwards Roderick, Edward/MaXx Images; 163 m, © 2003 Norbert Wu/www.nobertwu.com; 163 mr, Wolfgang Kaehler Photography; 164 tr, AFP/Corbis; 165 m, Art Directors/Fiona Good; 166 b, Robert Patrick/Corbis/Sygma; 167 br, M. & E. Bernheim/Woodfin Camp & Associates; 167 tl, Dave Bartruff/Danita Delimont; 168 tr, Dave Bartruff/Danita Delimont; 168 tl, Kal Muller/Woodfin Camp & Associates; 170, Discovery Channel School; 170 ml, Robert Caputo/Aurora Photos; 170 br, Reuters; 173 t, Kwame Zikomo/SuperStock; 174, Discovery Channel School; 175 tr, Howard Davies/Corbis; 176 bl, Eric Draper/White House/Getty Images, Inc.; 177 tr, Art Directors/Andrew Gasson; 177 br, David Pluth/Fotografx; 178 b, Robert Burch; 179 tr, Michele Burgess/MaXx Images; 179 b, Discovery Channel School; 181 mr, Betty Press/Woodfin Camp & Associates; 182 tl, DigtalVision/Artbase Inc.; 183 tr, Dave Bartruff/Danita Delimont; 183 m, Robert Burch; 186 br, Paul Souders/Getty Images, Inc.; 187 tr, PhotodiscRed/Artbase Inc.; 188 bl, Jeremy Woodhouse/Masterfile Corporation; 189, Tololwa M. Mollel

Chapter Seven

190–191, Eric Nathan/Alamy Images; 192 t, Discovery Channel School; 192 b, Volkmar Wentzel/Getty Images, Inc.; 194 tr, AFP/Corbis; 194 tl, Max-Planck-Institut Seewiesen; 200 Jason Lauré/Lauré Communications; 201 b, Patrick Roberts/Corbis/Sygma; 202 bl, Bettmann/Corbis; 204 t, Discovery Channel School; 204 bl, Artbase Inc.; 205 tr, Reuters/Corbis; 206 tl, Photodisc/Artbase Inc.; 206 ml, Photodisc/Artbase Inc.; 206 bl, Photodisc/Artbase Inc.; 207 m, Paula Bronstein/Impact Visuals; 208 bl, Charles O'Rear/Corbis; 209 br, TimeLifePictures/Getty Images, Inc.; 210 br, AP/WideWorld Photos; 211, Discovery Channel School; 212 tl, Owen Franken/Corbis; 213 ml, Artbase Inc.; 213 mr, AP/WideWorld Photos

Projects

216, Heini Schneebeli/Bridgeman Art Library

Reference

217, PhotoEdit

Glossary of Geographic Terms

234 t, A. & L. Sinibaldi/Getty Images, Inc.; 234 b, John Beatty/Getty Images, Inc.; 234–235 b, Spencer Swanger/Tom Stack & Associates; 235 t, Hans Strand/Getty Images, Inc; 235 m, Paul Chesley/Getty Images, Inc.

Gazetteer

237, SuperStock, Inc.

Text

Chapter One

21, Excerpt from "Where Hospitality is an Oasis," by Christine Negroni, *The New York Times,* January 19, 2003. 26, From *Cocoa Comes to Mampong,* by Dei Anang. Copyright © 1949. Reprinted with the permission of Methodist Book Depot. 93, Excerpt from "Swahili Coast: East Africa's Ancient Crossroads," by Robert Caputo, *National Geographic,* October 2001.

Chapter Three

96, From "African Statesman Still Sowing Seeds for Future," by James C. McKinley, Jr., *The New York Times.*

Chapter Five

144, From *Ghana in Transition,* by David E. Apter. Copyright © 1955, 1963, and 1972 by Princeton University Press.

Chapter Six

172, 173, From "Three Leaders," by Andrew Meldrum, *Africa Report,* September–October 1994. Copyright © 1994 by *Africa Report.* 182, From "Back to No Man's Land," by George Monbiot, *Geographical Magazine,* July 1994. Copyright © 1994 by *Geographical Magazine.* 186, From *A Promise to the Sun* by Tololwa M. Mollel. Text Copyright © 1991 by Tololwa M. Mollel.

Chapter Seven

207, Excerpt from "Nelson Mandela's Statement After Voting in South Africa's First Democratic Election, Inanda, Kwazulu Natal, 27 April 1994," by Nelson Mandela, the African National Congress. 208, Excerpt from "Preamble: Constitution of the Republic of South Africa by the Constitutional Assembly," Policy and Law Online News.

Note: Every effort has been made to locate the copyright owner of material used in this textbook. Omissions brought to our attention will be corrected in subsequent editions.